Chr̶̶̶̶̶on: Plays One

Christopher Hampton was born in the Azores in 1946. He wrote his first play, *When Did You Last See My Mother?*, at the age of eighteen. His work for theatre, television and cinema includes *The Philanthropist*, his adaptation of *Les Liaisons Dangereuses* by Laclos, adaptations from Ibsen and Molière and the screenplays *Dangerous Liaisons*, *Carrington* and *The Secret Agent*.

CHRISTOPHER HAMPTON

Plays One

Total Eclipse

The Philanthropist

Savages

Treats

Introduced by
the Author

faber and faber
LONDON · BOSTON

This collection first published in 1997
by Faber and Faber Limited
3 Queen Square London WC1N 3AU

Photoset by Parker Typesetting Service, Leicester
Printed in England by Mackays of Chatham plc, Chatham, Kent

A CIP record for this book
is available from the British Library
ISBN 0–571–17834–0

Contents

Introduction

The first of the plays here collected, chronologically speaking, is *Total Eclipse*, which was written in 1967 and which I now tend to think of, quite inaccurately, as the start of my career. This may be because my earlier writings, as schoolboy or student, were tentative experiments produced with the fluency and unselfconsciousness of an amateur, whereas this was a commissioned play more than likely to be professionally produced in front of paying customers; or because I had always considered my first play, *When Did You Last See My Mother?*, given a Sunday-night production by the Royal Court Theatre and kindly (no doubt too kindly) received by the critics, to be a kind of dry-run for this much more ambitious piece; or even because the beginnings of a literary career and the potentialities of a writer's life were in a sense the very subject I was examining in the play.

Language students at Oxford are given the option of extending their course for a year in order to work abroad and thus improve one or other of their languages. The amount of time I had spent in my second year mounting my plays, first in Oxford and then in London, combined with a no more than vestigial ability to speak German, made this in my case a necessity. My sympathetic and resourceful tutors found me a post in one of those vast municipal theatres which, then as now, possessed the resources to spend more money making armour for a single production than a comparable English theatre might receive in a year. So it was in Hamburg that I began writing the play, on 1 April to be precise, which seemed an appropriate date for so foolishly ambitious an undertaking.

My days in Hamburg were numbered. I had not enjoyed my time in the city: but, more to the point, there had been a misunderstanding about the nature of my *Studienstelle*, which turned out to be an honorary rather than a salaried position. I used this difficulty as an excuse to make an early getaway to Paris: where, under far more congenial circumstances, supporting myself with a translation job I was lucky to find, I pressed on into the summer with the play, which I eventually completed back in England in September.

Second plays were somewhat easier to place in those days than in the present, colder climate; still, production was by no means a foregone conclusion. The play had been commissioned by Michael Codron for the West End, but he soon decided, I'm sure correctly, that its dubious commercial prospects could never justify its expensive requirements, in terms of size of cast and number of locations. The Royal Court's initial response, meanwhile, was cautious. I began to be tormented by the idea that the piece, which had been at the forefront of my mind now for a number of years, would never be performed. Then, one day, unexpectedly, Robert Kidd (who had directed my first play) and William Gaskill (Artistic Director at the Royal Court) arrived in Oxford and asked me to read the play to them. They settled into the only two chairs in the room: I sat up on the bed and read. At the end there was a long silence, before Bill said, 'All right, we'll do it.'

This was not his only act of generosity towards me, as I'm happy to be able to acknowledge here. He also invented a job for me, which was given the resonant title of Resident Dramatist in the (successful) hope of attracting support from the Arts Council. And so, two weeks after graduating, I arrived for the start of rehearsals on *Total Eclipse* and a formative two years' work at the Royal Court.

The play was tepidly received at the time, but has since had more productions, I would guess, than any of my others; it seems to speak to a limited audience, but to speak to them loud and clear. Enthusiastic strangers have told me how much the play means to them in Utah and in Tokyo. For me, it was a means of posing a number of questions around a central puzzle, namely, what does it mean to be a writer? What could one reasonably hope to achieve? What were the pleasures and torments and what, if any, the responsibilities? Might one change the world, or would it prove beyond one's abilities even to change oneself? I still, of course, have no settled answers to these questions; but at that time it seemed that by examining two writers, Rimbaud and Verlaine, who had reached diametrically opposite conclusions on all these issues, despite their strong influence on one another, despite even the fact that they were lovers, some kind of fruitful internal debate might be triggered. For reasons I couldn't have explained then and still can't now, it seemed important to include the barest minimum of literary discussion in the play; to contemplate, in other words, only their lives and to leave with a scene which emphasized, despite the violence of their opposition, their fundamental solidarity as writers. Except in that final scene, I stuck firmly to the known facts ('Did you plunder my book?' Enid Starkie asked me when we met to discuss the play and seemed delighted when I admitted that I had), in the belief that reality will always yield more in the way of unexpected twists and poetic illumination than the most extravagant fictions.

Because the play is so central to me, I have had the greatest difficulty leaving it alone: consequently, there are four different published versions, two British and two American, of which I have chosen, for publication here, the third version, published after the revival at the Lyric, Hammersmith, in 1981, directed by David Hare. The fairly extensive changes for this production were made with David's help and encouragement and I haven't yet repented of them: but I still can't guarantee that this will remain my final version of *Total Eclipse*.

Molière was one of my special subjects at Oxford; and as I worked on *Le Misanthrope*, it occurred to me that in the climate of abrasive candour which characterized the late 1960s, Alceste would have been quite at home: whereas his opposite, a man concerned above all to cause no offence and be an unfailing source of sweetness and light, would very likely succeed only in raising hackles wherever he went. This notion was the germ from which *The Philanthropist* grew. As a setting which might be a modern equivalent of Molière's world, in which clever and envious people with a startling amount of leisure time sit around demolishing their colleagues, thoroughly insulated against any external pressures or upheavals, the university naturally suggested itself. Nowadays, no doubt, the bubble has burst and universities are as subject as the rest of us to the harsh rigours of market forces; but in 1968, as campuses erupted all over Europe, Oxford seemed as sleepy as ever, cocooned and self-regarding.

These are the factors which anchor *The Philanthropist* to its time; but I was also interested in applying Molière's method (comedy in which a character is examined in the light of a defining trait, such as hypocrisy or lust or avarice) to the study of what might technically be described as a virtue rather than a vice: compulsive amiability.

I began writing the play in February 1969, but pressure of work at the Royal Court, where I was now running the literary department, slowed me down and it was not until August, by which time I had agreed to stay on another year and acquired an assistant (and successor) in the shape of David Hare, that I was able to deliver. As with *Total Eclipse*, it was almost a year before the play reached the stage. During this time, I was happily employed providing new versions of *Uncle Vanya* (for Anthony Page at the

Court) and *Hedda Gabler* (for Peter Gill at Stratford, Ontario), but *The Philanthropist*'s lack of progress was a constant source of anxiety. It was too soon for the Court to have refined what later became one of its deadlier techniques, refusal to produce the Resident Dramatist's play, but *The Philanthropist* was being passed from one distinguished director to another, without ever arriving at one whose dates or casting requirements or overall reservations about the play would allow him to sign the necessary bit of paper. Robert Kidd, meanwhile, fired from the Court, so he very plausibly claimed, for having received better reviews than he deserved, was in Manchester, working off a nine-month contract with Granada TV.

Eventually Robert was free, an exceptionally strong cast was quickly assembled and despite a quite serious outbreak of last-minute management jitters about the viability of the play, it opened on an early August evening in 1970, so sweltering that some unfortunate patron noisily passed out near the beginning of the second act: which made it particularly satisfying that the play's success (Michael Codron moved it to the West End, where it became, as far as I know, the Court's longest-running straight play) largely contributed towards the installation of the theatre's air-conditioning system. The week after the opening my time at the Court was up and I was on my own.

The text used here is the second edition, published to coincide with a revival of the play in Chichester in 1985. Apart from a certain streamlining, amounting to perhaps five minutes of cuts, it remains identical to the first edition, not to say the first draft of the play.

On 23rd February 1969, the *Sunday Times* Colour *Magazine* published an article by Norman Lewis called 'Genocide', which dealt with the destruction of the Brazilian Indians. Among the many appalling examples of systematic extermination discussed by Mr Lewis and ranging from the sixteenth century to the present day was one which involved the slaughter of large numbers of the Cintas Largas tribe, supervised by one Francisco de Brito, 'general overseer of the rubber extraction firm of Arruda and Junqueira of Juina-Mirim near Aripuanã, on the river Juruena' in the early sixties.

'It was seen as essential', Mr Lewis writes, 'to produce the maximum number of casualties in one single devastating attack, at a time when as many Indians as possible would be present in the village, and an expert was found to advise that this could best be done at the annual feast of the "Quarup". This great ceremony lasts for a day and a night, and under one name or another it is conducted by almost all the Indian tribes whose culture has not been destroyed. The "Quarup" is a theatrical representation of the legends of creation interwoven with those of the tribe itself, both a mystery play and a family reunion attended not only by the living but by the ancestral spirits. These appear as dancers in masquerade, to be consulted on immediate problems, to comfort the mourners, to testify that not even death can disrupt the unity of the tribe.

'A Cessna light 'plane used for ordinary commercial services was hired for the attack, and its normal pilot replaced by an adventurer of mixed Italian-Japanese birth. It was loaded with sticks of dynamite – "bananas" they are called in Brazil – and took off from a jungle airstrip near Aripuanã. The Cessna arrived over the village at about midday. The Indians had been preparing themselves all night by prayer and singing, and now they were all gathered in the open space in the village's centre. On the first run packets of sugar were dropped to calm the fears of those who had scattered and run for shelter at the sight of the 'plane. They had opened the packets and were tasting the sugar ten minutes later when it returned to carry out the attack. No-one has ever been able to find out how many Indians were killed, because the bodies were buried in the bank of the river and the village deserted.'

It is this incident which forms, and which I knew as I read the article would form, the climax of this play. How this insistent image developed over the next four years into the finished play is a long and irrelevant story I need not go into here, except to mention that it involved first a realisation that it would be impossible to deal with the 'Indian problem' at all adequately without taking into account the current political situation, and second a journey to Brazil, which confirmed much of what I had researched in England, as well as providing one or two of those revelations which seem so obvious in hindsight, notably that the average urban Brazilian has far too many difficulties in his life to allow himself the luxury of worrying about the Indian of the interior, of whose existence he is in fact largely ignorant.

The legends spoken by West are based, respectively, on myths of the Kayapo-Gorotire, Macuxi, Arekuna, Xipaya, Xerente and Tukuna tribes. Two of them ('The Origin of Music' and 'The Life After Death') I found in Vol. 11 of the immense *Mythology of All Ages* (ed. Alexander), and the rest are from the first two volumes of Claude Lévi-Strauss's *Mythologiques* – *Le Cru et le Cuit* and *Du Miel aux Cendres*. The geographical area covered by these tribes is enormous – from the Xingu to the Colombian border to and perhaps even across the borders of Venezuela and Guyana – but I felt no necessity to choose myths from a specific area of Brazil, any more than I felt restricted when I was informed by various anthropologists and friends that strictly speaking the Cintas Largas tribe could not have been performing a 'Quarup', as this is a ceremony limited to the Xingu area. The point is, as Norman Lewis says, that 'this great ceremony . . . *under one name or another* . . . is conducted by almost all the Indian tribes whose culture has not been destroyed'; and since what is in question is not only the fate of individual tribes, but the survival of an entire race, I haven't hesitated to sacrifice scrupulous anthropological accuracy to what seemed to me to be most appropriate dramatically.

As to the political background of the play it is perhaps enough to say that an American-backed military coup took place in Brazil on 1st April 1964; that a serious urban guerrilla movement under the leadership of Carlos Marighela of the A.L.N. (Ação Libertadora Nacional) was established in 1968; that the military dictatorship consolidated its position in December 1968 with the notorious Fifth Institutional Act, designed to suppress all political and civil opposition; that between September 1969 and December 1970 ambassadors and embassy officials from the U.S.A., Japan, West Germany and Switzerland were kidnapped and exchanged for varying numbers of political prisoners; and that the urban guerrilla movement began slowly to fall apart after Marighela had been killed by the police in November 1969. The West-Carlos section of the play is set in early 1971 – in other words at a time when intense police pressure and the widespread use of torture was undermining and destroying the revolutionary movement: the event is fictional but the circumstances and outcome are, I think, not too unlikely.

Treats was the last of the five plays I wrote for the Royal Court. It was also the shortest, the one which took longest to write and, by a considerable margin, the one which was least well received by the critics. It had its origins in two disparate ideas, one visual and one literary. First, I was haunted by the simple notion of a set which would represent a half-furnished room; and second, while I had naturally been delighted by the success of a translation I had made of *A Doll's House*, which had opened in New York in 1971 and caught the crest of the Women's Liberation wave, in retrospect there seemed something disturbing about this fashionable endorsement. Ibsen, after all, had designed the play to provoke; now it seemed the last word in social orthodoxy. And yet, as everybody knew, there were still just as many women trapped in unsatisfactory, restrictive and degrading relationships as ever there could have been in the 1870s.

Inclining my head to tradition, I began writing the play on 1 April 1974. It tormented me for almost a year, during which, at various times, I rented rooms in Oxford and London in order to try to knock it on the head. Finally, early in 1976, it reached the stage.

An author who sets out to provoke can hardly complain if his aim is achieved. And, in any case, slightly to our amazement, the play broke a box-office record at the Royal Court and went on, again with Michael Codron's help, to a respectable run in the West End. Strangely enough, I found the critical reception rather bracing. All the same, the play formed a full-stop to the first phase of my career. I kept in touch with the theatre by writing translations, but I wanted to explore other avenues and it was more than five years before I attempted another original play. And then it was not for the Royal Court: I had a conviction it was a theatre for new writers, a description to which I could no longer lay claim. Still, it should be clear from the above that the plays in this volume were largely influenced by things I learned and supported by friends I made at the Court.

The version of *Treats* published here is the original text. Whether or not the memory of the agonies and mathematical rigours of its construction has caused me to shy away from the effort of revision, I can't say. In any event, the revival of the play at the Hampstead Theatre in 1989 made no changes. The critical response was noticeably mellower, but I was pleased to see the piece had not entirely lost its capacity to irritate.

CHRISTOPHER HAMPTON

TOTAL ECLIPSE

For Harry and Lynn
and in memory of work and friendship
with Robert Kidd and Victor Henry

This new production of *Total Eclipse* opened at the Lyric
Theatre, Hammersmith on 5 May 1981. The cast was as
follows:

Paul Verlaine Simon Callow
Mme Mauté de Fleurville Eileen Page
Mathilde Verlaine Lynsey Baxter
Arthur Rimbaud Hilton McRae
M. Mauté de Fleurville Tim Seely
Charles Cros William Sleigh
Étienne Carjat Tim Seely
Jean Aicard Peter McKriel
Judge Théodore T'Serstevens Tim Seely
Clerk Peter McKriel
Eugénie Krantz Judith Barker
Barman William Sleigh
Isabelle Rimbaud Anna Nyghe

Directed David Hare
Designed Hayden Griffin

The first performance of *Total Eclipse* was given at the
Royal Court Theatre on 11 September 1968. The cast was
as follows:

Mme Mauté de Fleurville,
Verlaine's mother-in-law Kathleen Byron
Mathilde Verlaine, Verlaine's wife Michele Dotrice
Arthur Rimbaud Victor Henry
Paul Verlaine John Grillo
Charles Cros Malcolm Ingram
M. Mauté de Fleurville Nigel Hawthorne
Étienne Carjat Nigel Hawthorne
Ernest Cabaner William Hoyland
Jean Aicard Stanley Lebor
Clerk Stanley Lebor
Judge Théodore T'Serstevens Nigel Hawthorne
Eugénie Krantz Ursula Smith
Isabelle Rimbaud, Rimbaud's sister Gillian Martell
Barman William Hoyland
Maid Judy Liebert
Artists, customers in cafés etc.

Directed Robert Kidd
Designed Patrick Procktor

Act One

SCENE ONE

Verlaine's Voice Sometimes he speaks, in a kind of tender dialect, of the death which causes repentance, of the unhappy men who certainly exist, of painful tasks and heart-rending departures. In the hovels where we got drunk, he wept, looking at those who surrounded us, the cattle of poverty. He lifted up drunks in the black streets. He had the pity a bad mother has for small children. He moved with the grace of a little girl at catechism. He pretended to know about everything, business, art, medicine. I followed him, I had to!

During this, the lights go up on the drawing-room/ conservatory of the Paris home of the Mautés de Fleurville at 14, Rue Nicolet. It's the 10th September, 1871. Indications of discreet affluence. **Mme Mauté de Fleurville,** *a handsome middle-aged woman, is trimming flowers and handing them to her daughter,* **Mathilde Verlaine,** *who arranges them in a vase. Mathilde is an attractive girl of 18, now 8 months pregnant.*

The women continue working for a moment in silence; then a strange, incongruous figure enters the room and stands for a moment, waiting in the shadows, watching them. Neither of them notices him. He is **Arthur Rimbaud.** *His appearance is striking. He is not quite 17 and looks his age. His hands are large and dirty. His tie hangs loose round his neck like a piece of old string. His trousers are too short and end an inch above his blue socks. His boots are filthy. He's extremely good-looking: thin lips, cold, grey eyes. Eventually he speaks, startling the women considerably.*

5

Rimbaud Evening. I'm looking for M. Paul Verlaine.

Mme M. de F. Are you . . . M. Rimbaud?

Rimbaud Yes.

Mme M. de F. Oh, M. Rimbaud, I am Mme Mauté de Fleurville, M. Verlaine's mother-in-law. And this is Mme Verlaine, my daughter.

Rimbaud smiles frostily, nodding to the two women.

Mme M. de F. You're not with M. Verlaine?

Rimbaud No.

Mme M. de F. Only he went to the station to meet you. I suppose he must have missed you.

Rimbaud Yes, well he doesn't know what I look like, does he?

Mme M. de F. Er, how did you get here?

Rimbaud Walked.

Silence.

Mme M. de F. Perhaps . . . would you like a wash?

Rimbaud (*considers this a moment*) No thanks.

Mme M. de F. Did you give your luggage to one of the servants?

Rimbaud I didn't meet any servants.

Mme M. de F. Well, then, it's in the hall, is it?

Rimbaud What?

Mme M. de F. Your luggage.

Rimbaud I haven't got any luggage.

Mme M. de F. No . . . luggage?

Rimbaud No.

Mme M. de F. Oh.

Silence.

Mathilde Won't you sit down, M. Rimbaud?

Rimbaud does so, slouching back in the chair and reaching into his pocket to find a repulsive old clay pipe and some matches. He lights the pipe, sucking noisily.

Rimbaud Mind if I smoke?

Mme M. de F. (*with obvious distaste*) Not at all.

Silence.

M. Verlaine and I were very impressed by your poetry.

Rimbaud He let you read it?

Mme M. de F. Oh yes, I'm a fervent admirer of the Muse. We're great friends with M. Victor Hugo, you know. He's an utterly charming gentleman.

Rimbaud He's getting a bit senile.

Mme M. de F. I don't think so. He still has perfect command of his faculties. Naturally to the young he seems a little elderly. But then the young must always be revolutionary.

Mathilde You're even younger than we thought you were.

Rimbaud Oh, yes?

Mathilde How old are you?

Mme M. de F. Darling, it's not very polite to ask people their ages.

Mathilde I'm sorry. I was just so interested.

Rimbaud, ignoring this exchange, has risen and crossed

to the window. He stands, looking out at the garden.

Rimbaud Pleasant view.

Mme M. de F. Yes, charming, isn't it?

Rimbaud Pleasant.

Rimbaud picks up a china animal, considers it with distaste, puts it down and turns back to the window. At this moment, Paul Verlaine hurries in. He's 27, bearded, but already going bald. He's well-dressed and looks like a civil servant with private means – which is what he is. He doesn't at first notice Rimbaud.

Verlaine I combed the station but no sign of him.

Rimbaud (*without turning round*) He's here.

Verlaine M. Rimbaud?

He advances towards Rimbaud, hand outstretched, then, as Rimbaud turns towards him, hesitates for a moment, apparently transfixed by Rimbaud's appearance.

Rimbaud M. Verlaine.

They shake hands.

Verlaine You found your own way here. What initiative.

Mme M. de F. Good, well, I must see about organizing some dinner. I expect M. Rimbaud must be hungry.

Rimbaud Starving.

Mme M. de F. Yes. (*to Mathilde*) Come along, dear. You can give me a hand and the men can have a little chat.

She leaves with Mathilde.

Verlaine Well, this is . . .

8

Rimbaud nods.

Verlaine How old are you, if you don't mind my asking?

Rimbaud I do.

Verlaine Oh, sorry.

Rimbaud Sixteen.

Verlaine Sixteen? Are you sure?

Rimbaud Of course I'm sure.

Verlaine It's just that in your letter you said you were twenty-one.

Rimbaud You never want to believe what I say in my letters.

Verlaine I'm amazed. I thought those poems you sent me were remarkable for someone of twenty-one. For someone of sixteen, they're – unprecedented.

Rimbaud That's why I told you I was twenty-one. I didn't want you to feel patronizing before you'd read them.

Verlaine Of course, it all becomes clearer now. The fact that your mother kept you at home with no money. If you're sixteen. You've left school, have you?

Rimbaud Yes.

Verlaine I suppose your mother must be very angry with me.

Rimbaud No, once she found out you'd sent me my train fare, she seemed quite happy.

Verlaine I'm sorry I wasn't there to meet you at the station. The thing is, your train arrived at the emerald hour. The hour of absinthe. (*He grins, gesturing at the room.*) I don't suppose this is quite what you expected. My

9

wife and I did have a flat on the Quai de la Tournelle when I was working. But what with one political upheaval and another I decided I was too sensitive for the Civil Service. So I couldn't afford to keep on the flat. Then Mathilde's father, rot his guts, very generously offered us a floor of this house. I thought it might be a good idea, Mathilde being pregnant and everything.

Rimbaud And wasn't it?

Verlaine Yes, yes, except for my loathsome father-in-law. Fortunately for you, he's away at the moment. On a shooting party. Where I sincerely hope he will meet with a fatal accident. My daily devotions are entirely directed to that end. (*He sighs.*) I suffered for that girl, you know. I had to wait over a year before I could marry her. The fates were against it. It was delayed so many times. By pestilence and war. Literally. She caught smallpox at the last minute. I thought, Mary mother, have I waited all this time to get married to a flayed hedgehog? Fortunately she was quite unmarked. Two days before the wedding one of my best friends committed suicide. Then, the next day, the final indignity, I got called up. But I was immune to all the portents. I even squirmed out of that – and I married her.

It's just that being pregnant's had a bad effect on her. She's only a child.

Rimbaud So am I.

Mme Mauté de Fleurville comes in with Mathilde, who crosses to Verlaine and kisses him on the cheek. Then she smiles at Rimbaud, who doesn't respond, but fills and relights his pipe.

Mme M. de F. Dinner's almost ready.

Rimbaud Good, I'm famished.

Silence.

Mme M. de F. You come from the Ardennes, don't you, M. Rimbaud? Charleville?

Rimbaud Yes.

Mme M. de F. Pleasant town, Charleville, isn't it?

Rimbaud The last place on God's earth.

Mathilde And what does your father do?

Rimbaud Drinks mostly, I believe. We haven't seen him for ten years.

Mathilde I'm sorry.

Rimbaud No need to be. He's very well out of it.

Silence.

Mme M. de F. Perhaps you'd like to read something to us after dinner?

Rimbaud I don't think so.

Mathilde Oh, why not?

Rimbaud I don't want to.

Mme M. de F. M. Rimbaud's probably tired, dear.

Rimbaud No. I never read out my poetry.

Mathilde Oh, but all the other poets do it. We have soirées here and . . .

Rimbaud I'm not interested in what all the other poets do.

Verlaine Don't you think poets can learn from one another?

Rimbaud Only if they're bad poets.

Mathilde I'm sure you'd enjoy our soirées. We had a

lovely one last week. Poetry and music. Musset and Chopin.

Rimbaud Musset?

Mathilde Yes. Don't you like Musset? He's my favourite poet. Except for Paul, of course. Daddy was at school with him.

Rimbaud Slovenly facile rubbish. The most objectionable and least talented of all the miserable buffoons of this dreary century. A poet for schoolboys and women.

Verlaine Ah, but what about his plays?

Rimbaud The theatre is beneath contempt.

Verlaine Your opinions are firm.

Rimbaud Shouldn't they be?

Silence.

Listen, I must have a piss. Can you tell me where it is?

Verlaine leads him across the room, murmuring directions. Then, when Rimbaud has left, he turns back to the others.

Mme M. de F. Well.

Mathilde He's not how I imagined him.

Verlaine He's all right.

Curtain.

SCENE TWO

The same; 25th September, 1871.
  Rimbaud walks into the empty room, smoking his pipe. He looks round the room, then, after a moment's

*consideration, goes over and picks up the china animal we
have already seen him handle in Scene 1. He contemplates
it briefly, then deliberately drops it on the floor and
smashes it. He's moving away, back towards the door,
when* **M. Mauté de Fleurville** *appears. He's an imposing
man of 64, with a white beard. He's startled to see
Rimbaud, who by contrast, seems remarkably calm.*

Rimbaud (*hospitably*) Morning. Everyone's out, I'm
afraid. They should be back soon. Unless you've come to
see the old boy.

M. de F. The old boy?

Rimbaud M. Mauté de Fleurville. You're not a friend of
his, are you?

M. de F. Er . . . no.

Rimbaud No, I didn't think you were. As far as I can
gather he doesn't have any friends.

M. de F. (*faintly*) Really.

Rimbaud Yes. Apparently he defeats all comers with an
impregnable combination of tediousness and avarice. It is
darkly rumoured that he cannot resist rifling the pockets
of those who fall stunned by the monotony of his
anecdotes.

*M. de F. is beginning to show signs of impending fury.
He utters one or two indeterminate sounds, but
Rimbaud interrupts him, suavely changing tack.*

You wouldn't like to buy a crucifix by any chance, would
you? (*He produces one from an inside pocket.*) Because I
happen to have one with me which I can let you have on
extremely reasonable terms. It's ivory, I think.

*M. de F. stares at the crucifix, which he recognizes as his
own, with rage and incomprehension.*

Tempted?

M. de F. Who the hell are you?

Rimbaud I might ask you the same question. Except I'd be more polite.

M. de F. I am Mauté de Fleurville.

Rimbaud Morning.

He exits smartly. M. de F. gapes after him. Then he hurries out the other side of the room. Hiatus. Verlaine and Mathilde appear, the former looking considerably more rumpled than in the first scene and already somewhat drunk.

Verlaine All I'm saying is, if he goes, I go.

Mathilde That's just silly.

Verlaine We can't just put him out on the street, he's only a boy.

Mathilde He's met all your friends. One of them will give him a bed for a while.

She sits down on the chaise longue and puts her feet up, grunting slightly with the effort.

Verlaine People don't understand him. I'm the only one who understands him.

Mathilde Well, Daddy certainly won't understand him.

Verlaine I'm tired of being ordered about by that old bastard. He has no sympathy at all for my position. None of you seem to realize we had a revolution this year, which I supported. I could have been shot. If I hadn't been thrown out of my job, do you suppose I'd have accepted his bloody charity for one moment?

Mathilde No, but it's . . .

Verlaine I've been very tolerant with him, but this time I'm putting my foot down. Now do I make myself clear?

Mathilde Yes.

Verlaine And you're going to give me your full support?

Mathilde Yes.

Verlaine I know you, the minute he comes back, you'll start agreeing with him.

Mathilde No. I won't.

Verlaine It's not asking much, for God's sake, all I'm doing is helping a friend. I don't know why we have to go through all this. I'm your husband.

Mathilde I'm sorry, Paul.

Verlaine Are you trying to annoy me?

Mathilde No.

Verlaine Well, don't.

Silence.

Mathilde Why is it you like him so much?

Silence. Rimbaud slips into the room. He looks cheerful.

Rimbaud I'm off.

Verlaine No, look, you don't have to go. We're going to have it out with him when he gets back.

Rimbaud He's back.

Verlaine What?

Rimbaud We met. I don't think he's best pleased.

Verlaine Did he ask who you were?

Rimbaud It wasn't that kind of conversation.

15

Verlaine Well, look, we've decided you must stay. (*to Mathilde*) Haven't we?

Mathilde (*hesitates fractionally*) Yes.

Rimbaud It doesn't matter.

Verlaine Of course it matters. Why should we let the old sod treat us like this?

Rimbaud It's his house.

Verlaine Right, well, I'm going to say either we all stay or we all leave together, what about that?

Rimbaud smiles at Mathilde, a touch ironically.

Rimbaud Suits me.

Verlaine I mean, what could he do?

Mathilde He could cut off our allowance.

Rimbaud Ah.

Verlaine He wouldn't do that. Yes he would. Well, what the hell, eh, don't you think?

Rimbaud It's entirely up to you.

Verlaine Look, why don't we discuss this over a few drinks? Then . . . er . . . I mean, look, go down and order one up for me, I'll join you in a minute. Actually . . .

Rimbaud What?

Verlaine I do know someone who has a spare room going. What's the joke?

Rimbaud Nothing.

Verlaine Listen, if you'd rather . . .

Rimbaud No, no. I'll go and order you a drink. (*He starts moving towards the door, then stops, turns back and* *produces a piece of paper out of his pocket.*) I've got a list here of the books I want from Mauté's library, I thought you might nick them for me, not all at once, one by one will do. They'll obviously be more use to me than they are to him.

He hands the list to Verlaine. As he does so, M. de F. sweeps into the room followed by Mme. M. de F. He's about to speak, but falls silent when he sees Rimbaud. Silence. Rimbaud grins.

Rimbaud (*to Verlaine*) Don't be long.

He leaves, bowing to the Mautés. Silence.

M. de F. Since when have you had the right to invite people to stay here without my permission?

Verlaine Since you had the kindness to offer the second floor of your house to Mathilde and me, I've treated it as our home.

M. de F. So it is, your home, not a guest house.

Verlaine If I can't put up one guest in my home when I feel like it, I might as well live somewhere else.

M. de F. If you weren't so idle, you might be able to afford to.

Verlaine Now, listen, you know very well, that since the Commune . . .

M. de F. Any excuse.

Verlaine I don't notice you working your fingers to the bone.

M. de F. Now look here, Verlaine, I want that hooligan out of my house. Is that clear?

Verlaine (*roars at him*) He's already left!

Silence.

M. de F. And when you see him next, you'll kindly ask him to return all the objects he's pilfered.

Verlaine What are you talking about?

M. de F. I'd hardly stepped in the door when he tried to sell me one of my own crucifixes. (*to his wife*) Come along, dear.

Mme M. de F. I think perhaps I'd better stay and have a word with them.

M. de F. Will you come with me!

Cowed by his tone, Mme M. de F. follows her husband out of the room. Verlaine is still furious.

Mathilde You'd better get him to give back Daddy's crucifix.

Verlaine What?

Mathilde You must get it back from him.

Verlaine I've no intention of doing anything of the sort. If your father's capable of throwing that boy out without a penny he deserves to lose more than a few religious knick-knacks. He's got no right to have Christ hanging all over his walls. You people don't understand what poverty is. Do you realize that in Charleville, whenever Rimbaud wanted a book, he had to go and steal it off the bookstall.

Mathilde That proves what sort of a person he is.

Verlaine bounds across the room, seizes Mathilde by the ankles and drags her off the chaise longue. She crashes heavily to the floor. He stands over her as she struggles to her feet, then punches her hard in the face. She goes over again, bringing down a small table as she falls. Brief silence. She moans softly. Verlaine starts forward and lifts her off the floor.

Verlaine I'm sorry . . . I'm sorry, love . . . sorry. You shouldn't have said that. (*He helps her over towards the chaise longue.*)

M. and Mme. M. de F. hurry in.

M. de F. What's going on? (*Silence.*) Mm?

Mathilde Nothing.

M. de F. What was all that noise then?

Mathilde I . . . knocked the table over.

Mme M. de F. Are you all right, dear?

Mathilde nods, very pale. M. de F. turns to Verlaine, and speaks in a venomous undertone.

M. de F. There's nothing more contemptible than a man who maltreats a woman.

Verlaine Unless it be a man who maltreats two.

He storms out.

Curtain.

SCENE THREE

A small attic room in the Rue de Buci; 7 November 1871.
Rimbaud is lying on a divan and Verlaine is sitting in an armchair.

Verlaine You see, I didn't think it really mattered who I married. I thought anybody would do. Anybody within reason.

Rimbaud I don't know why you wanted to get married in the first place.

Verlaine I was tired of it all. I was living with Mother then. Only because I was too lazy to live by myself and look after myself. She did everything – and to an extent it was all right. I did what I liked and only went home to sleep or to eat or to change. But in the end it began to wear me down, the office was so boring and home was so boring, and I started to drink more and more and I had to keep slipping off to the brothel, things got worse and worse. Day after day I'd wake up fully clothed, covered with mud or with all the skin off my knuckles, feeling sick and nursing a dim memory of $3\frac{1}{2}$ minutes with some horrible tart who hadn't even bothered to take her shoes off.

This can't go on, I said.

It has to stop.

One day I went round to see Sivry, who was doing the music for a farce I was going to write and as he was showing me up to his room we passed through the Mautés main room, you know, and there she was, standing with her back to us, looking out of the window. I think we startled her because she turned round very quickly. I was stunned, she was so beautiful. She was wearing a grey and green dress and she stood in the window with the sun going down behind her. Sivry said, had I met his half-sister, Mathilde, and I said, no, unfortunately I hadn't. So he introduced me and said I was a poet and she smiled and said how nice, she was very fond of poets.

I tell you, that was it.

A week later, I was in Arras, I woke up in bed with the most grisly scrubber you can imagine, sweaty she was, snoring, I was trying to tiptoe away when she woke up and called me back.

I went back.

Later on that morning I wrote to Sivry and told him I wanted to marry Mathilde.

I thought she was ideal. Plenty of money. Well enough brought up to have all the wifely virtues. Innocent.

Beautiful. Sixteen. She would look after me. And be there every night in my bed.

I had to wait over a year before I could have her. It was agony. Delicious. I used to go there every evening and look at her. When the wedding was put off for the third time, I practically went berserk. And when it finally took place, I couldn't believe it. I felt giddy all day.

The next few months were marvellous, you know. I didn't care about the war, the Prussians could do what they liked as far as I was concerned. I was otherwise engaged. I can't tell you how wonderful it was. It was a kind of legalized corruption. She was impossibly coy at first, she didn't like it, she didn't understand it, it hurt. And then slowly she began to take to it, she relaxed, she became . . . inventive. And then one night, when I was very tired, she suggested it.

Silence.

Rimbaud And now you have a son.

Verlaine And now I have a son.

Silence.

Rimbaud What happened last night, anyway?

Verlaine Well, I . . . can't remember it very clearly. As you know I wasn't quite myself when I left you last night. My idea was to go to bed with her, as I think I mentioned to you.

Rimbaud Many times.

Verlaine Yes, well I thought, it's a week since the child was born, it ought to be all right by now. I said I'd be careful, but, I mean, it's been such a long time. Anyway, it was no good, she wouldn't.

Rimbaud So what happened?

Verlaine I don't know, God knows.

Rimbaud Did you hit her again?

Verlaine No, no, not this time. I woke up, as in Arras, with my boots on the pillow, and tiptoed away. But she didn't call me back.

Rimbaud So you're still frustrated?

Verlaine nods. Silence.

Why don't you leave her?

Verlaine What?

Rimbaud Leave her.

Verlaine Why?

Rimbaud Because she's no good to you.

Verlaine What do you mean?

Rimbaud Do you love her?

Verlaine Yes, I suppose so.

Rimbaud Have you got anything in common with her?

Verlaine No.

Rimbaud Is she intelligent?

Verlaine No.

Rimbaud Does she understand you?

Verlaine No.

Rimbaud So the only thing she can give you is sex?

Verlaine Well . . .

Rimbaud Can't you find anyone else?

Verlaine I . . .

Rimbaud You're not that fussy, are you?

Verlaine No.

Rimbaud Anyone within reason would do, wouldn't they?

Verlaine Within reason.

Rimbaud What about me?

  Silence. Rimbaud laughs.

Are you a poet?

  Silence. Verlaine smiles uneasily.

Verlaine (*cautiously*) Yes.

Rimbaud I'd say not.

Verlaine Why?

Rimbaud Well, I hope you wouldn't describe that last volume of pre-marital junk as poetry?

Verlaine I most certainly would. Very beautiful love poetry, that is.

Rimbaud But you've just admitted that all you wanted to do was to go to bed with her.

Verlaine That doesn't make the poems any less beautiful.

Rimbaud Doesn't it? Doesn't it matter that they're lies?

Verlaine They're not lies. I love her.

Rimbaud Love?

Verlaine Yes.

Rimbaud No such thing.

Verlaine What do you mean?

Rimbaud I mean it doesn't exist. Self-interest exists.

Attachment based on personal gain exists. Complacency exists. But not love. It has to be re-invented.

Verlaine You're wrong.

Rimbaud Well, all right, if you care to describe what binds families and married couples together as love rather than stupidity or selfishness or fear, then we'll say that love does exist. In which case it's useless, it doesn't help. It's for cowards.

Verlaine You're wrong.

Rimbaud When I was in Paris in February this year, when everything was in a state of chaos, I was staying the night in a barracks and I was sexually assaulted by four drunken soldiers. I didn't like it at the time, but when I got back to Charleville, thinking about it, I began to realize how valuable it had been to me. It clarified things in my mind which had been vague. It gave my imagination textures. And I understood that what I needed, to be the first poet of this century, the first poet since Racine or since the Greeks, was to experience everything in my body. I knew what it was like to be a model pupil, top of the class, now I wanted to disgust them instead of pleasing them. I knew what it was like to take communion, I wanted to take drugs. I knew what it was like to be chaste, I wanted perversions. It was no longer enough for me to be one person, I decided to be everyone. I decided to be a genius. I decided to be Christ. I decided to originate the future.

The fact that I often regarded my ambition as ludicrous and pathetic pleased me, it was what I wanted, contrast, conflict inside my head, that was good. While other writers looked at themselves in the mirror, accepted what they saw, and jotted it down, I liked to see a mirror in the mirror, so that I could turn round whenever I felt like it and always find endless vistas of myself.

However, what I say is immaterial, it's what I write that counts.

If you help me, I'll help you.

Verlaine How can I help you?

Rimbaud By leaving your wife. As far as I can see, it's the only hope there is for you. Not only are you unhappy as you are, it's not even doing you any good. What are you going to do, write domestic poetry for the rest of your life? Bringing up baby? Epics of the Civil Service? Or will you be forced, you, Verlaine, to write impersonal poetry? Foolish plays and feeble historical reconstructions? If you leave her and come with me, both of us will benefit. And when we've got as much from one another as we can, we split up and move on. You could even go back to your wife again.

It's just a suggestion, it's up to you.

Verlaine You seem to forget that I have a son now.

Rimbaud On the contrary, that's what makes it so ideal. If you leave your wife now, you won't be leaving her alone. She can spend all her time bringing up her son. That's what my father did, he just upped and left us one day, he couldn't have done a wiser thing. Except he'd left it a bit late.

Verlaine But how would we live?

Rimbaud You've got some money, haven't you?

Verlaine Ah, now I understand. I help you by supporting you, and you help me by renewing my rusty old inspiration. Is that it?

Rimbaud Not altogether.

Verlaine Well, how else are you going to help me, then?

Rimbaud You name it.

Long silence.

Curtain.

SCENE FOUR

The Café du Théâtre du Bobino; 20th December, 1871.
A dinner of the Vilains Bonshommes, a poetry society.
Five of the guests are visible to the audience, arranged in
such a way as to suggest a much larger gathering. At one
end, although placed as if in the centre of the table, is the
featured poet, **Jean Aicard***, a portly and respectable figure,*
now somewhat nervously sorting through his papers. Next
to him is Étienne Carjat*, 43, a dapper figure with a goatee,*
who is talking to **Charles Cros***, 29, a languid dandy with*
frizzy hair and a lugubrious moustache. Next to Cros is
Verlaine, somewhat the worse for drink and, next to him,
Rimbaud, slouched back in his chair and wearing a
battered top hat. The scene opens with two simultaneous
conversations: between Cros and Carjat and between
Rimbaud and Verlaine. In addition, there's the buzz of
general chatter.

Cros The principle is very much like photography. Only
instead of photographing a man's face, you photograph his
voice. Then twenty years later, just as you might open the
photograph album, you simply put the relevant cylinder
into the paleophone and listen to him reading his poem or
singing his song.

Carjat And you think you could invent a machine like
that which worked?

Cros Perfectly possible.

Carjat Why don't you get on with it then?

Cros I don't know. I can't be bothered with all the organization and effort.

Carjat You're an idle bugger.

Cros I'm a man of ideas.

Rimbaud For Christ's sake, let's get the fuck out of here.

Verlaine We can't, he's just about to start reading.

Rimbaud Who?

Verlaine Aicard. Over there.

Rimbaud I don't think I'm going to like his stuff much.

Verlaine You won't, it's dreadful. Best we can hope for is to get a bit of sleep while he's at it.

Rimbaud And another drink. (*He calls offstage.*) Oy! Any chance of another drink?

Carjat What about your colour photographs? How are you doing with them?

Cros There's no money in it.

Carjat (*leaning across to Rimbaud*) Are you interested in photography?

Rimbaud No.

Carjat Only I was wondering how you'd like to be photographed.

Rimbaud Not particularly.

Carjat Because I'd like to photograph you. I find your appearance very striking. You have a very fine bone structure.

Rimbaud Really?

27

Carjat Yes. I don't think much of your poetry, but I love your bone structure.

Rimbaud Why don't you think much of my poetry?

Carjat Well, it's very promising of course. But it seems to me that all that ingenuity is rather marred by . . . well, not exactly a juvenile urge to shock, but something of that sort.

Rimbaud And were you shocked when you read it?

Carjat No, I . . . no, of course not.

Rimbaud Then why should you suppose that I intended you to be?

Carjat Well . . . that's not really the point.

Verlaine Seems fair enough to me.

Carjat I . . . I could object to your technical approach.

Rimbaud I could object to your tie.

Carjat Well, if you're going to take that attitude . . .

Verlaine He doesn't like discussing his poetry.

Carjat I see.

Cros I don't think you're being quite fair to the boy. I like his work. Especially that one about the girl spending the night before her first communion in the lavatory with a candle. My word. Magnificent stuff.

Rimbaud (*coldly*) Thank you.

There is now a general ripple of applause, as Aicard rises to his feet. Cros and Carjat applaud, Verlaine and Rimbaud do not. Cros then turns away from Rimbaud and murmurs to Carjat, as Aicard begins speaking.

Aicard Thank you very much, gentlemen. I should like to

start by reading a poem from a collection I am planning for children.

> *As he continues to speak, Rimbaud fetches a small phial out of his waistcoat pocket and empties the contents into Cros's beer, which immediately begins to bubble and fizz.*

I would ask you to bear in mind that the poem is written expressly for children, although, as with all worthwhile work for children, it is hoped that what is said is not entirely without relevance to adults.

> *Cros turns back to the table, reaches for his beer, lifts it almost to his lips, then does a horrified double-take and puts the glass down hurriedly. He speaks to Rimbaud in an urgent whisper.*

Cros What have you put in it?

Rimbaud Sulphuric acid.

Cros What?

Aicard (*simultaneously*) The poem is called 'Green Absinthe'. (*He clears his throat.*) 'Green Absinthe'.

> *Cros, appalled, continues to stare at Rimbaud, but the latter has turned his attention to Aicard, and bursts into ironic applause.*

'Green absinthe is the potion of the damned . . .'

> *Rimbaud belches.*

'A deadly poison silting up the veins,
While wife and child sit weeping in their slum . . .'

Rimbaud (*distinctly*) I don't believe it.

> *A certain sensation. Aicard soldiers on.*

Aicard 'The drunkard pours absinthe into his brains.'

Rimbaud Shit.

Aicard 'Oh! Drunkard, most contemptible of men . . .'

Rimbaud Shit.

Aicard (*his voice cracking*) 'Degraded, fallen, sinful and obtuse . . .'

Rimbaud It is! It is! Authentic shit!

Aicard 'Degraded, fallen, sinful and obtuse . . .'

Rimbaud I like it.

Aicard You scruple not to beat your wife and child . . .'

Rimbaud For trying to deprive you of the juice.

Pandemonium. Protests, laughter, shouting. Carjat springs to his feet.

Carjat Get out, you!

Silence falls.

Rimbaud Me?

Carjat Yes you, you offensive little bastard. Get out, or I'll throw you out. Who the hell do you think you are?

Rimbaud I think I may, may I not, be permitted to raise some objection against the butchering of French poetry?

Carjat No. You may not. Now apologize and get out.

He moves towards Rimbaud, who rises and grips Verlaine's sword-stick.

Verlaine Careful.

Rimbaud (*to Carjat, grim and pale*) Don't come any nearer.

Carjat If you think you can frighten me with that thing . . .

Rimbaud draws the sword.

(*ends weakly*) . . . you've got another think coming.

Deadlock. They watch each other venomously. Then Carjat attacks, and Rimbaud slashes out at him. Carjat stops, appalled, cries out, grasps his wrist. Blood flows. Chaos.

Verlaine Careful, I said.

Rimbaud (*turning to Aicard, with a great roar*) And now, you.

He bears down on Aicard, who, for a moment is transfixed with horror, before breaking and running for his life.

Miserable poetaster!

He pursues Aicard round the room.

Fucking inkpisser!

He slashes wildly at Aicard who manages to get the table between himself and Rimbaud. Meanwhile Rimbaud is resisting all attempts to disarm him by laying about him at anyone who comes too close.

In the days of François Premier, wise and benevolent giants roamed the countryside. And one, let me tell you, one of their . . . natural functions was to rid the world of pedants, fools and writers of no talent . . . (*he leaps up on to the table*) by . . . by pissing on them from a great height, and . . . and . . .

At this point he passes out, crashing spectacularly to the ground. Verlaine and Cros seize him and hurry out with him.

Curtain

SCENE FIVE

The Café du Rat Mort; 29th June, 1872.

The café is fairly empty. Verlaine and Rimbaud sit at a table, drinking absinthe. Throughout the scene, Rimbaud's behaviour is curious and distant, as if he has been taking hashish or drinking all night. Occasionally he shakes off this air of drugged or drunken fatigue for a time, only to relapse into dreamy contemplation when, for instance, Verlaine speaks at any length.

Rimbaud The first thing he did, it seems, when he was given the ring, a magic ring you understand, was to summon up a beautiful woman, the most beautiful he could imagine. And they were wonderfully happy and lived alone on a light blue southern island. Then one day he explained to her that with the ring he could grant her anything she wanted, and she asked him to build her a city. So he caused a city to grow up out of the sea, full of churches and echoing courtyards, and quite empty. She was so delighted with it that he granted her another wish, and she asked for a ship. So he gave her a magnificent galleon which needed no crew to look after the silk hangings and golden figurehead. It seemed to give her such happiness that he decided to grant her one more wish. 'One more wish,' he said. 'I will grant you one more wish.'

'Give me the ring,' she said.

He gave it to her. She smiled serenely at him and threw it into the sea. At once she disappeared, the ship disappeared, and the city slowly sank back under the water.

For a long time after that the man sat looking out to sea without moving. Finally he began to weep because he understood what he had done and that he would be alone for ever.

That was it. Something like that.

Colour is what's missing, colour. That's what this gives you, thick colours you can smell and hear. Otherwise everything is grey and dull. I want to go somewhere I can get it without this. South. Away from the dusty mantelpiece of Europe. If I may so express myself. (*He chuckles.*)

Let's leave. I've always wanted to see the sea. We can't possibly go on as we are. Can we? I mean . . . I mean, let's leave.

God, my hands are cold.

Can't we leave?

Verlaine Here?

Rimbaud Paris, Paris.

Verlaine Well . . .

Rimbaud We certainly can't go on as we are. It's been dragging on for months as it is. You can't keep sending me home whenever she threatens a divorce and summoning me back when the coast looks clear. What's needed, if . . . (*he blinks, concentrates*) if I may use a crude term I know you find distasteful, is a decision.

Verlaine Ah, decisions . . .

Rimbaud Yes.

Verlaine I always say, show me a decisive man and I'll show you a fool.

Rimbaud Wishful thinking.

Verlaine Anyway, she's not very well at the moment.

Rimbaud I'm not surprised, if you keep setting fire to her.

Verlaine (*indignantly*) I haven't set fire to her since May.

They both laugh.

33

It's not very funny.

They both laugh some more.

Rimbaud It's pathetic. (*He stops laughing, abruptly.*) Pathetic. Your acts of violence are always curiously disgusting.

Verlaine What do you mean?

Rimbaud They're not clean. You're always in a drunken stupor when you commit them. You beat up Mathilde, or hit me, or throw your son against the wall – and then you start apologizing and grovelling.

Verlaine I don't like hurting people.

Rimbaud Then don't. And if you do, do it coolly, and don't insult your victim by feeling sorry for him afterwards.

Silence.

Verlaine I don't think I ever told you about the most terrible of my little tantrums – when I attacked my mother and sisters.

Rimbaud I didn't think you had any.

Verlaine Oh, yes. Like you, I have one brother and two sisters. The difference between mine and yours is that mine are dead.

My mother had three miscarriages before I was born – and being of a rather morbid turn of mind, she kept the results in a cupboard in the bedroom, preserved, ominously enough, in alcohol. There they were, Nicolas, Stéphanie, and Elisa, stacked away on the top shelf in three enormous jars. I'll never forget the first time I came across them, when I was a small boy. I was fooling around in the bedroom, burrowing in the cupboard, which I'd never dared do before, when I saw these great jars. The light was pretty bad and I couldn't make out what was in them at first, so I got a chair and stood on it. I suddenly saw these three little puckered people, lined up, staring at me in a strangely knowing way.

I had no idea what they were. I dimly associated them with preserved plums, and for weeks after that my stomach turned over whenever we had roast.

When I found out they were my own flesh and blood, they assumed a monumental importance in my life. I used to watch Mother dusting them every Thursday, and consult them on all matters of moment. Not that they were very helpful. They remained expressionless and inscrutable at all times, and as the years wore on, I began to detect a certain superciliousness in their attitude, a kind of amused contempt for their younger brother, which came to be very wounding.

The older I got, the more I resented them.

They had a right to be complacent, I thought, because they'd had it very easy and didn't know any better. But they had no right to despise me for being less fortunate than they were. When Mother told me how difficult and dangerous my birth had been, I often felt there had been some terrible mistake and that my place was up there with them in a large glass jar, meditating quietly and being dusted on Thursdays. 'If any of you had lived,' I used to tell them, 'I wouldn't have had to. So it's all your fault.' They looked back at me, smug, sceptical and unblinking. And I envied their peace.

One night only a couple of years ago, I got very drunk indeed. I was really at the bottom of the pit, things couldn't have been blacker. As happens from time to time, I had a nasty attack of the vomits, racking out blood and bits and all the accumulated muck I'd been pouring into myself for years, I wished I was dead, you know how it is, the worst. That's when I get violent. When I see things as they really are.

I went to the cupboard and looked at Nicolas, Stéphanie and Élisa, sitting there comfortably, wise and gloating. And lifted my stick and smashed the jars.

Silence.

Rimbaud And?

Verlaine I remember being saturated in alcohol – and a glimpse of them grotesquely marooned in their broken jars before I passed out. The next day when I looked, they were back, just as before, in identical jars, and Mother never said a word about it. Were it not for the fact that I surprised a look of active dislike on their faces when I next visited them, I'd be inclined to write off the whole incident as a ghastly dream.

Rimbaud Few corpses can have led such eventful lives.

Verlaine laughs, summons the waiter.

Verlaine Two.

Silence.

Rimbaud You have digressed. Strayed from the point.

Verlaine We have all day and all night to get back to it. Whatever it was. Is.

Rimbaud It's time to leave.

Verlaine I've just ordered another drink.

Rimbaud Paris.

Verlaine Oh.

Rimbaud This is the time to go, the summer. We will be children of the sun and live in pagan pleasure. (*He smiles.*) The happiest times of my life were when I ran away from home. Walking through fields in the sun, or sheltering in a wood, sleeping under hedges, ham sandwich and a beer for supper, I just carried on until I had no money left, and even then it didn't seem to matter. I've never known such long and coloured days. Only I never got far enough. I wanted to follow a river to the sea, or walk to Africa and cross a desert. I wanted heat and violence of landscape.

But what I didn't have on those days often added to their harmony.

Verlaine (*a trace of irony*) It sounds idyllic.

Rimbaud It was. Much more idyllic than that filthy little room where I sleep when you're making love to Mathilde, and don't sleep when you're making love to me.

Verlaine You do sleep. I often watch you sleeping.

Rimbaud You often wake me up. (*Pause.*) Isn't it time you left Mathilde?

Verlaine Why? I love her.

Rimbaud You can't possibly.

Verlaine I love her body.

Rimbaud There are other bodies.

Verlaine That's not the point. I love Mathilde's body.

Rimbaud But not her soul?

Verlaine I think it's less important to love the soul than to love the body. After all, the soul may be immortal, we have plenty of time for the soul: but flesh rots.

Rimbaud laughs.

Do you find that amusing?

Rimbaud Not really.

Verlaine If people laugh at flesh it is because they do not

37

love its textures, or its shape and smell, as I do. Or its sadness.

Rimbaud (*coldly*) Quite possibly.

Verlaine It is my love of flesh which makes me faithful.

Rimbaud Faithful? What do you mean?

Verlaine It's possible to be faithful to more than one person. I'm faithful to all my lovers, because once I love them, I will always love them. And when I am alone in the evening or the early morning, I close my eyes and celebrate them all.

Rimbaud That's not faithfulness, it's nostalgia. If you don't want to leave Mathilde, it's not because you're faithful, it's because you're weak.

Verlaine If strength involves brutality, I prefer to be weak.

Rimbaud With you, weakness involves brutality as well. (*Pause.*) Don't expect me to be faithful to you.

Verlaine I don't.

Silence.

Rimbaud I'm leaving Paris next week. You can come with me or not, as you like.

Verlaine Where are you going?

Rimbaud I don't know. Just away. Are you coming?

Verlaine I . . .

Rimbaud Or are you staying with Mathilde?

Verlaine I don't know. The thought of losing either of you is unbearable. I don't know. Why are you so harsh with me?

Rimbaud Because you need it.

Verlaine Why? Isn't it enough for you to know that I love you more than I've ever loved anyone, and that I always will love you?

Rimbaud Shut up, you snivelling drunk.

Verlaine Tell me if you love me.

Rimbaud Oh, for God's sake . . .

Verlaine Please.

Silence.

Please. It's important to me.

Rimbaud Why?

Verlaine Please.

Silence.

Rimbaud I . . . you know I'm very fond of you . . . we've been very happy sometimes . . . I . . .

A very long silence. Rimbaud blushes deeply. He produces a large knife from his pocket, and picks at the table with it.

(*Almost inaudibly*) Do you love me?

Verlaine What?

Rimbaud Do you love me?

Verlaine (*puzzled*) Yes.

Rimbaud Then put your hands on the table.

Verlaine What?

Rimbaud Put your hands on the table.

Verlaine does so.

Palm upwards.

Verlaine turns his hands palm upwards. Rimbaud looks at them for a moment, and then with short, brutal hacks, stabs at both of them. Verlaine sits looking at his hands in amazement, as blood begins to drip down on to the floor.

The only unbearable thing is that nothing is unbearable.

Verlaine stares uncomprehendingly at him, then gets up and stumbles out of the café. Rimbaud watches him leave, then gets up himself and hurries out after him.

Curtain.

SCENE SIX

A room in the Hôtel Liégeois, Brussels; 22nd July, 1872.
Verlaine is lying half-in and half-on the rumpled bed. Mathilde stands with her back to the audience, getting dressed.

Verlaine That was wonderful, darling.

Silence.

Wonderful.

Mathilde Can you pass me my stockings? (*She indicates the chair by the bed, where they are neatly arranged.*)

Verlaine Why don't you come and lie down and relax for a bit? You don't have to get dressed right away, do you?

Mathilde It's getting late.

Verlaine Nonsense, it's only about half-past eight.

Mathilde Someone might come.

Verlaine Who?

Mathilde Mummy.

Verlaine I thought you weren't meeting her till lunch. Anyway, we're married aren't we, for God's sake?

Mathilde walks over to the chair, picks up her stockings, sits down on the bed, and starts to put then on.

Do you remember . . .

He leans forward and strokes her hair, then turns her face to him and kisses her. She submits briefly, and, it seems, without enthusiasm to his embrace.

. . . happier times?

Mathilde Yes. (*She continues dressing.*) Are you coming back to Paris with me?

Verlaine I . . . don't know.

Mathilde Why don't you want to?

Verlaine I do want to, it's just . . . it's just I don't think it's safe in Paris any more. I mean . . . I mean they're still arresting people connected with the Commune. Look what happened to Sivry. Four months in jail for practically no reason at all. And who gave him his job? I did. I had a very important job, you know. I was virtually in charge of the propaganda press.

Mathilde I know, but that was over a year ago.

Verlaine The police are slow, but methodical. They don't forgive and forget. I couldn't stand going to jail. (*Pause.*) That's why I think it's better if I play it safe and stay out of the country for a few months.

Mathilde With Rimbaud.

Verlaine Well . . .

Mathilde I suppose he's wanted by the police too.

Verlaine Er . . .

Mathilde Why don't you want to come back?

Verlaine I . . .

Mathilde Why do you prefer him to me?

Verlaine I don't, love, I don't. (*Pause.*) It's just . . . I'll tell you what it is. I can't stand living with your parents any more. I will not be pushed around by that stupid old man. I can't understand what makes you want to stay there.

Mathilde Because . . . because it's not safe anywhere else.

Verlaine What do you mean?

Mathilde You know what I mean.

Silence.

Verlaine It's only when I've been drinking, dear. It's only when I'm drunk, and it all becomes too much for me. It's only when things are impossible. You know I don't mean it.

Mathilde At the time you mean it.

Silence.

You know . . . you know Daddy wants me to get a divorce?

Verlaine I've told you before . . .

Mathilde He says if you go away with Rimbaud, you're deserting me and I can get a divorce. He says . . .

Verlaine (*shouting*) It's nothing to do with him. It's me you're married to, not him. (*more calmly*) Do you want a divorce?

Mathilde No. (*She begins to cry soundlessly, her body shaking with sobs.*)

Verlaine Don't cry, love. (*He puts his arms round her, and soothes her.*) That's better.

Mathilde Are you going to come with me?

Verlaine I don't know, love, I . . .

Mathilde Not home, I don't mean home, I mean abroad.

Verlaine Abroad?

Mathilde Yes, I had this idea, I thought of this idea, don't be angry. I thought we might . . . emigrate. To . . . Canada.

Verlaine Canada?

Mathilde Or New Caledonia. There are quite a lot of our friends out there, you know, Rochefort and Louise Michel, and I thought, as you said you wanted to write a book about the Commune, they might be able to help. And I've heard it's lovely out there, the country and the forests, and we could try again.

Verlaine What about the baby?

Mathilde Well, that's up to you, but I thought, if you wanted to that is, we could leave him behind, I mean, Mummy would be only too pleased to look after him for a couple of years, or however long . . . we wanted to stay.

Verlaine It's a nice idea . . .

Mathilde It's the best thing we could do, Paul. You could write, and be quiet, and . . . and it'd be like it was when we were first married, and . . .

Verlaine What?

Mathilde Doesn't matter.

Verlaine No, go on.

Mathilde Well, I . . . was only going to say you could stop . . . it would be easy for you . . . if you wanted to . . . stop drinking.

Verlaine You're frightened of me, aren't you?

Mathilde doesn't answer, Verlaine puts his arms round her again.

I do love you, you know. (*He kisses her.*) Don't think I like getting drunk. I mean I do like getting drunk, but I don't like being drunk. Or anyway . . . when I hit you or . . . do any of the things I do, I feel so terrible about it the next day, the only thing I can think of is to get drunk again and forget about it. I can't stop, there's no end to it. I'm not angry with you, when you mention it. Most of the time I want to give it up as much as you want me to. But it's as difficult as deciding to wake up when you're asleep.

Perhaps I could wake up out there. That's what I want most, you know, it's what I really want most. I want to live quietly, and work hard and well, and make love to you, and have children, would that be possible do you think? It should be easy, do you think it's possible?

Mathilde Yes, it's possible.

Verlaine Can you see us, can you see us living in a log cabin, or whatever they have?

Mathilde Why not?

Verlaine Then let's go, for Christ's sake, let's go. Before it's too late.

Mathilde We can go whenever you like.

Verlaine God, I love you.

He kisses her again, a long, clinging kiss, at the end of which he begins to undress her. She pulls away from him.

44

Mathilde No, not now.

Verlaine Why not?

She doesn't answer, attending to her clothes. Verlaine sits up and touches her shoulder.

Come on.

Mathilde No.

Verlaine Why not?

Mathilde I'm very tired. I've been in the train all night, and I didn't sleep very well.

Verlaine Please.

Mathilde Look, I'm supposed to be meeting Mummy for breakfast, and I'm late already. Why don't you get dressed and come with me?

Verlaine I don't want breakfast, I want you.

Mathilde There'll be other times.

Verlaine Will there?

Mathilde Well, of course. Help me with this, will you?

Verlaine helps her into her stern, billowing dress.

Verlaine What's this meeting Mummy for breakfast?

Mathilde I promised to. I think she hopes you'll come too.

Verlaine Tell her I don't feel like breakfast today.

Mathilde Can I tell her it's all right about Canada?

Verlaine What's it got to do with her?

Mathilde Well, she's got to be told, hasn't she?

Verlaine Now?

Mathilde Well, it *is* all right, isn't it?

Verlaine I . . . don't know.

Mathilde But, you just said . . .

Verlaine I know, I know what I said.

Silence.

Mathilde If it's money you're worrying about, Daddy's already said he'll pay the fare . . . (*She stops dead, realizing that she has made a bad mistake.*)

Verlaine What?

Mathilde Nothing.

Verlaine What did you say?

Mathilde Nothing.

Verlaine Go on, you'd better go and have breakfast. You can tell her it's all right.

Mathilde Can I really?

Verlaine Yes.

Mathilde That's wonderful.

Verlaine Here. Give us a kiss.

She does so.

Now, off you go.

Mathilde 'Bye.

Verlaine Good-bye.

Exit Mathilde. Verlaine gets dressed, sunk in reflection. Suddenly Rimbaud walks in. He takes in the situation at a glance.

Rimbaud I see.

Verlaine What are you doing here?

Rimbaud Nice, was it? A scene of conjugal bliss? I thought she looked a bit flushed.

Verlaine How did you get here?

Rimbaud I waited until she came down, and went up.

Verlaine How did you know which room?

Rimbaud I was with you when you booked it.

Verlaine Oh, yes.

Silence.

Rimbaud Well, aren't you going to tell me all about it? You don't usually spare me the hideous details. What about those thighs, paradoxically both moist and silken? What recondite position did you you adopt this time?

Verlaine I think you'd better go.

Rimbaud Oh, I will. I'm more interested in what the position is than in what it was. Just explain it to me, and then I'll go.

Verlaine Well, look, not here, she might come back. Let's . . .

Rimbaud No. I want to hear it from you now, and I want you honest and I want you sober. The alternatives are simple. Either you stay in Brussels with me, in which case you send Mathilde back to Paris. Or you go back to Paris with Mathilde, in which case you will kindly leave me some money so that I can get back to France if I want to. That's all. Choose.

Silence.

Choose.

Verlaine I'm going back to Paris with Mathilde.

Rimbaud Right. (*He moves over to the door.*)

Verlaine Wait. Wait a minute. Give me a chance to explain.

Rimbaud Why should I? I don't need an explanation. I'm not going to waste my time trying to dissuade you, if that's what you want. It's your decision, you made it.

Verlaine Listen, don't go. I just want to explain it to you. Sit down a minute.

Rimbaud remains standing, but moves a little nearer to the centre of the stage.

Rimbaud She might come back.

Verlaine Never mind that. It doesn't matter.

Rimbaud smiles and slumps into a chair.

Well, she . . . she suggested that we emigrate. To Canada.

Rimbaud Did she?

Verlaine Yes.

Rimbaud Ah.

Verlaine Don't you think it's a good idea.

Rimbaud No.

Verlaine Why not? What difference does it make? Look, it's a chance for me. We've got friends out there, it'd be a quiet life, I could write and relax and stop drinking . . .

Rimbaud Leave behind all the bad influences of Europe . . .

Verlaine (*after a pause*) Yes. Enjoy the country . . .

Rimbaud Clean living. Back to Rousseau. The noble

48

savage. Paul and Mathilde and their dog Fidèle. Man against the elements. Her idea, was it?

Verlaine Yes.

Rimbaud Or Daddy's? Nefarious Daddy's?

Verlaine You don't care about my happiness, do you?

Rimbaud No, and neither should you.

Silence.

Verlaine I know I said I'd send her back. But you've never been able to understand how much I love her. She's so beautiful. I came in, this morning, I walked in without knocking and she was lying there, naked, on the bed. She looked so beautiful when I came in, she looked so young and confused . . .

He breaks off. Rimbaud is laughing helplessly.

Verlaine What's the matter?

Rimbaud Was she really lying naked on the bed when you arrived?

Verlaine Yes.

Rimbaud I like that, that's marvellous.

Verlaine What do you mean?

Rimbaud My estimation for her goes up a long way.

Verlaine Why?

Rimbaud For realizing what was required, and providing it.

Verlaine You are a cynical bastard. She was resting after the journey. She didn't know what time I was arriving.

Rimbaud Is she in the habit of lying about the place with no clothes on?

Verlaine No. (*Pause.*) Look, what does it matter, anyway?

Rimbaud It doesn't. (*Pause.*) She's your wife, you love her, go back to her. (*He gets up.*)

Verlaine Christ, I don't know what to do.

Silence. Rimbaud begins moving towards the door.

What do you think?

Rimbaud I think it's time I went. I think it's up to you.

Verlaine God.

Rimbaud I shall await your decision in the hotel.

Verlaine Don't go.

Rimbaud (*smiles*) Perhaps a few drinks would make the whole situation seem a bit clearer.

Exit Rimbaud. The light fades on Verlaine, who sits, staring morosely in front of him.

Curtain.

Act Two

SCENE ONE

Verlaine's Voice   How many night hours have I watched beside his dear sleeping body, wondering why he wanted so much to escape from reality. There never was a man with such an aim. I could see – let alone the effect on him – that he might be a serious danger to society. Did he perhaps know secrets *to change life*? No, he's only looking for them, I told myself. His kindness is enchanted. I am its prisoner.

> *During this the lights go up on a large Georgian room converted into a bed-sitting room at 34–5, Howland Street, London; 24th November, 1872.*
> *Verlaine is sitting at the table, writing a letter. Rimbaud is lying on or in the bed, reading, jotting down the odd note in an exercise book. The conversation is disjointed and sporadic, the atmosphere domestic.*

Rimbaud   What's your greatest fear?

Verlaine   Mm?

Rimbaud   I said what's your greatest fear?

Verlaine   I don't know. I wouldn't like to mislay my balls. (*He continues writing.*) Why, what's yours?

Rimbaud   That other people will see me as I see them.

> *Silence.*

What time is it they open?

Verlaine   Not till one o'clock. Ludicrous bloody country.

Rimbaud   I hate Sundays.

Verlaine Nothing but warm beer you have to drink standing up. What is it makes them so bloody respectable? Even the beggars have shiny shoes.

Rimbaud I've always hated Sundays. Even in Charleville I hated them. We used to march off to High Mass, like a . . . crocodile of penguins. First, Vitalie and Isabelle. Then, Frédéric and I. And bringing up the rear, Mother Rimbaud, the mouth of darkness. People used to point us out. She made us hold hands.

I've always felt, contrary to all evidence, that about five o'clock on Sunday evening must have been the time Christ died.

Silence.

Verlaine Chuck us a pear.

Rimbaud does so.

Shall I give Lepelletier your love?

Rimbaud No.

Silence.

I love this language. 'To put a spurt on',
'to lick the dust', 'to test the bottom of a dog'.
What do you suppose that means?

Verlaine It's what they have to do before they make their, what's it called, ox-tail soup. (*He picks up a bit of paper, reads.*) 'William George of Castle Street offers a large and varied selection of French letters.' Are we going to listen to George Odger this afternoon?

Rimbaud Who?

Verlaine George Odger, republican. (*He reads from a leaflet.*) '. . . will speak at Hyde Park on behalf of the discharged and imprisoned constables.'

Rimbaud Doesn't sound very interesting to me.

Verlaine At least it's free.

Silence. Rimbaud lights his pipe.

We're very short at the moment, you know.

Rimbaud So you keep saying.

Verlaine Don't you think it's time we took a job?

Rimbaud I've told you before, I'm not going to take a job. I've got better things to do with my time.

Verlaine I mean just a part-time teaching job or something?

Rimbaud No. There's nothing to stop you getting a job if you want to.

Verlaine I don't want to, I have to.

Rimbaud Well, I don't have to. Anyway . . . I'm not staying here much longer.

Verlaine Really?

Rimbaud It's best if I leave you for a bit.

Verlaine Why?

Rimbaud Look, do you want a divorce from Mathilde or not?

Verlaine Of course not.

Rimbaud Well, you're going to get one. They can give her one on desertion, you know, let alone desertion and sodomy.

Verlaine I know that.

Rimbaud I don't want to get mixed up in it.

Verlaine That's why it's better if you stay here. I mean, if you leave now, it'll be an admission of guilt, won't it? Obviously. The only answer is to bluff it out.

That's why I've told Lepelletier that if Mathilde's father likes we're ready to submit to a medical examination.

Rimbaud Are you mad?

Verlaine No, look, I've phrased it delicately . . .

Rimbaud What have you said?

Verlaine (*reads from the letter*) Rimbaud and I are quite prepared, if necessary, to let the whole gang of them look up our arses.

Rimbaud Suppose he takes you up on it?

Verlaine He won't.

Rimbaud I'm leaving next week.

Verlaine He couldn't possibly.

Rimbaud You don't think he made this accusation because he was looking for a way to liven up the long winter evenings, do you? He made it because he knows.

Verlaine Nonsense, it was a theatrical gesture.

Rimbaud You always judge people from a literary standpoint, which means that your assessment of their motives is usually inaccurate.

Verlaine Anyway, it's him that's in the wrong. How many times have I asked for my things back from that house, and he's still got them there.

Rimbaud You're in the wrong.

Verlaine (*suddenly coldly angry*) All right, I'm in the wrong, if you say so, then that's established, isn't it? Now perhaps you'll let me get on and finish my letter.

Silence. Verlaine writes for a while.

Rimbaud I shall leave next week.

Verlaine We'll discuss it later, shall we?

Rimbaud I doubt it.

Verlaine signs his letter with a flourish.

Verlaine Course it won't go today, even if I post it. The post is terrible in this country.

Rimbaud Are they open yet?

Verlaine Are we going to listen to Mr Odger?

Rimbaud Drinks first.

Verlaine Just a minute, I must line my stomach first. (*He pours himself a glass of milk and drinks.*) Ugh. It's horrrible. Want some?

Rimbaud shakes his head. Verlaine goes over to the window.

It's foggy. (*He puts on his overcoat, then wraps his long red scarf carefully round his mouth.*) The old nosebleed. (*He stuffs cotton wool in his ears and speaks as he does so, his voice muffled by his scarf.*) One evening, I set out to assassinate Napoléon III. I was rather drunk and I decided things had gone far enough. Unfortunately I never managed it.

They smile at each other with some tenderness.

Curtain.

SCENE TWO

8, *Great College Street, London; 2nd July, 1873.*
Drabber, anonymous bed-sitter. Verlaine is opening a bottle of wine, Rimbaud is lying on his bed, doing nothing.

Verlaine Any chance of you moving about at all today?

Rimbaud I've always liked the autumn.

Verlaine It's supposed to be summer. Not that you can tell the difference in England.

Rimbaud How long have we been in this hole?

Verlaine Not more than five weeks.

Rimbaud God, life will never end.

Verlaine pours wine into two glasses and takes one over to Rimbaud.

Verlaine A lot can happen in five weeks.

Rimbaud A lot can happen in ten minutes. But it rarely does.

Verlaine When I got married . . .

Rimbaud I thought you weren't going to mention that again.

Verlaine I was only . . .

Rimbaud Well, don't.

Verlaine I'm sorry.

Rimbaud More.

Verlaine goes over and pours him out some more wine.

Verlaine There have been good times, though, haven't there? I mean, we have been happy.

Rimbaud When?

Verlaine You know. Even you must grudgingly admit we've been happy sometimes.

Rimbaud I've told you before, I'm too intelligent to be happy.

Verlaine I remember you telling me once, when we were trying to get some sleep in a ditch in Belgium, that you'd never been so happy in your life.

Rimbaud Kindly spare us another bout of your lying and utterly revolting nostalgia.

Verlaine Why do you take such pleasure in being unhappy?

Rimbaud I assure you I get no more pleasure from pain than I do from pleasure.

Verlaine You've become perversely addicted to pessimism.

Rimbaud More.

Verlaine Get it yourself.

Rimbaud You're getting a bit assertive in your old age.

Her gets up to pour himself some more wine. Verlaine wanders over to the window.

Verlaine It's still raining.

Silence.

You're right about old age. I shall be thirty next birthday. Thirty. What a horrible thought.

Rimbaud Disgusting.

Verlaine And you're getting on. Nearly nineteen.

Rimbaud I begin to despair.

Verlaine Why?

Rimbaud When I was young and golden and infallible, I saw the future with some clarity. I saw the failings of my predecessors and saw, I thought, how they could be avoided. I knew it would be difficult, but I thought that all I needed was experience, and I could turn myself into the philosopher's stone, and create new colours and new flowers, new languages and a new God, and everything to gold. Thou shalt, I said to myself, adopting the appropriate apocalyptic style, be reviled and persecuted as any prophet, but at the last thou shalt prevail.

But before long I realized it was impossible to be a doubting prophet. If you are a prophet you may be optimistic or pessimistic as the fancy takes you, but you may never be anything less than certain. And I found I had tormented myself and poked among my entrails to discover something that people do not believe, or do not wish to believe, or would be foolish to believe. And with the lyricism of self-pity, I turned to the mirror and said Lord, what shall I do, for there is no love in the world and no hope, and I can do nothing about it, God, I can do no more than you have done, and I am in Hell.

Not that I haven't said all this before.

I have, and clearly a new code is called for. And in these last few weeks when you may have been thinking, I've just been lying here in a state of paralysed sloth, you've actually been quite right. But bubbling beneath the surface and rising slowly through the layers of indifference has been a new system. Harden up. Reject romanticism. Abandon rhetoric. Get it right.

And now I've got it right and seen where my attempt to conquer the world has led me.

Verlaine Where?

Rimbaud Here. My search for universal experience has led me here. To lead an idle, pointless life of poverty, as the minion of a bald, ugly, ageing, drunken lyric poet, who clings on to me because his wife won't take him back.

Silence. At first Verlaine is too astonished to speak.

Verlaine How can you bring yourself to say a thing like that?

Rimbaud It's easy. It's the truth. You're here, living like this, because you have to be. It's your life. Drink and sex and a kind of complacent melancholy and enough money to soak yourself oblivious every night. That's your limit. But I'm here because I choose to be.

Verlaine Oh, yes?

Rimbaud Yes.

Verlaine And why exactly?

Rimbaud What do you mean, why?

Verlaine Why exactly did you choose to come back to London with me? What was the intellectual basis of your choice?

Rimbaud This is a question I repeatedly ask myself.

Verlaine No doubt you regarded it as another stage in your private Odyssey. Only by plunging ever deeper, if I may mix my myths, will you attain the right to graze on the upper slopes of Parnassus.

Rimbaud Your attack is unusually coherent this morning.

Verlaine My theory differs from yours. My theory is that you are like Musset.

Rimbaud What?

Verlaine Rather a provocative comparison, don't you think, in view of your continual attacks on the wretched man?

Rimbaud Explain it.

Verlaine Well, I simply mean that like Musset or one of Musset's heroes, you tried on the cloak of vice, and now it's stuck to your skin. You came back here with me because you wanted to, and because you needed to.

Rimbaud Well now, that's quite original for you, even though you have made your customary mistake.

Verlaine What's that?

Rimbaud Getting carried away by an idea because it's aesthetically plausible rather than actually true.

Verlaine Oh, there are less subtle reasons for your putting up with me.

Rimbaud Such as?

Verlaine Such as the fact that I support you.

Silence.

Rimbaud Your mind is almost as ugly as your body.

Silence. They look at each other. Verlaine struggles with himself for a moment, then, suddenly, his face goes blank and he strides across the stage.

(*uneasily*) Where are you going?

Verlaine To the kitchen. It's lunchtime.

Exit Verlaine. Rimbaud pours himself a drink rather shakily, and swallows it. He seems puzzled. A moment later, Verlaine enters again, carrying in one hand, a herring, and in the other, a bottle of oil. Rimbaud looks at him, then bursts out laughing. Verlaine scarcely responds.

Rimbaud God, you look such a cunt.

Verlaine doesn't answer. Instead, he puts the herring and the bottle of oil down on the table, and strides across the stage, away from the kitchen.

Where are you going?

Exit Verlaine.

Where are you going? (*He looks frightened and vulnerable.*)

   Curtain.

SCENE THREE

A room in the Hôtel de Courtrai, Brussels; 10th July, 1873.
   Rimbaud is packing. He looks tired and rather sad. The door bursts open and Verlaine enters. He is drunk, which in his case means overexcitement and a certain belligerence, rather than incoherence or physical unsteadiness.

Rimbaud Where have you been?

Verlaine Out. I went, I went to the Spanish Embassy again, to see if they would change their minds. But they wouldn't, it's ridiculous, it's bloody ridiculous. I'm willing to fight, I said, and die for your cause, you can't afford to turn away volunteers. But they said they weren't taking on any foreigners. Then, I said, you deserve to lose the bloody war, and I hope you do.

Rimbaud And were you at the Spanish embassy all morning?

Verlaine No.

Rimbaud You're drunk.

Verlaine I have yes had a few drinks.

   Silence. Verlaine notices that Rimbaud is packing.

What are you doing?

Rimbaud I'm packing.

61

Verlaine Where are you going?

Rimbaud I've told you already, I'm going back to Paris. And if you'll kindly give me some money for the fare, I shall leave this evening.

Verlaine No, listen, listen, we're going back to London.

Rimbaud We are not going back to London.

Verlaine Yes, look, I've been thinking it over this morning, it's by far the best idea.

Rimbaud Then why did you go to the Spanish Embassy?

Verlaine I didn't.

Silence.

Rimbaud I am going back to Paris.

Verlaine It won't happen again, look, I'll never walk out on you again like that, I promise.

Rimbaud No you won't, I'm not giving you the chance. What did you expect me to do on my own in London with no money? Mm? I ran along the quayside shouting for you not to leave me and you just turned your back on me.

Verlaine What was I supposed to do, jump overboard?

Rimbaud Now you want me to forgive and forget.

Verlaine I was very hurt.

Rimbaud I can't think why. God knows, I've said far worse things to you than that. Anyway you really did look a cunt.

Verlaine bridles, then controls himself.

Verlaine Don't go. Just wait another day or two and think it over.

Rimbaud I've thought it over.

Verlaine Or else, what about this, I had another idea this morning. I thought I might go to Paris.

Rimbaud What?

Verlaine I thought I might go to Paris and try to find Mathilde.

Rimbaud (*after considering this*) Well, all right, I don't mind travelling with you.

Verlaine No, no, you would stay here in Brussels.

Rimbaud Are you mad?

Verlaine No, don't you see, it would be absolutely fatal if you came back with me. She'd never take me back.

Rimbaud I doubt she will anyway.

Verlaine Well then, I'll come back to Brussels, and we can go back to London.

Rimbaud You're out of your mind.

Verlaine Do you realize what day it is tomorrow?

Rimbaud Friday.

Verlaine It's my anniversary, it's our third anniversary. And I haven't seen her, my wife, for almost a year. A year ago, here in Brussels, we made love, and I haven't seen her since. And I haven't seen my son for more than a year. She won't answer my letters. Do you know that I wrote to her last week, and told her if she didn't come to Brussels within three days, I'd commit suicide? And she didn't even answer.

Rimbaud Ah, but then you didn't commit suicide.

Verlaine I suppose you think that's funny.

Rimbaud No, it's pitiful. How many people did you write and tell you were going to commit suicide? I'm surprised you didn't send out invitations.

Verlaine How can you be so callous?

Rimbaud Callous? You abandon me in London and then summon me to Brussels and expect me to hang about while you decide whether you're going to go back to your wife, join the army, or shoot yourself. Then, when you fail to achieve any of these aims, as you undoubtedly will, you want me to go back to London again.

I'm not going to. It's all over. I'm leaving you.

Verlaine You can't. You can't. (*Paces up and down for a moment.*) Where's mother?

Rimbaud Next door, I suppose, in her room. I asked her to let me have some money, but she wouldn't give it to me until you came back. I'll go and ask her again.

Verlaine No, no, wait a minute. Look, I'll give you the money. I just want to talk to you a minute. (*He paces up and down, smiles nervously at Rimbaud.*) Hot, isn't it?

I think we can start again. I don't think it would be too difficult to go back to the beginning. I know it's my fault, all the trouble we've had recently, but it's only because of Mathilde, because I still loved Mathilde. It's finished with her now, I know I shall never see her again. Look, it's summer. Don't you remember last summer, when we set out, how wonderful it was? I remember evenings . . . There's no need to go back to London if you don't want to. We could go south. Late summer on the Mediterranean, we could live more cheaply there, we wouldn't need to work, we could dedicate ourselves to warmth. Or Africa, we could go to North Africa, I know you've always wanted to go to Africa. Just for a month and then make up your mind.

Look at the sun.

Long silence.

Rimbaud No.

Verlaine Why not?

Rimbaud (*gently*) I can't. It's no good. It's too late.

Verlaine No, it's not. I promise you it's not. You know if you leave me, you'll kill me. I can't bear to be alone. I don't exist without someone else. I don't care if you stay with me out of pity, as long as you stay.

Rimbaud I can't.

Verlaine Why not? What more can I say to make you stay? Don't you care? Have you no idea of what this means to me?

Rimbaud Oh, for God's sake, stop whining.

Silence. Verlaine goes over to look out of the window. He mops his brow with a handkerchief.

Verlaine It's very hot.

Rimbaud I should take your coat off.

Verlaine I will. (*He slips his coat off, walks over to the door, and hangs it up.*) I did some shopping this morning. (*He takes something out of his pocket, and turns towards Rimbaud.*) I bought a gun. (*He points a revolver at Rimbaud.*)

Rimbaud What for?

Verlaine For you. And for me. For everybody.

Rimbaud I hope you bought plenty of ammunition.

Verlaine moves a chair in front of the door, and sits astride it, pointing the revolver at Rimbaud over the back of the chair. Rimbaud leans against the opposite wall, smiling.

Verlaine I'm not going to let you go, you know.

Rimbaud Well, this is rather an entertaining number. We haven't seen this one before.

Verlaine (*cries out*) I'll kill you!

Rimbaud Oh, pull yourself together.

Silence.

Verlaine Have you forgotten what you said in your letter?

Rimbaud What letter?

Verlaine The letter you wrote me last week, the day after I left you.

Rimbaud It's of no relevance.

Verlaine Oh, yes it is. You apologized. You begged me to come back. You said it was all your fault. You said you loved me. You said it would be all right in the future. You said you were crying as you wrote. I could see your tears on the paper.

Rimbaud Well, I didn't have any money, did I? That was before I thought of pawning your clothes.

Verlaine springs to his feet, shaking with rage. He raises the revolver and fires at Rimbaud, then, apparently stunned at the noise of the retort, fires again into the floor. Rimbaud is clutching at his left wrist, and staring at it in amazement and horror, as the blood pours down over his hand. He shies away, as Verlaine moves towards him.

Verlaine Oh, God, I'm sorry, I didn't mean to.

Rimbaud Look what you've done.

Verlaine I'm sorry, I didn't mean to.

Rimbaud Look.

Verlaine bursts into tears. He tries to give Rimbaud the revolver.

Verlaine Oh, for God's sake, kill me, kill me, shoot me.

Rimbaud What?

Verlaine Shoot me.

Rimbaud How can I, you silly bugger, you've just blown a hole in my hand.

A furious banging at the door and a female voice shouting: 'Paul, Paul' . . . Verlaine drops the revolver. Rimbaud begins to laugh hysterically.

Verlaine Oh God, what have I done?

Rimbaud You missed.

Blackout.

Curtain.

SCENE FOUR

Brussels, 10th–19th July, 1873.
This scene is constructed from fragments of Verlaine's trial. On one side of the stage, Rimbaud lies in bed, his arm in a sling. Verlaine sits on the other side of the stage, in court. The magistrate, **Judge Théodore T'Serstevens,** *and his* **Clerk** *commute from one side of the stage to the other. When the scene opens, the Clerk is taking down Rimbaud's statement.*

Rimbaud . . . When the wound had been dressed, the three of us returned to the hotel. Verlaine asked me continually not to leave him and to stay with him; but I refused to agree and left the hotel about seven o'clock in the evening, accompanied by Verlaine and his mother. Not far from the Place Rouppe, Verlaine went on a few paces ahead, and then turned towards me: I saw him put his hand in his pocket to get his revolver, so I turned and walked away. I met the police officer and told him what had happened to me, and he invited Verlaine to accompany him to the police station.

If Verlaine had let me leave freely, I would have taken no action against him for the wound he inflicted on me . . .

Verlaine . . . I swear to tell the whole truth and nothing but the truth, so help me God and all His saints.

Judge Have you any previous convictions?

Verlaine No.

Judge What is the motive behind your presence in Brussels?

Verlaine I was hoping that my wife might come and join me here, as she had already done so on one occasion since our separation.

Judge I fail to see how the departure of a friend could have cast you into such despair. Did there not exist between you and Rimbaud other relations besides those of friendship?

Verlaine No; this is a suggestion slanderously invented by my wife and her family to harm me; I have been accused of this in my wife's petition for divorce.

Judge Both doctors have testified that on the basis of their examination they are satisfied that you have recently indulged in both active and passive sodomy.

68

Verlaine Yes.

Judge Then do you deny that you are a practising sodomist?

Verlaine The word is sodomite . . .

Pause. The Judge and the Clerk return to the court, where the Clerk reads Rimbaud's final statement, as the lights dim.

Clerk . . . I, the undersigned, Arthur Rimbaud, declare it to be the truth that on Thursday, the 10th inst., at the moment when M. Paul Verlaine fired at me and wounded me slightly in the left wrist, M. Verlaine was in such a complete state of drunkenness, that he had no idea of what he was doing.

I am utterly convinced that there was no criminal premeditation in his action.

I further declare that I am willing to withdraw from any criminal, correctional or civil action against him, and as from today renounce the benefits of any proceedings which may be brought against M. Verlaine by the Public Prosecutor arising from this matter . . .

Judge . . . The accused, Paul-Marie Verlaine, is committed for trial at the criminal court, charged under article 399 of the Penal Code, of grievous bodily harm. The preliminary examination is closed . . .

Clerk (*in the darkness*) Paul-Marie Verlaine, the court finds you guilty of grievous bodily harm and sentences you to a fine of 200 francs and 2 years' imprisonment.

Curtain.

SCENE FIVE

The Black Forest, near Stuttgart; 28th February, 1875.
The curtain goes up on an empty stage. The scene suggests a clearing in a wood by a river. Sounds of laughter offstage. Presently Rimbaud enters, a little better dressed than in previous scenes. It is evening. Moonlight.

Rimbaud This way.

He laughs. Verlaine enters.

When was this, anyway?

Verlaine Earlier this month.

Rimbaud laughs again.

Rimbaud And they threw you out?

Verlaine Certainly not. After a week the Father Superior and I agreed that it wasn't really the life for me.

Rimbaud This'll do. (*He squats down on the ground and lights his clay pipe.*) And what led you to believe that you were cut out to be a Trappist monk?

Verlaine I don't know. Perhaps it was nostalgia for prison. It was terrible coming out, you know, I'd got used to the quiet and the routine, they treated me very well, and I was sober and able to do a lot of good work. Then, when I came out and couldn't even get to see Mathilde's lawyer, let alone Mathilde, I thought the best thing to do might be to . . . withdraw. To a monastery, to live a quiet, simple life with God.

Rimbaud But it turned out to be a teetotal order.

Verlaine I told you I got used to being sober in prison.

Rimbaud I'm pleased to see the situation is not wholly irreversible.

Verlaine Well, tonight is different. Tonight is a celebration. It's really . . . wonderful to see you again. (*Pause.*) After all this time. (*Pause.*) I hope you never thought . . . that I was angry with you.

Rimbaud No.

Verlaine I mean, I know you had no idea that I might get put away for so long, I certainly . . . forgave you for it.

Rimbaud Did you?

Verlaine Oh, yes.

Rimbaud I didn't forgive you.

Verlaine What for?

Rimbaud For missing.

Verlaine laughs uneasily. Silence.

Verlaine It's very pleasant here.

Rimbaud Im Schwarzwald.

Verlaine How is your German?

Rimbaud Flourishing.

Silence.

Verlaine Not very warm, is it?

Rimbaud Why did you come here?

Verlaine What?

Rimbaud I want to know your reason for coming here.

Verlaine Well . . . to see you, of course. I wanted to talk to you, to discuss certain things with you.

Rimbaud You want us to love each other in Jesus, am I right?

Verlaine Well . . .

Rimbaud All right, I'm listening, tell me about it.

Verlaine It's very difficult to talk seriously if you're going to be so aggressive. I've changed, you know.

Rimbaud Go on, talk seriously, never mind what I say. A missionary should be prepared to meet aggression from the unenlightened. Tell me about your conversion. Was it a bit of an occasion? Was there a celestial voice?

Verlaine Recently it occurred to me that your anger and disgust prove how ready you are for conversion. And anyway I often think you do believe in God. Even in the old days, when you used to paint up 'Sod God' in the urinals in Paris, you must have had some faith. You can't blaspheme if you don't believe.

Rimbaud No, you're wrong. You couldn't blaspheme if nobody believed. Your own feelings have nothing to do with it.

Verlaine I just want you to follow my example. The day of my conversion was one of the happiest of my life. It was the day the governor came and told me Mathilde had been granted a legal separation. I lay down and looked at my life, and there was nothing, nothing. It seemed to me the only thing I could do was submit myself to God, and ask Him to forgive me, and help me to face my situation. And He did. I promise you He did.

Rimbaud (*kindly*) Don't let's talk about it any more.

Verlaine Why not?

Rimbaud It's dangerous.

Verlaine But I want you to find some direction to your life. I want God to help you to achieve your aims.

Rimbaud Aims? I have no aims.

Verlaine Well, I mean your writing.

Rimbaud I've stopped writing.

Verlaine What?

Rimbaud I have stopped writing.

Verlaine I don't understand . . .

Rimbaud Well, let me put it another way: I no longer write.

Verlaine Yes, but why not?

Rimbaud Because I have nothing more to say. If I ever had anything to say in the first place.

Verlaine How can you say that?

Rimbaud laughs at Verlaine's unhappy choice of words.

How can you?

Rimbaud Well, as you know, I started life as a self-appointed visionary, and creator of a new literature. But as time wore on, and it took me longer and longer to write less and less, and I looked back at some of the absurdities of my earlier work, at some of the things I thought were so good when I wrote them, I saw it was pointless to go on. The world is too old, there's nothing new, it's all been said. Anything that can be put into words is not worth putting into words.

Verlaine The truth is always worth putting into words.

Rimbaud The truth is too limited to be interesting.

Verlaine What do you mean? – Truth is infinite.

73

Rimbaud If you're referring to the truth that was revealed to you in prison by an angel of the Lord, you may be wrong. After all, what makes you think it's any truer than the rather different views you asserted with equal confidence three years ago?

Verlaine Well, obviously one develops.

Rimbaud And have you developed?

Verlaine Yes.

Long silence.

Rimbaud Then, here in the wilderness, I offer you an archetypal choice – the choice between my body and my soul.

Verlaine What?

Long silence.

Rimbaud Choose.

Verlaine Your body.

Silence.

Rimbaud See, the ninety-eight wounds of Our Saviour burst and bleed.

Verlaine Please.

Rimbaud So you didn't come here to convert me.

Verlaine No.

Rimbaud And the iron glove conceals a velvet hand.

Verlaine moves towards Rimbaud, touches his shoulder.

Don't.

Silence.

74

So God turned out to be a poor substitute for Mathilde and me, suffering, as he does, from certain tangible disadvantages.

Verlaine Surely my sins are a matter for my own conscience.

Rimbaud They would be if you had one.

Verlaine Anyway, why should it worry you?

Rimbaud Because I hate your miserable weakness.

Verlaine Is overcoming my conscience weakness? Or strength?

Rimbaud Don't be absurd.

Silence.

Verlaine But I see no clash between loving God and loving you.

Rimbaud Come on, let's go back.

Verlaine No, listen, I sat in my cell and thought how much love I had in me, and how happy we could be, it should be easy, it should be the easiest thing in the world, why isn't it?

Rimbaud It never worked with us. And it will never work for either of us.

Verlaine Of course it will. Why should you think that? Why are you so destructive?

Rimbaud Probably because I no longer have any sympathy for you.

Verlaine Don't you feel anything for me?

Rimbaud Only a kind of mild contempt.

Verlaine But how can you change like that? How is it possible?

Rimbaud I don't know.

Verlaine I wanted us to go away together.

Rimbaud Yes.

Verlaine What are you going to do?

Rimbaud I'm going to finish learning German. And then I'm going to leave Europe. Alone.

Verlaine What about me?

Rimbaud You'll have to go away and find somebody else.

Verlaine I can't. Please.

He puts his arms round Rimbaud.

Please.

Rimbaud Let me go.

Verlaine clings on to him. Rimbaud speaks, as he has done throughout this last exchange, with great weariness.

Let go.

Verlaine Please.

Rimbaud hits Verlaine hard, stunning him. He hits him again, carefully and methodically, until he collapses in an untidy heap. Rimbaud straightens him out almost tenderly, then stands looking down at him for a moment.

Rimbaud (*quietly*) Good-bye. (*He exits.*)

Curtain.

SCENE SIX

A café in Paris; 29th February, 1892.
  It is early evening and the rather squalid café is not very full. Presently Verlaine enters. He is now 47, but looks much older, a derelict carnal hulk. His clothes are correct, much as they were in the first scene of the play, but worn and shabby. He has a walking-stick, and limps heavily, dragging his left leg behind him. He is accompanied by **Eugénie Krantz**, *who is about fifty and a semi-retired prostitute. Her accent sounds like a crude parody of Rimbaud's.*

Verlaine Evening.

  A few muttered replies. He and Eugénie sit at one of the tables.

Absinthe, please. Two.

  *The **Barman** nods, pours drinks behind the bar.*

God, I'm tired.

Eugénie (*sniggers*) Not surprised.

Verlaine You're beautiful, Eugénie.

Eugénie I know. (*She laughs raucously.*)

Verlaine Don't let anyone tell you different. If I think you're beautiful, then you're beautiful.

  The Barman brings the drinks.

Barman Someone been in to see you this afternoon, M. Verlaine.

Verlaine Who?

Barman A young lady. She didn't leave her name.

Verlaine A young lady?

Barman Well, in her thirties, I suppose. She seemed very keen to see you, so I said you'd be sure to be in later, and she said she'd come back. She said it was quite important.

Verlaine Thanks.

The Barman turns away.

Just a minute . . . What did she look like?

Barman Oh, not bad, monsieur, not bad.

Verlaine Thanks.

Silence.

Eugénie Who is it?

Verlaine What?

Eugénie Who is it?

Verlaine How should I know?

Eugénie It can't be Esther, it's too young for her. So it must be someone else.

Verlaine I told you I haven't seen Esther since I came out of hospital.

Eugénie You told me! Who is it?

Verlaine I don't know.

Silence.

It must be some business matter.

Eugénie Business, eh?

Verlaine Yes. I'd appreciate it if you'd let me talk to her alone when she comes.

Eugénie Oh, charming, that is. Lovely. I'm supposed to go

78

and sit on my own, am I, while you talk to your new girlfriends?

Verlaine I promise you, I don't know who it is, and if it's a business matter, I'd rather talk to her alone.

Eugénie (*a threat*) I shall go and talk to that gentleman over there.

Verlaine Well, you must do as you like.

Eugénie Perhaps he'll turn out a bit more respectful than you are.

Silence.

Verlaine Two more, please.

The Barman comes over, and pours the drinks.

Can you let me have some money, please?

Eugénie Eh?

Verlaine I haven't any money on me.

Eugénie Well, don't ask me for money.

Verlaine Look, Eugénie, I'm not feeling very well, and I don't want to argue with you. Now will you kindly give me some money.

Eugénie You haven't done any work today.

Verlaine I haven't been feeling very well.

Eugénie Well, if you don't do any work, you can't expect to be paid.

Verlaine Look, it's my money.

Eugénie It wouldn't be much longer if I let you get your hands on it.

Verlaine I just want a few . . .

79

Eugénie No.

> *Isabelle Rimbaud enters. She is 31, very respectably dressed in mourning, and already something of an old maid. There is some resemblance between her and her brother, but this is most noticeable when she speaks – with Rimbaud's soft, provincial accent. She goes over and has a word with the Barman, who points out Verlaine to her. He is still arguing with Eugénie in a violent undertone.*

Verlaine Now, listen, Eugénie, if you don't give me some money at once, there'll be trouble, do you understand?

Eugénie I haven't got any money with me. So you'll have to do without, won't you?

Verlaine You're making me very angry.

Eugénie Anyway, here comes your girl-friend, by the look of it. So I'll be leaving you. (*She gets up, then leans forward and speaks in a venomous whisper.*) And if you don't come back tonight, you'll find your things in the street.

> *She leaves him, and while he is speaking to Isabelle, she joins one of the men sitting at a table at the back of the stage. Verlaine rises, turns to meet Isabelle.*

Isabelle (*tentatively*) M. Verlaine?

Verlaine At your service, mademoiselle.

Isabelle I am Isabelle Rimbaud.

Verlaine Pardon? (*He sinks into his chair.*)

Isabelle I am Isabelle Rimbaud. I am M. Arthur Rimbaud's sister.

Verlaine Of course, er, of course, please sit down, mademoiselle. You must excuse me for being so rude, but I find it difficult to stand.

Isabelle sits.

I heard, we heard the tragic news a couple of months ago. I could hardly believe it, he was so young. And then, he'd been reported dead before, you know, earlier. I was deeply . . . affected by his death, although I hadn't seen him for so long.

Isabelle I didn't know whether you'd heard.

Verlaine Is it true . . . is it true he had to have his leg amputated?

Isabelle Yes.

Silence.

I'll get straight to the point, M. Verlaine, I don't have very much time.

Verlaine You look a bit like him, you know. Your eyes . . . are not unlike his.

Isabelle So I've been told.

Verlaine Would you like a drink?

Isabelle No thank you very much. It's really a business matter I want to discuss with you. M. Vanier said you might be able to help me.

Verlaine Well, I'll do what I can.

Isabelle On the day my brother died, a volume of his poems was published in Paris, wasn't it?

Verlaine You mean *The Reliquary*?

Isabelle That's right. The publication was completely unauthorized, and there was an anonymous preface full of the most outrageous and libellous statements, which claimed to be a biography of my brother. My mother and I were very upset by it.

Verlaine Yes, well, er, I believe M. Genonceaux is the man you should see about this. He's the editor.

Isabelle I know. I haven't been able to get hold of M. Genonceaux.

Verlaine Anyway, the book's now been withdrawn from circulation.

Isabelle I know. But my mother and I are anxious to prevent anything like this from happening again. And M. Vanier said you might be able to help us.

Verlaine I? How?

Isabelle Well, I understand you have a large number of my brother's manuscripts.

Verlaine I have . . . some, yes.

Isabelle My mother and I would be very grateful if you'd return them.

Silence.

Verlaine I've always . . . used the utmost discretion in everything concerning your brother. I think I can say that I've always defended his interests. Since his name began to be well known, various newspapers and magazines have printed forgeries, you know, and I've made myself responsible for putting a stop to it and making sure that everything that comes out under his name is his work. I'm quite fanatical about it, it's very important to me. We did our best work when we were together, you know, both of us. Since then, as far as I'm concerned, it's all been just one long footnote.

Isabelle I didn't know his name was all that well known.

Verlaine Oh, yes.

Isabelle That makes it even more vital that we collect up

82

all his manuscripts. Perhaps I should explain our intentions to you. Did you know he was converted before he died?

Verlaine Converted?

Isabelle Yes. I reasoned with him and prayed for him for weeks while he was ill and about a fortnight before he died, he asked to be confessed. After that, we prayed together every day, and the chaplain said that he had never encountered faith as strong as Arthur's. Do you know, in spite of the tragic circumstances, the day Arthur asked for the chaplain was one of the happiest of my life.

Verlaine So he took the last Sacraments?

Isabelle No, unfortunately they weren't able to give him communion, because he couldn't keep anything down, and they were afraid there might be an involuntary sacrilege. But I know his soul was saved.

Verlaine (*without irony*) That must be a great comfort.

Isabelle Yes. Anyway, you'll appreciate now how important it is for my mother and I to get hold of his writings.

Verlaine Er . . .?

Isabelle The point is, M. Verlaine, to speak frankly, a number of the poems he wrote in extreme youth were rather . . . indecent, and in some cases even profane. He would never have wished to be remembered for them. My mother and I plan to as it were separate the wheat from the tares, and destroy those of his works which we feel he would have destroyed himself.

Verlaine I see.

Isabelle We were amazed, in fact, that the poems in *The Reliquary* were thought to be worthy of publication. We supposed that they could only have been published for motives of profit. I'd be very interested to know who pocketed the author's royalties.

Verlaine (*guiltily*) Yes . . . well, er, I couldn't tell you.

Isabelle Here's my mother's card. Perhaps you could send the manuscripts to this address.

Verlaine As a matter of fact, Vanier and I were planning an edition of Rimbaud's complete works.

Isabelle Yes, M. Vanier told me.

Verlaine Well, don't you think that there's . . . a place for the works you mentioned in our edition? I mean, surely his conversion becomes even more striking if it's seen against . . . some of the things he wrote when he was young.

Isabelle I'm sure these considerations will be borne in mind.

Verlaine Yes, yes, of course . . .

Isabelle I wonder if you could give us your address, so that I can get in touch with you if it's necessary.

Verlaine Well, I . . . don't really have an address, mademoiselle. I spend a lot of time in hospital, you see, and my address seems to . . . change quite often.

Isabelle I see. Well, I think that's about all, M. Verlaine.

Verlaine It occurs to me, that if you want Rimbaud's manuscripts, my wife might be able to help you.

Isabelle Your wife?

Verlaine Yes. I still think of her as my wife, although I'm told she's taken advantage of the Gospel according to the Civil Service, and married someone else. I haven't seen her since before . . . for about twenty years. I spent years trying to get her to send me Rimbaud's manuscripts and letters.

Isabelle Yes. Thank you.

Verlaine She's a spiteful and wicked woman. Do you know that my son will be twenty-one this year, and I haven't seen him since he was eight?

Isabelle I think I should be going, M. Verlaine, I'd like to get back to my hotel before it gets dark.

Verlaine Wait. Please. Just a minute. I wonder if you could, before you go, just tell me something about . . . your brother. You see, the last time I saw him, in Stuttgart, must have been about seventeen years ago, when he was over there learning German. After that, the reports were so vague. We heard he was in Abyssinia, we heard he was dead, and later that he was alive, and all kinds of rumours. I wonder if you could just . . . fill in the details a little, that's all.

Isabelle I don't know that there's very much to tell. He travelled. He was a building consultant in Cyprus for some time, then he moved on to Aden and got a job with a trading firm. He established a new depot for them in Abyssinia about five years ago, which he managed and ran himself.

Verlaine But how did he die?

Isabelle He had a tumour on his knee.

Verlaine That's very strange.

Isabelle Why?

Verlaine Because that's what I have, a . . . tumour on my knee.

Isabelle It would have been all right if he'd done

85

something about it sooner, if he hadn't been so conscientious about his work. There was no doctor there, but he insisted on staying until the pain became unbearable. After that, it took him two months to get back to Marseilles, and they amputated his leg . . . but by that time it was too late to do anything for him.

Verlaine How terrible.

Isabelle In fact, after the operation it was worse. They tried to fit him with a wooden leg, but he couldn't manage it. They'd had to amputate too high and the stump couldn't take the weight. He said, after the operation, he kept saying, that if he'd known what it was going to be like, he'd never have let them amputate. He hated the hospital so much, that at the end of July he left and came home.

Verlaine Was he alone in Marseilles?

Isabelle Oh yes. Mother went down for the operation, but she couldn't afford to stay with him, because it was getting near to harvest-time.

A burst of raucous laughter from Eugénie.

When he got home things weren't too bad at first, but before long he lost the use of his right arm, and the pain spread and increased. The doctor gave him drugs to stop the pain, and he became delirious. I remember one night, I was woken up by a terrible crash from his room. I rushed up there and found my brother lying face down on the floor, naked. He told me he had opened his eyes and it was dawn, and time to go, to lead his caravan of ivory and musk to the coast. He said, he kept saying, that he wanted to go back to the sun, and that the sun would heal him, and eventually he left for Marseilles and I went with him. He intended to travel on from there to Aden, but when he got there he was too ill, and he went back into hospital.

The paralysis gradually spread, and a large tumour appeared on the inside of his stump. I think God kept him alive long enough to repent, so that he could be saved.

Verlaine Yes. The last time we met, in Stuttgart, we spoke of religion. I had just been converted, and I tried very hard to convince him of the truth. Perhaps I helped him in some small way.

Silence. Eugénie exits on the arm of the man she has been talking to.

Verlaine Did he . . . I don't suppose he ever mentioned me?

Isabelle No.

Verlaine It was a long time ago.

Isabelle It's getting dark. I must go.

Verlaine But still . . .

Isabelle stands up, and Verlaine, at first startled by her movement, drags himself painfully to his feet.

Isabelle Good-bye, M. Verlaine.

They shake hands.

Verlaine Won't you let me see you to your hotel?

Isabelle No, it's quite all right.

Verlaine Are you sure?

Isabelle (*formally*) It was an honour to meet such a distinguished poet.

Verlaine It was a great pleasure to meet you, mademoiselle.

Isabelle You have mother's card there, don't you? Don't forget to send us Arthur's manuscripts.

Verlaine No.

Isabelle Good-bye, monsieur.

Verlaine Good night.

Exit Isabelle. Verlaine sits down. For a moment there is absolute silence. Then he tears up Mme Rimbaud's visiting card, smiling a little to himself.

Eugénie? Where are you?

Absinthe. Two, please.

The Barman pours two absinthes into the two glasses already on the table. Verlaine drinks.

It was a long time ago. But I remember the first time I saw him. That evening in the Mautés' main room. When we walked in, he was standing with his back to us, looking out of the window. He turned round and spoke, and then I saw him, and I was amazed how beautiful he was. He was sixteen.

Since he died I see him every night. My great and radiant sin.

Rimbaud enters, dressed as he was in the first scene, but moving with more confidence, smiling, handsome, lithe. He sits down at the table next to Verlaine and they smile at each other.

Tell me if you love me.

Rimbaud You know I'm very fond of you. We've been very happy sometimes.

Silence.

Do you love me?

Verlaine Yes.

Rimbaud Then put your hands on the table.

Verlaine What?

Rimbaud Put your hands on the table.

Verlaine does so.

Palm upwards.

Verlaine turns his hands palm upwards. Rimbaud looks at them for a moment, and then bends forward and kisses them. Then he gets up, smiles at Verlaine, and exits. There is a long silence.

Verlaine We were always happy. Always. I remember.

Verlaine sits alone in a pool of light, which gradually dims as he speaks.

Eugénie?

What I love in old, sad flesh is the youth which whispers around it. I love its memories of youth.

I remember our first summer, how happy it was, the happiest time of my life. Wandering across Belgium, eating turnips and huddling in ditches. He's not dead, he's trapped and living inside me. As long as I live, he has some kind of flickering and limited life. It's always the same words and the same gestures – the same images: I walk behind him across a steep ploughed field; I sit, talking to him in a darkening room, until I can barely see his profile and his expressive hand; I lie in bed at dawn and watch him sleeping and see how nervously his hand brushes at his cheek. I remember him of an evening and he lives.

Absinthe.

Are you there? Eugénie? Are you there?

Darkness.

Curtain.

Appendix
Extract from one of Rimbaud's last letters to his sister:

Marseilles, 15th July, 1891

My dear Isabelle,

. . . I spend day and night torturing myself, trying to think of ways to get about. I want to do all kinds of things, live, get away from here: but it's impossible, at least, it'll be impossible for months, if not for ever. All I can think about are these damn crutches: without them, I can't take a step, I can't exist. I can't even get dressed without the most terrible gymnastics. It's true I can run now with my crutches; but I can't go up or down stairs, and if the ground isn't level, shifting the strain from one shoulder to the other is very tiring. I still have very painful neuralgia in my right arm and shoulder, and in addition to this, the crutches cut into my armpits. My left leg is very painful as well – and the worst thing is having to behave like an acrobat all day to have any sort of existence at all.

My dear sister, I've been thinking about what really caused my illness. The climate in Harar is cold from November to March. I never used to wear many clothes – just a pair of canvas trousers and a cotton shirt. Also I quite often used to walk 15 to 40 kilometres a day, leading lunatic processions across steep, mountainous country. I think I must have developed some arthritic trouble caused by fatigue and the heat and the cold. It all started with a kind of hammer blow which used to strike me under the kneecap every so often. The joint was very dry and my thigh was stiff. The next thing was the veins all round the knee swelled up, which made me think they were varicose. I kept on going for walks, and working harder than ever, I thought it was just a chill. Then the pain inside my knee

got worse, every step I took, it was like a nail being driven
in. I was still walking, but it got more and more difficult;
so I used to ride, and whenever I dismounted, I felt
completely crippled. Then the back of my knee swelled up,
my kneecap got very fleshy, so did my shin. The blood
wasn't circulating properly, and my nerves throbbed from
my ankle right the way up to my back. I couldn't walk
without a heavy limp, and it was getting worse and worse.
But I still had a lot of essential work to do. I started
bandaging the whole of my leg, massaging it, bathing it,
and so on, but it was no good. I lost my appetite. I was
suffering from stubborn insomnia. I got weaker and lost a
lot of weight. About the 15th March, I decided to stay in
bed between my desk and papers and the window, so that
I could keep an eye on the scales at the end of the yard,
and I paid people to keep the business going, while I lay
there with my leg stretched out. Every day the knee
swelled up more until it was like a large ball. I noticed that
the back of the shin bone was much bigger at the top than
on the other leg. I couldn't move the kneecap, it was
soaked in the muck which formed the swelling, which, I
was horrified to see, turned as hard as bone within a few
days. A week later, my whole leg was stiff, I couldn't bend
it at all; I had to drag myself along the ground to the
latrines. In the meantime my calf and my thigh got thinner
and thinner, while the knee joint swelled, hardened, and
seemed to turn into bone; and my physical and mental
weakness increased. At the end of March, I decided to
leave. I sold up everything in a few days – at a loss; and as
the stiffness and pain prevented me from riding a mule or
even a camel, I had a litter made with a curtain roof, and
hired 16 men, who took a fortnight to get me to Zeyla. On
the second day of the journey, we went on far ahead of the
caravan, and were caught in a rainstorm in the middle of
the desert. I lay for 16 hours in the pouring rain, with no
shelter and no possibility of movement; this did me a great

deal of harm. On the way I was never able to get out of the litter. They set up the tent above me wherever they'd happened to put me down. I used to dig a hole with my hands near the edge of the litter, crawl over to it with great difficulty, relieve myself into it, and then fill it with earth again. In the morning they'd take the tent away, then they'd take me away. I arrived at Zeyla exhausted and paralysed. I had only four hours' rest before the steamer left for Aden. They bundled me on to the bridge on my mattress, having hoisted me aboard in my litter, and I had to endure three days at sea without eating. Then I spent a few days settling things with M. Tian and left for the hospital where the English doctor advised me, a fortnight later, to push off back to Europe.

I'm absolutely certain that if the pain in the joint had been treated at once it could easily have been cured and would have had no consequences. But I had no idea how serious it was, and I ruined everything by insisting on long walks and hard work.

Why don't they teach medicine at school, at least enough to prevent people from making such stupid mistakes?

If anyone, in the condition in which I then found myself, came to me for advice, I would say to him: however bad it is, never let them amputate. If you die, it will be better than living with a missing limb. People often refuse, and if I had another chance, I would. Better to suffer the tortures of hell for a year than to let them amputate!

Anyway, they have. And this is the result. Most of the time I'm sitting down, but every so often, I get up, hop a hundred yards or so on my crutches, and then sit down again. My hands can't grip. When I'm walking, I can't take my eyes off my only foot and the end of the crutches. My head and shoulders bend forward and I look like a hunchback. I'm frightened of things and people moving around me, in case they knock me over and break my other leg. People watch me hopping and snigger. When I sit down again, my hands are limp, my armpits are bruised, my expression is vacuous. I despair; and I sit here, completely powerless, snivelling, and waiting for the night, which will bring me the same endless insomnia until the dawn of a day still more miserable than the last. So it goes on.

I will write again soon.

All best wishes,
RIMBAUD

Selected Bibliography

Album Rimbaud: ed. Pierre Petitfils and Henri Matarasso,
Bibliothèque de la Pléiade, 1967
Rimbaud: *Oeuvres Complètes*, ed. Roland de Renéville
and Jules Mouquet, Bibliothèque de la Pléiade, 1965
Verlaine: *Oeuvres Poétiques Complètes*, ed. Jacques Borel,
Bibliothèque de la Pléiade, 1965

Delahaye, Ernest: *Souvenirs Familiers*, Messein, 1925
Lepelletier, Edmond: *Paul Verlaine, sa vie, son oeuvre*,
Mercure de France, 1907
Martino, Pierre: *Verlaine*, Boivin, 1924
Mouquet, Jules: *Rimbaud raconté par Verlaine*, Mercure
de France, 1934
Porché, François: *Verlaine tel qu'il fut*, Flammarion, 1933
Rimbaud, Isabelle: *Reliques*, Mercure de France, 1922
Starkie, Enid: *Arthur Rimbaud*, Faber & Faber (3rd ed.),
1961
Verlaine, Ex-Madame: *Mémoires de ma vie*, Flammarion,
1935
Wilson, Edmund: *Axel's Castle*, Charles Scribner, 1931
(Fontana, 1961)

THE PHILANTHROPIST

A Bourgeois Comedy

For Laura

C'est que jamais, morbleu! les hommes n'ont raison
                    Molière, *Le Misanthrope*

Characters

Philip
Donald
John
Celia
Braham
Elizabeth
Araminta

The first performance of *The Philanthropist* was given at the Royal Court Theatre, London, on 3 August 1970. The cast was as follows:

Philip Alec McCowen
Donald Dinsdale Landen
John David Ashton
Celia Jane Asher
Braham Charles Gray
Elizabeth Tamara Ustinov
Araminta Penelope Wilton

Directed Robert Kidd
Designed John Gunter

The play was set in the near future and its characters are aged between 23 and 35.

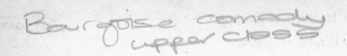

SCENE ONE

Philip's room. The room of a bachelor don, comfortable but not well-furnished, ordered but not tidy. Philip and Donald sit, relaxed but attentive, one in an armchair, one on the sofa perhaps. John, a younger man, is sitting in a wooden chair, a pile of papers on his knee. He holds a revolver.

John You needn't think I'm not serious. Because I am. I assure you I am. Can't you see that? I've come here this evening because I think both of you are responsible for this and I think you deserve it as much as I do. If you hate me for doing it, that's your problem. It won't concern me. I just want you to have one vivid image of me, that's all, one memory to last all your life and never vanish, to remind you that if you won, I lost, and that nobody can win without somebody losing. Good-bye. (*He puts the revolver to his head.*) Bang. (*He smiles uneasily at them.*) Curtain.

   Silence.

Do you like it?

Philip Very good. Would you like another drink?

John Oh, yes, thanks, er . . . Philip.

   Philip pours a drink.

Philip Ice?

John Please.

   Exit Philip.

John He doesn't like it, does he?

Don Oh, I don't know.

John He doesn't. I can tell.

Don I'm sure he does like it.

John Do you?

Philip returns with the ice.

Don Well. Yes and no. I mean there are some enormously promising things in the play. Obviously it's basically a conversation piece, but you do try to give the customers a bit of everything – a touch of melodrama, the odd *coup de théâtre*, humour, tragedy, monologues and pastoral interludes, yes, yes, I like that, generous. But on the other hand I think there are certain . . . lapses, which, you know, detract from the play as a satisfying whole.

John You mean it's stylistically heterogeneous?

Philip I think Don prefers to see it as an unsatisfying whole. (*He laughs merrily and alone.*) Sorry. Would you like a chocolate?

John No thanks.

Philip Don? I think I'll have one.

He helps himself to one, as he is to throughout this scene.

John Tell me what you don't like about it.

Don Well, one thing is that character who appears every so often with a ladder. The window cleaner. What's his name?

John Man.

Don Yes. Well, I take it he has some kind of allegorical significance outside the framework of the play. I mean I don't know if this is right, but I rather took him to signify England.

John No, no, erm, in point of fact he signifies man.

Don Ah.

John Yes.

Don Hence the name.

John Yes.

Don I see.

John Although now you come to mention it, I suppose he could be taken to represent England.

Philip Is that two ns?

John What?

Philip In Man.

John No, one.

Philip Ah, well, you see, I thought it was two ns. As in Thomas.

John Thomas?

Philip Thomas Mann.

John Oh.

Philip So I thought he was just meant to represent a window cleaner.

John Well . . .

Philip Under the circumstances, I think you've integrated him into the plot very well.

John Thank you. (*He seems displeased.*)

Don I always think the beginning and the end are the most difficult parts of a play to handle, and I'm not sure you've been entirely successful with either.

John Aren't you?

Don I can't really say I like that Pirandello-style beginning. It's been done so often, you know. I mean I'm not saying that your use of it isn't resourceful. It is. But the device itself is a bit rusty.

John Yes, perhaps you're right. I'm not really very happy about the beginning myself. (*to Philip*) What do you think?

Philip I liked it.

John Why?

Philip No special reason, I just liked it. You shouldn't take any notice of me, though, I'm not really qualified to comment.

John You do lecture in English, don't you?

Philip Yes, but in philology, not literature.

John Philology? Don't you find that incredibly tedious?

Philip No, it's exactly the right subject for me. I'm fascinated by words.

John Individual rather than consecutive.

Philip Yes. My only advice to writers is: make the real shapes.

John Pardon?

Philip It's an anagram of 'Shakespeare' and 'Hamlet'.

Don He's obsessed by anagrams.

John (*coldly*) Really. (*Pause.*) What's your objection to the end of the play?

Don It just doesn't convince me. It seems artificial. Do you really think he'd commit suicide in front of them like that?

John Yes. Why not?

Don It doesn't seem to tie in with his character as we've seen it in the rest of the play.

Philip I don't know. I liked it.

John You don't have to say that, you know. I'd much prefer to have honest criticism than your, if you don't mind me saying so, rather negative remarks.

Philip Please take no notice of what I say. I always like things. I get pleasure from the words that are used, whatever the subject is. I've enjoyed every book I've ever read for one reason or another. That's why I can't teach literature. I have no critical faculties. I think there's always something good to be found in the product of another man's mind. Even if the man is, by all objective standards, a complete fool. So you see I'd like a play however terrible it was.

John So you think my play is terrible.

Philip I didn't say that, I . . .

John I'm not an idiot, you know, I can take a hint.

Philip Please don't get angry.

John (*furious*) I am not angry! I just don't think there's any point in our discussing it any more, that's all. It's different with Don, Don has some constructive criticisms to make, which will probably be very helpful.

Philip But I like the play more than Don does, I think it's very good.

John There's no need to be hypocritical.

Philip I . . .

John I have no illusions about this play, you know . . .

Philip I . . .

John But I do think it has a little more merit than you give it credit for.

Philip I'm sorry.

John Never mind.

Silence.

Philip Would you like a chocolate?

John No.

Silence.

John (*to Don*) Now, what were you saying?

Don I was just wondering whether the suicide is altogether justified.

John Oh, I think so. Given the kind of man he is. I think it could be quite powerful. I think perhaps he might put the revolver in his mouth. Then, if the back wall of the set was whitewashed, they could use some quaint device to cover it with great gobs of brain and bright blood at the vital moment. And just the two of them sitting there gaping. That would be wonderful.

> *To illustrate, John puts the revolver into his mouth and presses the trigger. Loud explosion. By some quaint device, gobs of brain and bright blood appear on the whitewashed wall. Philip and Don sit gaping. Long silence.*

Don Jesus.

> *John has slumped back into the chair. Philip rushes*

abruptly from the stage. Don gropes shakily for the telephone and begins to dial.

Blackout.

The first movement of the 2nd Brandenburg Concerto.

SCENE TWO

A few days later. Philip, alone, laying the dinner-table for six. A knock at the door. Don enters.

Don Hello. Am I too early?

Philip No.

Don I wondered if there was anything I could do to help.

Philip No, it's all under control. Help yourself to a drink.

Don pours himself a Scotch.

Don For you?

Philip No, thanks. Not just yet.

Don sits down.

Don Where's Celia?

Philip In the kitchen.

Don Are you all right?

Philip Yes. Why?

Don I don't know, you seem a little morose.

Philip I am a bit.

Don Why? You're not still upset about John, are you?

Philip Well . . .

Don I can't think why. You hardly knew the man.

Philip That doesn't make any difference.

Don Well, it should do. He was my friend, not yours. And I haven't been sitting around brooding about it for days. You're too sensitive, Philip, really. I mean, the whole thing was just a grotesque accident.

Philip I've never seen anyone dead before. I've never seen anyone die.

Don I don't know, the whole evening was a complete disaster. I mean, apart from that. I only suggested we had it here because I knew I'd hate the play, and I wanted someone around who'd say something nice to him. I don't know why he got so ratty with you.

Philip Well, I was very tactless.

Don Nonsense, he was absurd. A sad case in many ways. There's no doubt he was very intelligent, but he had no idea how to write. That play was no good at all.

Philip I rather liked it.

Don I know you did, but it was no good. The ideas were there, but not the technique, it was far too cerebral.

Philip Under the circumstances, I think that's a uniquely unfortunate adjective.

Don What? Oh, oh yes. (*He laughs.*) Anyway, I see you've managed to get him off the wall.

Philip Don.

Don Sorry.

Silence.

Philip Celia wasn't very sympathetic either. The first thing she said when I rang her up and told her about it was: 'I'm not surprised, he's always been ludicrously absent-minded.'

Don Did she?

Philip Yes.

Don Come to think of it, absent-minded's even more unfortunate than cerebral. (*He laughs, recovers, shakes his head.*) No, it was a terrible thing to happen, really. (*He tries to look solemn, but is suddenly overcome by helpless laughter.*) Sorry.

    Celia enters.

Celia What's the joke?

Don John.

    She puts some mats on the table.

Celia It's all very well for you to laugh, you didn't have to clean him up. He was all over the place.

Philip Please, love . . .

Celia Philip had to throw away his Picasso print, didn't you?

    She heads for the door.

Philip Can I do anything in the kitchen?

Celia I've yet to see any evidence of it. (*Celia goes out.*)

Don Who's coming this evening?

Philip Liz.

Don Good.

Philip Erm . . . Araminta, do you know her?

Don Oh, really, where did you pick her up?

Philip I didn't pick her up. She's one of the few people I come into contact with who has any interest in my subject at all. She seems quite intelligent, so I asked her.

Don I don't think it's your subject she's interested in.

Philip Oh?

Don Haven't you heard about her?

Philip No.

Don The quickest drawers in the faculty. Old Noakes was telling me the other day he literally had to beg her to leave him in peace.

Philip Did he really?

Don Yes. So I should keep your hand on your ha'penny if I were you. (*Pause.*) Who else?

Philip Braham Head.

Don The novelist?

Philip Yes. He's up here for a couple of weeks. Celia met him at some party and wanted to ask him. Do you know him?

Don Slightly.

Philip What's he like?

Don Incredible prick. He's one of those writers who've been forced to abandon the left wing for tax reasons.

Philip I quite like one or two of his books.

Don They're dreadful. Dreadful. The man hasn't a glimmer of talent. And he's so rude and loud.

Philip Oh.

Don He left his wife last year. He said to her: 'Darling, I hope you're not going to be bourgeois about this, but I'm going to leave you and the children for a few months.'

Philip What happened?

Don She divorced him. Best thing she could have done. Their whole relationship was soured by her failure even to attempt suicide, which he apparently regarded as unforgivable. He likes to think of himself as a Romantic.

Philip Surely he's not that bad?

Don Worse. Worse. (*He broods for a moment.*) What about the Prime Minister, then?

Philip What about him?

Don Haven't you heard?

Philip No.

Don He's been killed.

Philip What?

Don Assassinated.

Philip Has he?

Don They've had nothing else on the radio all day.

Philip How terrible.

Don Most of the Cabinet as well.

Philip Killed as well?

Don Yes.

Philip How did it happen?

Don Well, shortly after the debate began today, this rather comic figure came bowling into the courtyard of the House of Commons on a bicycle: an elderly and rather corpulent woman wearing one of those enormous tweed capes, you know, ankle-length. She parked her bicycle, dropped the front wheel into one of those slots they have, and puffed up to the gallery, where she sat for a bit, beaming amiably and sucking Glacier mints. Then, all of a sudden, she leapt to her feet, produced a sub-machine-gun out of nowhere, and mowed down the front bench.

Philip My God.

Don Yes.

Philip But . . . who was she?

Don A retired lieutenant-colonel.

Philip Salvation Army?

Don No, no, she was a man. He gave himself up afterwards. He's completely round the twist. He says he did it to save Britain from the menace of creeping socialism.

Philip But it's a Tory government.

Don Nevertheless, he feels, if you can believe it, that the party is slithering hopelessly to the left. Said he felt called to be his country's liberator. Apparently, he's been practising in his garden in Wolverhampton for months.

Philip God.

Don Nine of them he got, and several others wounded. He probably could have managed more, but he seemed to feel an adequate statement had been made, so he trotted down the stairs, gave himself up like an officer and a gentleman and sauntered off to the cells whistling the Dam Busters' March.

Philip But . . . what's going to happen?

Don Oh, I don't know, coalition government, another election, something like that. It's not going to make much difference, whatever happens.

Philip Isn't it?

Don Not to us, anyway.

Philip But . . . it's appalling.

Don Yes. (*Pause.*) Worse things have happened. (*Pause.*) I must say, I think it was rather boring of him to do it on November the 5th. I suppose in the Tory Party that's the kind of thing that passes for aesthetics.

Celia enters.

Celia Did you put the lemons in the 'fridge? I can't see them anywhere.

Philip Oh, God.

Celia Don't say you've forgotten them. Honestly, I ask you to get one thing . . .

Philip I'm sorry. I'll go and get them now.

Celia Everything's shut. We shall just have to have it without lemon, that's all.

Don I think I've got a couple of lemons.

Celia Have you?

Don Yes, in my rooms, in the fruit bowl, I think.

Celia Can I nip over and get them?

Don Yes, sure.

Celia Thanks.

She moves over to the door.

Philip Celia.

Celia Yes.

Philip Anything I can do to help?

Celia has sense of humour!

*— She is better cathar
him & she knows
this*

THE PHILANTHROPIST

Celia No.

Celia goes out. Philip looks unhappy.

Don When is it you're getting married?

Philip I, er, not sure really. Probably sometime in the vacation.

Don Are you looking forward to it?

Philip Well, yes, I think so. Why?

Don Just wondered.

Silence.

Philip You don't really think it's a good idea, do you?

Don I don't know, Philip.

Philip I mean, you don't really like her, do you?

Don It's not that I don't like her, that's not it at all. She's very amusing and intelligent and attractive – it's just I sometimes wonder whether she's your kind of person.

Philip What do you mean? You mean I'm not amusing and intelligent and attractive. *serious & paranoid*

Don Of course not. But you're rather... serious, aren't you?

Philip I suppose so.

Don And Celia isn't. In fact, she's rather frivolous.

Philip But I like that.

Don Oh, I'm sure you do. Sure you do. But it may cause you some trouble.

Philip She is very malicious sometimes. She does seem to hate a large number of people I find perfectly harmless. Intensely. At first, I didn't think she really hated them, but I'm not so sure now.

Don Have you ever thought about Liz?

Philip Liz?

Don Ever thought about marrying her?

Philip No. Why?

Don She's very fond of you, you know.

Philip Really?

Don Yes. I was talking to her about you the other day and I could see she was very fond of you.

Philip Why, what did she say?

Don Well, I can't remember exactly, nothing specific, it was just the way she talked about you. I'm sure she'd marry you like a shot if you asked her.

Philip Do you think so?

Don I'm sure of it.

Philip She hasn't said anything to me about it.

Don Well, she has her pride.

Silence. Philip broods.

Philip And you think I should marry her instead of Celia?

Don I didn't say that. I wouldn't dream of saying that.

Philip But you think it.

Don I'm just saying it would be possible if you wanted to do it.

Philip Well, I don't.

Don I know you don't. I'm sorry I mentioned it.

Philip That's all right.

Don I have this theory which I think is rather attractive. I think we're only capable of loving people who are fundamentally incompatible with us.

Philip That's horrible.

Don But attractive.

Philip It's not really a very helpful thing to say.

Don Take no notice. You know very well that unless you're a scientist, it's much more important for a theory to be shapely, than for it to be true.

Celia enters with the lemons, which she puts down on the table.

Celia Christ, I must have a drink. (*She pours herself a Scotch and sinks into a chair.*)

Don Did you find the lemons?

Celia Yes. Thanks.

Don Isn't she marvellous?

Philip eyes Don uneasily.

Philip I think so.

Celia So do I. I can't bear cooking: and I cook. I can't bear working: and I work. (*She smiles.*) And I can't bear Philip: and I'm marrying him.

Philip It's all part of one basic condition.

Celia What?

Philip You can't bear being a woman: and you are.

Celia bristles.

Celia What do you mean?

Philip It was a joke.

Celia Not a very funny joke.

Philip It was about as funny as yours.

Celia Mine?

Philip Yes, when you said you couldn't bear me and you were marrying me.

Celia You think that was a joke?

Philip I . . .

Celia (*laughing*) Your trouble is you have no sense of humour.

Philip is bested.

Philip Sorry.

A knock at the door and **Braham** *enters. He is a tall, good-looking man, fashionably and expensively dressed. He carries a large paper bag.*

Braham I hope I've come to the right place. (*He sees Celia.*) Ah, hello love. (*He turns to Don.*) You must be Philip.

Philip No, I'm Philip.

Don I'm Don.

Braham Oh, yes, we've met, haven't we? Well, I'm Braham. Very nice of you to invite me.

Philip It's kind of you to come.

Braham (*Turning to Celia*) I went down to the market to buy you some flowers, my love, but they didn't seem to have any. So I got you this instead. (*With a flourish, he produces a cauliflower from the paper bag.*) As a token of my esteem.

Celia (*dubiously*) Thanks.

Braham I'm sure you'll be able to find a niche for it.

Celia takes it from him.

Celia I'll put it in the kitchen.

Braham Just the place.

Celia goes out.

Philip Can I get you a drink?

Braham Lovely girl.

Philip Sherry or Scotch?

Braham (*abstractedly*) Yes, please.

He looks over towards the kitchen, as Philip stands by the drinks table, helpless with indecision.

Lovely. She tells me you're getting married.

Philip Yes. Erm . . .? (*His courage fails him.*)

Braham What?

Philip Nothing.

He decides on Scotch and pours it shakily. Braham sits down.

Braham Well well well.

Silence. Philip hands him the glass.

Braham I observe that you are left-handed and that your maternal granny stands, or rather stood, six foot three in her socks.

Philip Er . . .

Braham How can I tell, I hear you cry.

Philip exchanges a slightly desperate glance with Don as Braham sips his drink. Philip smiles weakly.

I can see it in your . . . Did I ask for Scotch?

Philip Well . . .

Braham Funny, I thought I said sherry.

Philip Let me . . .

Braham No, no, never mind, never mind. Think nothing of it.

Silence. Philip takes a cigarette box from the table and offers one to Braham.

Philip Do you smoke?

Braham takes one.

Braham Thank you.

Philip hands one to Don. Then closes the box and lights their cigarettes as he speaks, nervously.

Philip I gave up last summer. It was months before I could make up my mind, but I finally decided I was more nervous about dying of cancer than I would be if I gave up smoking.

Braham Well, naturally.

Philip No, no, what I mean is that I decided that the degree of nervousness I suffer in everyday life under normal circumstances without smoking although it was alleviated by smoking together with the added nervousness caused by the threat of ultimate cancer came to a sum total of nervousness it seemed to me in the end after lengthy as I say consideration greater than the original nervousness which had in the first place prompted me to take up smoking. If you follow my meaning.

Celia has re-entered during this speech.

Braham I'm not sure I do.

Philip No, well, I'm not expressing myself very well. I just mean it was paradoxical that I took up smoking because I thought it would be good for my nerves and discovered that even though it was I was more nervous after I'd taken it up than before because of the . . .

Celia What are you burbling about?

Philip I'm not, I'm not expressing myself very well. I don't know what's the matter with me.

Braham I should have a cigarette if I were you.

Blackout.

Aria: 'Be joyful in the Lord' from Handel's 'Jubilate'.

SCENE THREE

After dinner. Philip, Don, Braham, Celia, Liz and Araminta are relaxing, talking, drinking coffee, brandy, etc., and smoking. Araminta, a rather large girl with a dramatically low-cut dress, sits on the floor, drinking crème de menthe. Liz, a quiet, reserved girl (she does not in fact speak during the course of the scene) is dressed more soberly and sits watching, smiling to herself from time to time.

Braham Tell me, what is the official line on Christ's navel?

Araminta On what?

Braham Christ's navel. When I went down to London on the train the other day, I fell into conversation with this priest, a very sprightly old gent, who told me that one of his proudest achievements was a polemic he'd written some years before against the view, which he said was widely held, that Christ had had no navel.

Celia Why shouldn't he have had a navel?

Braham Oh, well, it's all to do with the mysterious circumstances of his birth.

Celia Oh, I see.

Braham Anyway, he was a marvellous old boy. Marvellous. He said he lamented the passing of the closed compartment, no-corridor train and I asked him why and he told me that years and years ago, before he'd taken up the cloth and was sowing the occasional wild oat, he'd managed to strike up an acquaintance with a boy, seduce him and suck him off, all in the course of a journey between Bognor Regis and Littlehampton.

Don Really?

Braham Yes.

Araminta Wonderful.

Philip Er, shall we have the ten o'clock news?

Braham Why?

Philip Well, I was just wondering what's happened about the Prime Minister and the government, you know . . .

Braham Oh, no, I think that would be unnecessarily depressing.

Philip I just thought . . .

Braham In the car on the way over I heard them say the Queen had sent for the Minister of Sport.

Araminta What for?

Celia Her trampoline needs restringing.

Araminta Who is the Minister of Sport, anyway?

Don Edith somebody, isn't it?

Araminta Why's she been sent for?

Braham Well, presumably she's the senior uninjured Minister.

Araminta They're not going to make her Prime Minister, are they?

Braham No, they can't possibly. I don't know, though, it might be rather diverting if they did. I must say, the great thing about all this is it shows we're accepting our decadence with a certain stylishness.

Don What do you mean?

Braham Well, I think most people would agree that this has become a fairly sophisticated country. But I've always thought of sophistication as rather a feeble substitute for decadence. I mean I'm not saying everyone should go round assassinating people, but you must admit the way this man went about it did show a kind of rudimentary dramatic flair.

Don I'd say he was a lunatic.

Braham Oh, yes, very probably. But like a lot of lunatics he's got one or two very shrewd ideas rattling around in his head.

Don Like what?

Braham Like accepting our decadence without trying to go on pretending we're morally superior to the rest of the world. Like realizing that socialism is about as much use to this country as . . . a pogo-stick to a paraplegic.

Don That's an extraordinarily repulsive image.

Braham What? Oh, yes, I suppose it is, really. Sorry, it just sprang to mind.

Araminta I thought it was very expressive.

Braham Thank you, Araminta.

Don Do you really think that? About socialism?

Braham My dear chap, what I think about socialism is neither here nor there. Listen, when I was younger, I was a passionate Lefty writing all kinds of turgid, earth-shaking stuff which was designed to set the world to rights and which no publisher would have touched with a pitchfork. But eventually I realized, and what a moment of five-star disillusionment that was, that it wasn't going to work. Governments would not tumble at the scratch of my quill. I was just one little person in this enormous bloody world. God, in his infinite wisdom, had given me the ability to create essentially frivolous entertainments, which were enjoyed by enough essentially frivolous people for me to be able to amble comfortably through life. Naturally, it distresses me that people are wasting their energies killing each other all over the world, and of course I'm sorry thousands of Indians starve to death every year, but I mean that's their problem, isn't it, if they will go in for all this injudicious fucking. I actually used to think that in some obscure way it was my fault.

Don You've got over that now, have you?

Braham Well, I have, yes. Nowadays, if I get one of those things through my letter-box telling me I can feed an entire village for a week for the price of a prawn cocktail, I tear it up, throw it in my waste-paper basket, go out to my favourite restaurant and order a prawn cocktail.

Don And do you find that amusing?

Braham Oh, come now, the next thing you're going to say is what if everybody was like me. Fortunately for the world and even more fortunately for me, not everybody is. Look, if I actually get a concrete chance to help people, then I do.

Araminta Yes, I saw that TV appeal you did a few weeks ago.

Don What was that for?

Braham Twenty-five guineas.

Don I meant, on behalf of whom.

Braham I know you did.

Don Well?

Braham (*playing up*) Oh, I don't know, it was an appeal on behalf of spavined children. Or something equally sordid.

Don And did it raise much money?

Braham Enough to cover my fee.

Don I'm sorry . . . I must say I find that rather disgusting.

Braham That's perfectly all right. Most people do. (*Pause. He turns sharply to Philip.*) Do you think I'm disgusting?

Philip Er . . . no, I don't think so, no.

Braham (*to Araminta*) Do you?

Araminta Oh, no.

Braham (*to Liz*) You?

   Liz shakes her head.

Braham (*to Celia*) What about you?

Celia (*smiling*) No.

Braham (*turning back to Don*) There you are, you see, that's quite a good average. Obviously, my living depends on disgusting a certain percentage of people. If I didn't disgust at least a substantial minority, I wouldn't be controversial, and if I wasn't controversial, I wouldn't be rich.

Don That's the way it works, is it?

Braham More or less.

Don And that's the purpose of it all, to be rich?

Braham I don't know whether it's the purpose or not, but it's the result. I used to feel terribly shifty about all the money I was making, but then I realized I belonged to that small class of people who make exactly what they deserve. I'm a product. If the public stop wanting me, I stop earning.

Celia But you're all right for the time being.

Braham Oh, yes.

Araminta What's the best thing about being a writer?

Braham Ah, well, the real bonus comes when one actually discovers one or two moral precepts lurking about at the back of one's head. Then one can base a book on them and enjoy the illusion that one has bought one's E-type with a couple of really valuable insights, golden truths, you might say. (*He laughs heartily.*)

Don Well, at least no one could accuse you of being self-righteous.

Braham No, but I think one would be forced to admit I was pretty complacent. What I mean is there's no point in feeling guilty about these things, there's only two alternatives, keep it or give it all away, and that's a very interesting proposition, as the rich man said to Christ, but don't call me, I'll call you.

Celia And egotistical too, I suppose that's necessary.

Braham Oh, absolutely. Self-obsession combined with the ability to hold opposite points of view with equal conviction. The marvellous thing is that if the internal logic is coherent, I know that even if I'm wrong, I'm right. Makes me what you might call an existentialist's nightmare.

Don Or a hypocritical creep, some might have it.

Braham Yes. (*He shakes with laughter.*) Oh, God, I did upset some poor little journalist the other day. 'How would you describe your job?' she said, and I said, 'Well, I suppose you might describe it as a kind of subsidized masturbation.'

Don Don't you really think any better of it than that?

Braham Certainly not. I hope you're not implying there's anything wrong with masturbation.

Don Well, I, no, not exactly . . .

Braham I should hope not. Masturbation is the thinking man's television. Don't you agree?

Don I can't say I really remember.

Braham You shock me.

   He turns to Philip.

You're not like that, are you?

Philip No. I mean, well, occasionally, sometimes, I do.

Braham I'm pleased to hear it. It's extremely good for you, you know. Ah, many's the time I've had to lay down the pen and slip off to the bog for a quick one. Always remembering the Dunkirk spirit. Never forgetting that Waterloo was won in the dormitories of Eton. Any more brandy, is there?

Philip pours Braham a brandy, then sees to the other guests.

Celia (*to Don*) Wasn't that your pupil's problem?

Don Who?

Celia The one who's just been sent down.

Don Who, Boot? No, no, no, I don't think it was sexual fantasy that finished him off, it was the failure of his political fantasies.

Braham Ah, well, there you are, you see, that's what I mean.

Don Very sad case, was Boot. James Boot. His first year he was very quiet, very shy, and all his work was carefully done and scrupulously on time. Good, solid, second-class stuff. Then, the beginning of this term, he didn't turn up when we were fixing the schedules, and one of the others told me he was in bed. So I sent him a note telling him when to come for the first tutorial and what to do. But when the time arrived I got a note from him saying he couldn't come, he was in bed. I naturally assumed he was ill, so when I was next in college I thought I'd call in on him to see how he was. He's got one of those nasty new modern little rooms, and I knocked on the door and went in. It was about four o'clock in the afternoon, he was in bed, the curtains were drawn, the fire was on and the stench was incredible. We talked for a bit. He offered me a biscuit. Then, anxious to beat a hasty retreat, I said I hoped he would be better soon. Then he told me there was nothing wrong with him.

It seems he'd spent the long vacation studying various political and economic works which had plunged him into such a state of total despair, that he had decided to devise some kind of final solution. At the beginning of term he had laid in enormous supplies of soup, cornflakes, biscuits, coffee and sugar – and then gone to bed. Since then, he'd been in bed twenty-two hours a day, brooding, only getting up to fix himself a meal, and never leaving the room except for the odd trip to the lavatory. 'But, Boot,' I said, 'but

Boot, why this sudden interest in politics? It's not even your faculty. Can't you, don't you think it would really be better, to turn your attention back to Wordsworth?' Wordsworth, he said, with some passion, had nothing to do with anything, and his work, like all art, was a lot of self-indulgent shit which had no relevance to our problems and was no help at all to man or beast. I must say, the way he put it, it sounded quite convincing. I said to him: 'Look, it's not necessary to upset yourself like this. No one's expecting you to come up with an answer to all the problems of Western democracy.' 'Yes, they are,' he said, 'I am.' Further discussion seemed pointless. So I left him.

Celia And what happened?

Don Well, he stayed in bed for the next six weeks, sending polite notes whenever he was supposed to be turning up somewhere, and I did nothing about it, because, because I rather admired him. And finally he reached a decision. He arrived at a conclusion.

He got out of bed one afternoon, took all his books down from the shelves, and piled them up in the middle of the room. Then he added all his papers and notes, wrapped the whole bundle up in his gown and set fire to it. He also set fire to the curtains, and turned the gas on. Then he put his dressing-gown on and left the building. A couple of his friends saw him wandering about and asked him jovially what he was doing up at that time of day. He told them he'd just set fire to the college. They carried on their way with much merry laughter. A moment later his windows blew out.

Braham Was there much damage done?

Don His room was gutted. A little later they came to take him away. He's been formally sent down, which I think was quite unnecessary. I understand that since he's been admitted, he's been quite unable to move.

Celia I think that's very sad.

Braham I'd say he has a promising career ahead of him.

Araminta What as?

Braham A literary critic.

Don I should think that's highly unlikely.

Braham I don't know. He sounds ideal. Do you know, I was actually forced to write a letter to some wretch a few weeks ago. He said my novel was too clever by half. So I wrote and said judging by the prose style of your review, I am forced to conclude, sir, that on the contrary, you are too stupid by half. (*He laughs.*)

Don I really don't see what that has to do with Boot.

Braham Now you come to mention it, I suppose there is no logical connection. I forgot we were subject to the austere disciplines of academic tradition. I hope you're not going to give me fifty lines.

He makes a mock appeal to Celia.

Are they all like this?

Celia No, Don is in a class of his own. He's the only one of my tutors who hasn't made a pass at me.

Braham Really?

Celia Yes. I don't count Philip, of course. Anyway, he doesn't teach me.

Philip You're not going to tell me Professor Burrows made a pass at you?

Celia Ah, no, well I've made an interesting discovery about Professor Burrows. Professor Burrows is actually dead.

Philip What do you mean?

Celia Well, I happened to see him with his wife just before one of those lectures he's been giving for decades, and she had her hand up inside his gown. Strange, I thought, and it was only later that it dawned on me what she was doing: she was winding him up. After that everything became clear – his voice, his colouring, the fact that he never takes any notice of what anyone says in seminars. He's been dead for years. They've installed a tape-recorder between his ears, and Mrs B. stacks him away in the 'fridge every night. That's it. It explains everything, the syllabus, everything. He's a contemporary of Beowulf.

Don Who does that leave?

Philip Johnson.

Don Oh, inevitably.

Celia (*to Braham*) Johnson is the Young Lion. He's a six-before-breakfast man. He lectures on Keats with such vigour and verve that the sticky young girls in the front row believe he is Keats. He's your typical Establishment misfit.

Don And was he stylish about it?

Celia Stylish? It was one of the clumsiest gropes I've undergone for a long time. At the beginning of the tutorial, he poured me a drink and came and sat next to me on the sofa, and I thought this is it, fasten your seat belts. But he was just terribly nervous, he sat there looking strained and burbling on about the Romantics for three-quarters of an hour, and then suddenly he grabbed my further shoulder and wrenched me round so abruptly I emptied my sherry all over his camel-hair trousers. That threw him for a second. But he obviously had the sentence all worked out and he told me he thought I was very beautiful, and would

I have dinner with him. I said I thought he'd better go and change his trousers before the next tutorial or his pupils would think he'd been at the Swinburne again.

Braham How did he handle that?

Celia Badly. Poor man, he was desperately embarrassed. He's never stopped apologizing ever since. I quite like him now. Rather him than Noakes any day.

Don Noakes? (*He is amused at the thought.*)

Celia (*to Braham*) Noakes, I must tell you, is not one of the world's ten best. In fact, he looks as if he's escaped off the side of Notre Dame. His face is enormous. And he sweats profusely, which makes him a very . . . shiny man. Ice-hockey matches could be played on his forehead. He's also kind of Neanderthal, I mean his knuckles scrape along the pavement as he walks. I must say, though, his grope was a great deal more thorough than Johnson's. Fortunately, his palms are so slimy, he wasn't able to get a proper purchase, as they say. But it was very nasty. He is, in every sense, oleaginous.

Araminta I think he's rather sweet.

Celia *Chacun à son goût.*

Araminta What do you mean?

Celia (*feigning innocence*) Nothing.

Braham He certainly sounds extraordinarily repulsive.

Araminta I think she's exaggerating.

Braham No, no, he sounds very familiar to me. (*to Philip*) What do you think about all this?

Philip What?

Braham All your colleagues leching after your fiancée.

Philip Oh, well, I think it's quite understandable. I don't really mind.

Braham Don't you? I'm sure I would.

Philip I don't know, you know . . .

Braham How come you don't teach her? Is there some fifteenth-century statute against seeing your betrothed in school hours?

Philip No, the thing is, I teach philology, which is sort of optional, and old texts and things like that, which she doesn't do because she's a graduate.

Braham Philology?

Philip Yes.

Braham My God, I thought that went out years ago.

Philip No.

Braham I seem to remember it as the only subject which cunningly combined the boredom of the science faculties with the uselessness of the arts faculties.

Philip Well . . .

Braham The worst of both cultures.

Philip Most people seem to think that way. But I . . . find it interesting.

Braham Why? How?

Philip Words. Words as objects. The development of words. Abuse of words. Words illustrating civilization. I mean, I can't go into it now, but all this new work that's being done in structural linguistics, I find absolutely fascinating.

Braham Structural linguistics, what's that, a yet more

complicated method of over-simplification?

Philip You might say so.

Braham You say you can't go into it now. Does that mean you don't think I could grasp it?

Philip I'm sure you could grasp it, I just don't think it would interest you very much.

Braham Yes, you may be right.

Philip But it does make me notice things. For instance, you're supposed to be, I mean you are, a successful writer, you make your living out of stringing words together. So it's very interesting for me to try to see how your language is formed.

Braham And how is it formed?

Philip Well, I noticed just now you said something was extraordinarily repulsive, and I thought that was very revealing because it was a phrase Don used a few minutes ago.

Braham What are you getting at?

Philip Well, it shows your ability for picking out and retaining striking phrases, subconsciously of course, but . . .

Braham Actually, as a matter of fact . . .

Philip (*enthusiastically*) See, that's another thing, the word 'actually', you use it a great deal.

Braham Why shouldn't I?

Philip No reason why you shouldn't, you just do.

Braham I think you're being subtly insulting.

Philip No, not at all, I . . .

while all this is going on Celia is loving it [handwritten]

Braham Yes, you are, go on, why don't you admit it?

Philip I'm not.

Braham I think there's nothing cruder than an excess of subtlety.

Philip No, look, I'm only making an observation. Like what you just said. That's something else. Your use of paradox. You've got it down to a fine art, it's a reflex action. You've digested that it's an extremely simple and extremely effective technique.

Braham You are being insulting!

Silence. Braham is angry, Philip somewhat upset. The others are becoming embarrassed.

Philip No.

Silence.

Celia He's not. He's just obsessed with the way people talk, that's all. Sometimes I think he's more interested in that than in what they actually say.

Braham What they what?

Celia Actually say.

Braham (*triumphantly, to Philip*) See, I'm not the only one.

Philip No, I know. Celia uses it quite often as well.

Braham (*to Celia*) You're obviously my kind of person.

Don Actually . . . (*He stops dead.*) Er, no, I mean, shit, yes, why not, actually . . . God, fuckit, I've forgotten what I was going to say now. (*Pause.*) Oh, yes, I was going to say Philip is quite remarkable with words. He can give you an anagram of any word or phrase, if there is one, in about two minutes, working it out in his head.

Braham Really?

Don Yes.

Celia Try him.

Philip No, I don't think . . .

Braham Ah, no, you're not going to get away with it as easy as that. I want an example of this. Give me an anagram of . . . give me an anagram of 'La Comédie Française'.

Silence. Philip concentrates.

Philip In French?

Braham (*magnanimously*) No, no, English will do. (*Pause. He returns his attention to the others.*) I always go there when I'm in Paris. God knows why. All that French classical theatre. Terrible camp old rubbish.

Araminta It's so stylized, isn't it?

Braham (*ignoring her*) Mind you, the French never go there. Wouldn't go near it. It's full of Americans and Germans. Last time I went, I had this enormous American lady sitting next to me, and just as the lights went down, mark you, and they were banging that thing on the stage, she leant across and said, 'Excuse me, I haven't had time to read my programme, would you mind telling me what the play is about, because I just can't understand a word they're saying.' So I said, 'Well, madam, it's about a man who hates humanity so much that he would undoubtedly refuse to explain the plot of a world-famous play to an ignorant tourist.'

Araminta You didn't really?

Braham She thanked me. Profusely.

Araminta Which play was it?

134

Braham (*coldly*) Three guesses. (*He broods for a moment.*) Anyway, I hate the Frogs.

Philip A defence o' racialism.

Braham What?

Philip A defence o' racialism. It doesn't quite work. There's an f missing. But it's the best I can do.

Braham (*sourly*) Wonderful.

Philip Thank you.

Braham Now perhaps you'll oblige us with a fart.

Don It's exceptionally difficult to do, that. You should try it sometime.

Braham What?

Don That anagram game.

Braham Oh, no, if we must play games, for God's sake let them be simple.

Don Shall we play a game?

Araminta Oo, yes, let's. What about murder?

Celia (*maliciously*) Postman's knock.

Braham I think it's a bit late for all that. I'm for a quick hand of Emptying the Brandy Bottle, and then I must be on my way.

Philip (*vaguely*) I've got some carpet bowls somewhere.

Braham (*handing Philip his glass*) Some other time, perhaps.

> Silence. Philip pours brandy for Braham, Celia and Don, crème de menthe for Araminta. Liz covers her glass with her hand.

135

Araminta Are you writing a new novel?

Braham Yes, I am. It's nearly finished.

Araminta What's it about?

Braham It's about a social worker, who, after years of unremitting toil, finally sees the light, and renounces everything to become a merchant banker. I'm going to give it a really unfashionable happy ending. It's going to finish with his marriage to a sensitive film star.

Araminta Sounds intriguing.

Braham If it does as well as the last one, I'm going to have to leave the country.

Araminta Why?

Braham Tax. The tax system is absolutely iniquitous. What do they do with it all, I don't know. You'd think they'd make some sort of reasonable allowance. After all, I am a dollar-earner.

Araminta But the system's always been weighted against artists, hasn't it?

Braham Yes, all that's in the book. Although it's mainly, as I say, about this self-sacrificing character who gives up the comforts of moral superiority for the harsh realities of high finance. Should bring foam to the lips of the progressives. It'll be one up the noses of all the self-appointed salt of the earth who preach the revolution in the happy and comfortable knowledge that it'll never come.

Don There are some people who believe in it, you know.

Braham (*acidly*) There are some people who believe in God.

Silence.

Don I don't really see what that has to do with it.

Braham No, well, never mind, perhaps you're right. (*He empties his glass.*) In any case, I must be getting along. It's been a delightful evening. (*He looks over to Celia.*) Can I give anyone a lift? Only one of you, I'm afraid, because it's only a two-seater.

Araminta Yes, please.

Braham Er, right, OK, where do you live?

Araminta Just round the corner, actually.

Braham Oh, well, that's all right, if it's very nearby, you can squeeze in the back, and I can take someone else. (*To Celia*) Where do you live?

Celia Bradley Road.

Braham Is that far?

Celia About half an hour's walk.

Braham OK, fine.

Celia I think perhaps I should stay and clear up a bit.

Philip No, that's all right, love, I'll do it.

Celia (*meaningfully*) But I'd like to stay.

Philip No, it'll be quite all right, you've done enough work for this evening.

Don Come to think of it, Araminta, it'd probably be easier if you come with me. I shall be driving Liz back.

Philip I'm sorry I haven't got my car. I lent it to a friend this evening.

Braham Right, good, that's all settled then. (*He gets up, turns to Celia.*) Shall we be off?

Celia (*to Philip*) Are you sure you don't want me to stay?

Philip Quite sure.

Celia Right then.

Braham and Celia move over to the door.

Braham Thanks again. Lovely to meet you. And may all your troubles be lexicological ones.

Philip I'll show you out.

Braham Good night.

Araminta Good night.

Don (*charming*) Good-bye.

Philip shows them out amid general salutations.

Don Miserable bugger. (*Pause. He gets up.*) Are we all ready, then?

Liz gets up, Araminta remains seated.

Araminta Perhaps . . . it's a terrible mess. Perhaps I'll stay and give him a hand.

Don It's a kind thought. I don't suppose he'd let you.

Araminta I don't know, I might be able to persuade him.

Philip re-enters.

Philip You going as well?

Don Yes, I think we'd better.

Araminta I'm going to stay and help you clear up.

Philip Oh, no, that's all right.

Araminta Then you can walk me home. How's that for a bargain?

Philip Well . . .

Araminta Fresh air will do you good.

Philip Well, all right, that's very kind.

Don and Liz are by the door. Philip goes over and shows them out. Sounds of leave-taking from the hall. Araminta starts piling plates in a fairly desultory way. Philip returns.

Philip It's very good of you, this.

Araminta Nonsense. You just sit down.

Philip sinks down on to the sofa, sighing.

Philip Just stick them in the kitchen. My man will do them tomorrow.

Araminta Tired?

Philip Exhausted.

Araminta It was a great success.

Philip smiles wanly. Silence. Araminta pauses in her work.

Araminta What time does he come in?

Philip Who?

Araminta Your man.

Philip (*uneasily*) About eleven, usually.

Silence. Araminta leaves the table and moves round behind the sofa to look out of the window. Philip seems anxious. After some hesitation, he steals a glance at her.

Philip Not raining, is it?

Araminta No.

Philip Oh, good.

Araminta wanders across until she is directly behind Philip. Then, she leans forward and begins to massage his temples gently. This has the effect of making him seem even less relaxed. After a time, she moves round and sits on his knee.

Araminta Hello.

Philip Erm, hello.

She kisses him.

Araminta Is that nice?

Philip Very. Could you, could you just move down a bit?

She does so, and Philip's look of intense pain changes to one of acute anxiety.

Araminta Better?

Philip Yes.

She kisses him again.

Araminta Shall we go to bed?

Brief silence.

Philip I'll . . . just go and get my coat.

Araminta stares at him for a moment in blank incomprehension, then realizes what he means. She stands up.

Araminta I meant together.

Philip Oh, I wasn't quite sure.

Panic overcomes him. He looks at his watch, stares fixedly at it for a moment.

Araminta Well?

Philip Well . . .

Araminta Don't be too enthusiastic.

Philip It's just . . . it's just . . .

Araminta What?

Philip (*clutching at a straw*) I haven't any, haven't got any . . .

Araminta Not necessary.

Philip Oh.

Araminta If you don't want to, just say so . . .

Philip No, no, I do, I do.

Araminta . . . and I'll go home . . .

Philip No.

Araminta . . . it's not a matter of life or death to me, you know.

   Philip stands up.

Philip I know, I'm sorry, it just took me a bit by surprise, that's all.

   He kisses her.

Araminta Didn't look like a very pleasant surprise.

Philip Please. (*He kisses her again.*) It's just that I'm shy, that's all.

Araminta I know. I love shy men.

Philip All right now?

Araminta Yes.

   They embrace.

Araminta Is that the bedroom, through there?

Philip Yes.

She moves across to it, turns at the door.

Araminta Don't be long.

Philip smiles weakly at her, as she exits, then sinks down on to the sofa again. A moment later he gets up, moves over to the table, takes a cigarette from the cigarette box, and puts it in his mouth, where it hangs limply for a moment. Then he returns it to the box, and sighs deeply.

Philip God help us all.

He exits wearily and reluctantly into the bedroom, leaving the stage empty.

Curtain.

Aria: 'O wie ängstlich' from Mozart's 'Die Entführung aus dem Serail', followed, during the interval, by the aria: 'Dies Bildnis ist bezaubernd schön' from 'Die Zauberflöte', and the aria: 'Wenn der Freude Tränen fliessen' from 'Die Entführung'.

SCENE FOUR

The opening of Purcell's ode: 'Welcome, welcome, glorious morn'. The next morning. Araminta is sitting at the table with a cup of coffee and a cigarette, reading the newspaper. The music fades. There is a knock at the door. She looks up, startled. Celia walks in, sees Araminta and stops dead. Araminta gets up, quickly. It takes her a moment to regain her composure.

Araminta Er, hello.

Celia Good morning. Is Philip in, by any chance?

Araminta I believe he's in the bath.

Celia Oh, really? (*The shock is beginning to leave her.*) Alone?

Araminta I think so.

Celia You're slipping. (*She helps herself to a cigarette, lights it.*) Well, I must say, I am surprised.

Araminta Why?

Celia I never thought you'd manage to add Philip to your collection.

Araminta What do you mean?

Celia You know, I sometimes think, although I can never quite bring myself to accept it, that you really are as thick as you pretend to be.

Araminta You're very offensive this morning.

Celia I'm very offended. I don't know why you couldn't have left him alone. Do you write all their names up in a Book of Remembrance, or something? Do you give every hundredth one a pair of gold cuff-links with some discreetly erotic motif? Are you thinking of turning professional?

Silence.

Araminta Would you care for some coffee?

Celia No, I would not.

Araminta Don't be like that.

Celia Why not?

Araminta It wasn't serious.

Celia Why did you bother, then?

Araminta That's an absurd question. I just felt like it.

Celia Didn't you stop to consider the consequences?

Araminta There are no consequences. At least, there wouldn't have been, if you hadn't walked in just now. The idea was, you see, that you weren't going to find out about it.

Celia Well, all I can say is, there's no accounting for taste.

Araminta What, his taste or my taste?

Celia (*flustered*) His taste.

Araminta You should know, you're engaged to him.

Celia That's my business.

Araminta I know. I hope he gives you better service than he gave me.

Celia What do you mean?

Araminta Never mind.

Celia How can you be so cheap and disgusting?

Araminta Practice makes perfect.

Celia Yes, apparently.

Araminta And where did you spend last night?

Silence.

Celia Look, will you, will you please tell Philip that I called . . .

Araminta Why don't you wait and tell him yourself?

Celia . . . and that I won't be calling again.

Araminta That's ridiculous, you can't mean that, I can't tell him that.

Celia (*moving to the door*) Don't, then.

Araminta There's no need to be like that about it, honestly. I promise you I won't be coming back for more. If that's the word.

Celia Well, neither will I.

Celia storms out. Araminta sits down, reflects for a moment, then returns to the paper. A moment later, Philip enters. He and Araminta greet each other warily. He pours a cup of coffee, sugars and stirs it, then moves over to the window.

Philip It's a good view, isn't it?

Araminta Yes, very nice.

Philip You can see the river. In the distance. When the tide's in. (*Longish pause.*) It's out at the moment. (*Pause.*) Look, I'm sorry about last night.

Araminta No need to be.

Philip Yes, it was awful. I mean, it must have been awful for you.

Araminta No, it wasn't.

Philip The thing is, I suppose I was a bit taken by surprise. It's the first time that's ever happened to me.

Araminta You're not . . . you're not trying to tell me you were a virgin?

Philip No, no. No, not that.

Araminta Oh, you mean it's the first time you've not been able to make it?

145

Philip Not that, either.

Araminta What then?

Philip It's just the first time I've ever been asked like that, point-blank. I think I must have found it rather disconcerting.

Araminta And that's why you were rather . . . disconcerted.

Philip Yes.

Araminta It doesn't matter at all. It happens more often than you might think. Especially the first time.

Philip Oh, does it?

Araminta (*breezily*) First-night nerves.

Philip What a . . . colourful description.

Araminta Nothing to worry about. If at first you don't succeed . . .

Philip smiles, appalled.

Philip Have you had some breakfast?

Araminta Coffee, I've had.

Philip Would you like something to eat?

Araminta I don't think so, thanks.

Philip I usually have an enormous breakfast.

Silence.

Araminta Don't worry.

Philip What about?

Araminta Anything. I don't mind. At least you're kind and gentle. It's more than can be said for most of them.

Philip What do you do it for?

Araminta Company. I like being with people. And if
you're with them, you might as well do it as not. Don't
you agree?

Philip I don't . . . disagree.

Araminta They tell me I'm a classic case, because my
uncle raped me when I was twelve. I've never quite been
able to see the connection, you'd think it would have put
me off, wouldn't you?

Philip Yes.

Araminta I suppose it did rather take the romance out of
things.

Philip Haven't you ever . . . been in love with anyone?

Araminta Not really. I did have an affair with a gypsy
when I was about fifteen. I used to climb out of the
window every night and cycle about three miles to meet
him. He never used to say very much. I was terrified of
him. It went on for about a month, then he moved on, and
I remember being very sad. But I don't know that I was in
love with him. I quite often hero-worship people, that
quite often happens, but it's difficult to go on with once
you know them a little . . . better.

Philip And are they often cruel to you?

Araminta Oh, yes, I'd say so, what I am seems to upset
them in some kind of way. I always seem to bring out the
worst in people. There was one who stole my clothes when
I was asleep one night and locked me in the bedroom of
his flat for about three weeks. He was the worst. He
hardly gave me any food. He used to threaten me with a
knife. Once he nearly strangled me.

Philip What happened?

Araminta Well, in the end he came and let me out. I was nearly going mad. There seemed no logical reason why I shouldn't be there, in that disgusting room, for ever. But finally he let me go. It was strange. He was so abject. He kept apologizing all the time, asking me to forgive him. Then, when I was leaving, he asked me to marry him.

Philip God.

Araminta I felt so sorry for him.

Philip Yes. (*Pause.*) It must have been terrible.

Araminta I could tell you things you would never forget.

Silence.

Philip Why . . . why do you do it all?

Araminta That's rather a silly question.

Philip Yes, yes, it is, sorry.

Araminta I get lonely. I hate sleeping alone. All that.

Philip Yes.

He smiles at her. She gets up.

Araminta Well, I suppose I'd better get dressed.

Philip Yes, I'll fix some breakfast. What would you like?

Araminta takes his hand.

Araminta Come on.

Philip What?

Araminta We'll be all right this time.

Philip hesitates. A moment of private dilemma.

Philip No.

Araminta No?

Philip Really.

Araminta lets go his hand.

Araminta Well, all right.

Philip No, listen, I think I'd better explain.

Araminta There's no point in explaining, love, you either want to or you don't.

Philip No, I mean about last night.

Araminta I've told you . . .

Philip I know it was my fault, I was very weak-minded.

Araminta Weak-minded, was it?

Philip I should never have agreed, I knew it would be a disaster.

Araminta Well, I could see you were thrown by the directness of my approach.

Philip It wasn't that, it was just, I didn't really want to.

Araminta I know, it's funny how important fidelity is to some people. I mean, it's something that never occurs to me.

Philip It wasn't that, the truth is, I don't really find you attractive.

Silence.

Araminta I see.

Philip No, don't be upset, it's my fault, my taste has always been terribly limited.

Araminta (*upset*) I'm not upset.

Philip No . . .

Araminta I don't know why you should think that.

Philip It's just . . .

Araminta I mean, I don't exactly find you irresistible.

Philip No. I'm sorry about it all.

Araminta So you should be.

Philip Yes.

Araminta It might have been easier if you'd said last night.

Philip Yes.

Araminta Don't you think?

Philip Yes.

Araminta I don't know, who do you think you are?

Philip Well . . .

Araminta Anyway, I shan't offend your sight much longer.

Philip You don't offend my sight . . .

Araminta I'll get dressed and leave you alone.

Philip . . . that's not it at all.

Araminta Won't take me a minute.

Philip Please.

Araminta A lot of people do find me attractive.

Philip I'm sure. It's just me. I can't seem to like women unless they're . . .

Araminta There's no need to go into it.

Philip No, all right.

Araminta Not that you did.

She moves off towards the bedroom.

Philip Can I get you some breakfast?

Araminta Will you please stop parroting on about breakfast?

Araminta exits. Philip stands disconsolately for a minute then pours himself a huge bowl of cornflakes, adding sugar and milk. He is about to begin eating when Araminta returns, having dressed with extraordinary speed.

Araminta There is just one other thing.

Philip Look, please don't go.

Araminta There is one other thing I should mention.

Philip What?

Araminta When you were in the bath.

Philip Yes.

Araminta Celia.

Philip What?

Araminta Called.

Philip God. Why didn't you tell me?

Araminta I just have.

Philip What . . . what did she say?

Araminta She seemed a bit put out.

Philip Put out?

Araminta Yes. She asked me to tell you she wouldn't be calling again.

Philip What?

Araminta That was it, I think.

Philip Why?

Araminta Well, as far as I could gather, it's not to do with your religious beliefs.

Philip What?

Araminta Why do you think, you half-witted buffoon?

Philip Because you were here.

Araminta does not answer.

Oh, God.

Araminta Passion.

Philip I don't know what to do.

Araminta No, I'm sure you don't. (*She moves over to the door.*)

Philip Wait. What did she say?

Araminta Well, naturally we discussed the weather. Then, as I remember, she became rather impolite.

Philip groans. Araminta softens.

Look, I'm sorry it happened. There was nothing I could do about it. I think I'd better go now.

She does so. Philip stands for a moment, uncertain. Then he picks up the 'phone, dials a five-figure number and waits. No answer. He puts the 'phone down. He wanders back to the table, sits down, picks up the bowl of cornflakes and starts eating.

Blackout.

Chorus: 'Vollendet ist das grosse Werk' from Haydn's 'Die Schöpfung'.

SCENE FIVE

Philip is sitting at his desk, working, later that day. A knock at the door. Celia walks in. Philip gets up quickly. They look at each other for a moment, distraught.

Philip Love.

Celia I just came back to tell you I wasn't coming back.

Philip I've been trying to 'phone you all day.

Celia I've been out.

Philip Working?

Celia No, of course not, what do you think I am?

Philip I . . .

Celia I suppose you've been working.

Philip Yes.

Celia Typical.

Philip I thought it would take my mind off things.

Celia And did it?

Philip No.

Celia Even more typical.

Philip Why?

Celia Did you hear what I said?

Philip What?

Celia When I came in.

Philip Yes, but listen . . .

Celia If you say 'I can explain everything', I'll punch your bloody teeth in.

Philip But I can.

Celia I suppose you were discussing morphology all night. Or checking her vowel sounds.

Philip No.

Celia It's so insulting, Philip. I mean you deliberately got rid of me.

Philip What do you mean?

Celia Well, I did ask you to let me stay.

Philip You didn't.

Celia Of course I did. I couldn't have made it much clearer if I'd started unbuttoning myself.

Philip But I thought you just wanted to help with the washing-up.

Celia You amaze me. You really do.

Philip Christ, I wish you had stayed.

Celia Why?

Philip I didn't realize you wanted to stay the night. Oh, God, I wish you had.

Silence.

Celia You're being cunning.

Philip I'm not.

Celia Don't. It's most unlike you.

Philip I'm not.

Celia Look.

Philip What?

Celia Why did you ask her to stay?

Philip I didn't. It's just she offered to help with the washing-up.

Celia If you didn't let me stay because you thought I wanted to do the washing-up, why did you let her stay when you thought she wanted to do the washing-up?

Philip She insisted.

Celia And more to the point, why did you let her stay when you realized she didn't want to do the washing-up?

Philip She insisted.

Celia And you gave in.

Philip Yes.

Celia Well, why?

Philip Because I didn't want to hurt her feelings.

Celia What about my feelings?

Philip You weren't there.

Celia If you go on saying things like that to me, do you really expect I'm going to marry you?

Philip I hope so.

Celia You're so incredibly . . . bland. You just sit there like a pudding, wobbling gently.

Philip Do I?

Celia You're about as emotional as a pin-cushion.

Philip I don't think that's true.

Celia Don't you?

Philip No, I don't think so.

Celia Only you would sit there pondering the pros and cons of a fairly conventional simile.

Philip It's more of a hyperbole really, isn't it?

Celia It's more of a fucking insult, that's what it really is, I think you'll find. Seeking a response, not a bloody inquest.

Philip Oh, well . . .

Celia Inviting a retort, not a sodding debate.

Philip I . . .

Celia You're talking about last night as if it were a conference on the future of the phoneme.

Philip Am I?

Celia You're not even sorry!

Philip Of course I am. Of course I am.

By now, Celia is angry and upset.

Celia I'm going.

Philip No, don't.

Celia I've said what I came to say.

Philip Don't go before I tell you what happened.

Celia I know what happened, I don't want to hear the squalid details. I don't want to listen to your pathetic attempts at self-justification.

Philip I'm not trying to justify myself. I just want to explain to you exactly what happened. Then you can make your mind up.

Celia All right, go on, tell me. (*Pause.*) Try to make it as entertaining as possible.

Philip Well . . . well . . . she asked me to go to bed with her, just like that. It took me so much by surprise, I could think of no delicate way to refuse. So I accepted. The whole thing was a complete fiasco. No good at all. Then, this morning she suggested we try again, and I had to tell her it was no use, because I quite honestly didn't find her attractive.

Celia Not many laughs in that.

Philip No. No, I suppose there weren't.

Celia What happened next?

Philip She left.

Celia Immediately?

Philip Yes. She seemed very angry.

Celia Fancy that.

Philip I handled it badly.

Celia You might say so. Sounds to me like a triumph of emotional incompetence.

Philip Well, that's how it happened.

Celia And I suppose you think that makes it all right, do you?

Philip What do you mean?

Celia I suppose you think because you were bullied into doing something you then failed to do anyway, it's as if the whole thing didn't happen.

Philip No.

Celia Did it never occur to you that I might prefer it if you brazened the whole thing out and said, yes, it was all planned, it was your final fling before we got married, or something like that?

Philip But it wasn't.

Celia You're so damn literal-minded. I mean you might have just said you'd done it and you were sorry and it wouldn't happen again – instead of saying all right, not to worry, I was an abject failure, so that doesn't count.

Philip I didn't say that.

Celia No, you didn't even say that.

Philip All I can do is tell you what happened and leave it up to you.

Celia Well, if you leave it up to me, I shall have to say I can't possibly undertake to spend my life with someone so hopelessly weak and indecisive, he's going to leave every major issue up to me.

Philip That's not very fair.

Celia We're not playing croquet, you know.

Philip No, but in this case I've made my half of the decision. I want to marry you. So it's only up to you in the sense that you haven't decided yet.

Celia Oh, you do make me so angry.

Philip Why?

Celia You never understand what I'm trying to say.

Philip Maybe not, but I think I usually understand what you do say.

Celia God, you're completely impossible.

Philip (*bewildered*) I'm sorry. (*Pause.*) I suppose I am indecisive. (*Pause.*) My trouble is, I'm a man of no convictions. (*Longish pause.*) At least, I think I am.

Celia starts laughing.

What's the joke?

Celia I am fond of you.

Philip (*lost*) Are you?

Silence.

Celia I'm afraid my plan didn't work at all.

Philip Plan?

Celia I was going to use it as an excuse. I mean it seemed like a perfectly good excuse.

Philip Use what as an excuse? What for?

Celia For . . . finishing.

Philip I don't understand.

Celia Well, I've been thinking, you see, really, for a long time, that we aren't really compatible.

Philip Oh.

Celia I always used to think you were just the sort of person I'd been looking for. Someone fairly intelligent and reliable and kind and safe and a little bit dull. Somebody who admired me and thought what I said was worth listening to, not just worth tolerating.

Philip But you were wrong.

Celia Yes, I think perhaps I was wrong.

Philip I see.

Celia And after what happened last night, I thought I'd better come over to discuss things with you. And when I found Araminta here, I thought that gives me an excuse not to discuss things with you, I can just leave you, and make you think it's your fault.

Philip (*confused*) How do you mean, what happened last night? You didn't know about it, did you?

Celia I mean what happened to me.

Philip Oh. What did happen to you?

Celia Braham took me back to his hotel.

Philip Oh.

Celia And I stayed the night there.

Philip But . . . why?

Celia I don't know, he went on at me. And I finally thought oh well, why not, I was still very angry about your not letting me stay. I don't know why. I felt dreadful this morning. He kept saying that creative artists had a much more consuming sexual urge than ordinary people. He told me that's why Bach had thirty children.

Philip And were you convinced by this argument?

Celia No.

Philip But you still . . .?

Celia Yes.

Philip Why? I don't see why.

Celia Well, he's so confident and self-assured, I don't know why. I just suddenly felt like it, don't go on about it.

Philip And is that what you want?

Celia I don't know, I suppose so. Not him, I don't mean him, he's awful, but something like that.

Philip What makes you think he's awful?

Celia Well, it was this morning, the way he behaved this morning, that really turned me off him. For one thing, he was so nasty about you.

Philip Was he?

Celia Yes, he really hates you. All the time yesterday evening, he thought you were taking the piss in a particularly subtle way.

Philip Really?

Celia And then when I'd argued with him a bit and told him that wasn't in your nature, he finally agreed and said, yes, come to think of it, he supposed you were far too boring to do anything as enterprising as that.

Philip Well, he's right there, isn't he?

Celia What do you mean?

Philip Isn't that what you think?

Celia Of course not, don't be so rude.

Philip I'm sorry, I thought that's what you just said.

Celia I think you get a perverse kick out of running yourself down.

Philip No, I don't. I don't think I do.

Celia Anyway, I defended you, even though I knew you wouldn't have defended yourself.

Philip Why did he hate me, I don't know, I didn't hate him.

Celia Didn't you?

Philip No, I thought he was quite amusing.

Celia And do you hate him now?

Philip No.

Celia Not even after everything I've told you?

Philip I don't suppose he's very happy.

Celia (*angrily*) And are you happy?

Philip No.

Celia Well then.

Philip Not at the moment.

Celia (*offended*) Oh, I see.

Philip I mean . . . I mean, I hope to be. I have been. I hope I will be. (*He moves over to the window.*) Look. The tide's in. It's a lovely day, look. (*Pause.*) It's very rare to have a day as fine as this in November.

Celia Yes.

Philip (*smiling*) Just when one was getting used to the idea of winter. (*Pause.*) I'm glad you defended me. I don't see what he has against me.

Celia That was only the beginning. He got far worse.

Philip In what way?

Celia It was when he read about R. J. Morris in the paper.

Philip What about him?

Celia Haven't you looked at the paper today?

Philip No, I couldn't, it was all full of stuff about the Prime Minister, I thought it would be too upsetting.

Celia Well, R. J. Morris was murdered yesterday as well.

Philip He wasn't!

Celia Yes, apparently there's some gang of lunatics about, whose intention is to knock off twenty-five of the most eminent English writers.

Philip What do they want to do that for?

Celia I don't know. They've formed this organization called the Fellowship of Allied Terrorists Against Literature – F.A.T.A.L. It seems R. J. Morris was their first victim. But they've sent copies of this letter to twenty-four others saying they're going to kill them off, one by one.

Philip How horrible!

Celia Yes. Anyway, Braham was transfixed by it.

Philip Was he?

Celia He wasn't one of the twenty-five. He didn't know whether to be relieved or insulted.

Philip Oh, I see.

Silence.

Celia He's asked me to go back and see him again this evening.

Philip And will you?

Celia Certainly not. I wouldn't dream of it.

Philip Come back, then. (*He smiles.*) All is forgiven.

Celia (*bristling*) What do you mean?

Philip I don't know. Joke, really.

Celia Oh.

Philip But, I mean, I mean it.

Celia I've thought about it a lot.

Philip I know . . .

Celia I've made up my mind.

Philip Why?

Celia I think we'd probably make each other very unhappy.

Philip Why?

Celia Because I don't think you'd be able to control me.

Philip Does that matter?

Celia I didn't think so at first. In fact, to begin with, I thought that was the great advantage. But I don't any more.

Philip Perhaps you're right.

Celia You see, that's the thing, you're so unassertive. Perhaps you're right! Is that the best you can do?

Philip All right, I'm not going to let you leave me!

Celia It's no good doing it now, is it, it's supposed to be spontaneous.

Philip Well, I only said perhaps you're right because I was trying to look at it from your point of view. I mean, it's quite obvious what I see in you, isn't it? It's much more of a mystery what you see in me, and if you don't see what you did see any more, then perhaps you *are* right. If you see what I mean.

Celia No.

Philip I'm not surprised you're having second thoughts, if all these people keep making passes at you all the time.

Celia What are you talking about?

Philip Well, you know, Noakes and Johnson and all those people you were talking about last night.

Celia Oh, that.

Philip Yes.

Celia None of that was true.

Philip What?

Celia You know I'm always making things up.

Philip Why?

Celia Well, you've got to say something, haven't you? Can't just sit there like a statue all evening. Like Liz. And lies are usually that much more interesting than the truth, that's all.

Philip Oh. (*Pause. Philip considers this.*) Well, if that's the case, can't we try to come to some arrangement? I mean, I could try – or pretend – to be firmer, and you could pretend not to mind my weakness so much.

Celia No. Of course not.

Philip Why not?

Celia What a monstrous suggestion.

Philip Why?

Celia Well, it's . . . it's so deceitful.

Philip laughs.

No, look, it's different telling a few stories to liven up the party, from basing your whole life on a lie.

Philip You just said lies were more interesting than the truth.

Celia You're being literal-minded again.

Silence.

Philip I don't know. I've always been a failure with women.

Celia Oh, please.

Philip But it's true. I remember, I remember the first girl I was ever in love with, Carol her name was, and I made the mistake, just as we were about to go to bed together for the first time, of telling her I was a virgin. Oh, well, then, she said, that was that, she wasn't going to be a guinea-pig for anyone. It was that phrase that did it. She became so entranced and horrified by the idea represented by her own quite fortuitous image, that I gave up, there was obviously no hope. Guinea-pig, 'I'm not going to be a guinea-pig', she kept on saying. So there it was. A whole relationship doomed by a random word-association. This is the same thing. You think I'm being sentimental and self-pitying just because I say I'm a failure with women. But I'm not. I'm just telling the simple truth, which is that I've never managed to give a woman satisfaction. I hope to. I hoped to with you. Given a bit of time. But in itself it's just a perfectly neutral fact. Like the fact I was a virgin when I was with Carol. (*He breaks off for a moment.*) She was very cruel. I adored her.

Celia You probably adored her because she was cruel.

Philip On the contrary, it was when she became really cruel that I stopped adoring her. Your interpretation is both perverse and banal.

Celia Oh, don't be so pompous.

Philip Sorry.

Celia You know something, you apologize far too often. You really oughtn't to, it's not very attractive.

Philip Yes, I know, I'm sorry.

Celia laughs, briefly, and Philip smiles as he realizes what he has said.

Celia What made you want to get married?

Philip You.

Celia Yes, I know, but apart from that.

Philip What do you mean?

Celia Well, you've been a comfortable bachelor for so long, I think you must have made some kind of abstract decision to get married, I mean quite apart from wanting to marry me.

Philip I suppose that might be true.

Celia Well, why?

Philip Perhaps it was because I'm beginning to get lonely.

Celia Go on.

Philip I don't know, I've been doing this job for about twelve or thirteen years now, and I'm beginning to realize that I'm not immortal. Another thing is, when I sit and remember the past, you know, involuntary memories, what I remember most is certain rooms, rooms I've lived and worked in, at different times, in different countries. I was thinking about some of them the other day, and I suddenly realized something that had never occurred to me before. They were all empty. I mean I remember them as if I'm sitting in them, furniture, ceiling angles, street noises, clock ticking, all very vivid. But never anyone else. It gave me rather a shock.

Celia Don't you like being alone?

Philip No, you know how gregarious I am. Look, who's the most boring person you know?

Celia I don't know. If you wait a few minutes, I could probably give you quite an impressive list.

Philip Well, whoever it is, I'd quite willingly spend an hour a day with him for the rest of my life. Rather than being alone.

Celia Do you think you want to get married because you're unhappy?

Philip I'm not unhappy. I mean, I am at the moment, but in general I've got no reason to be unhappy. In fact, I've got no right to be unhappy.

Celia That's never stopped anyone.

Philip I know, I know that, but when you consider how pleasant my job is, how well-fed and privileged and comfortable I am and how easy it is for me to be tolerant and compassionate, it does seem perverse to be unhappy as well, doesn't it? I mean, to be unhappy on top of all that does seem unreasonably self-indulgent, don't you think? It's not as if my life was a struggle. I sit in my study and read the latest journal, and occasionally I get up and change the record on my player, and sometimes I go abroad for a few weeks and wander round the galleries, and I play with words and make my anagrams and read the arts pages. And books, I must have read thousands of books, and seen hundreds of films and plays in my life. Not that many of them stay with me longer than an evening, but I'm grateful to all those people for whiling away my time. And that's all. Oh, yes, and I teach, and lecture, and write rather boring and pedantic articles, and from time to time, I suffer. Not often, I wouldn't like to exaggerate, but from time to time. A full life and an empty one.

He smiles. Celia assesses this for a moment.

Celia Sympathy, is it, you're after?

Philip Well, yes, perhaps, yes, I suppose so. I don't know. Perhaps not sympathy. Liking.

Celia At least you like everyone, that's half the battle anyway.

Philip Yes, that's half the battle. The wrong half, but there we go.

Celia 'And you're an optimist, that makes life pleasanter, doesn't it?

Philip I don't think I am. What makes you think that? You can like people without being an optimist. For instance, it's easier to like people if it occurs to you that they're going to die. It's difficult not to like a man if you can envisage his flesh falling from his bones.

Celia Oh dear, oh dear.

Philip What?

Celia Let us grow amorous, you and I,
Knowing that both of us must die.

Philip Who said that?

Celia Somebody must have.

Silence. Then, from the playing fields outside, a long, mournful whistle.

Philip Full time.

Celia What?

Philip Nothing.

Celia Not being lyrical, are you?

Philip (*shaking his head*) I . . .

Celia Let us eschew lyricism. Don't you think? I think lyricism should at all costs be eschewed.

Philip Stop it.

Celia Well, you started it. I never realized you had a morbid streak in you.

Philip Oh, yes, I suppose . . . (*He pauses, before deciding to go on with what he is saying.*) All my life, you know, I've been in a state of perpetual terror.

Celia Terror?

Philip I think that's more accurate than the word I normally use for it, which is concern.

Celia What do you mean?

Philip I mean, I mean that the basic feature of my character is an anxiety to please people and to do what they want, which leads to, that is, which amounts to a passion, and which is, in fact, so advanced that I can only describe it as . . . terror.

Celia In other words, it's not that you like people, it's just that you're afraid of them.

Philip No, there's no contradiction in that, the one is a consequence of the other.

Celia I don't believe that.

Silence.

Philip I'll tell you something I've never told anyone before, it's one of the most humiliating things that ever happened to me. When I was teaching in Hong Kong, I used to, walking from the lecture-hall to the car-park, I used to pass a hunchback, a, a cripple with an enormous head, who used to sit on the pavement and beg. After a time, I got into the habit of giving him a little money, every day, when I passed him. This went on for a bit, and then, to my great embarrassment, he started to clean my car. I tried to tell him not to bother one day when I found him at it, but he didn't understand, so I just left it, it seemed to be what he wanted to do. So every day, I would come out of my lecture, walk past him, press a little money into his hand,

shamefully little, now I come to think of it, get into my
beautiful, shiny car and drive off.

I used to keep a cache of small change handy to pay
him, but one day, for some reason, I found I had none left,
in fact, as I was leaving the building I found I had nothing
smaller than a ten-dollar note, which was obviously, I
thought to myself, far too much to give him. So, on this
particular day I walked hurriedly past on the other side of
the street, hoping he wouldn't see me, and crossed into the
car-park as quickly as I could. But I'd just got into the car
and put the key in the ignition, when I saw him hobbling
towards the entrance of the car-park on his crutches at
great speed, stopping occasionally to wave his duster at
me. No, I thought, I can't face this, so I started up, and put
my foot down, and raced out of the car-park. Now, I don't
know about this, I mean, I'm sure I wasn't anywhere near
him, but for some reason he panicked, and tried to jump
backwards – and I just had this appalling glimpse of his
crutches going up in the air as he overbalanced and fell on
to his back. Needless to say, I didn't stop.

After that, whenever he saw me coming, he used to get
up, move down the road a bit and go indoors. I hoped I'd
be able to make it up with him, but I never got a chance,
he never, he never let me get near him again.

No wonder they want our blood.

Celia Why are you telling me all this? I can't ever
remember you talking so much.

Philip I don't want you to go.

Silence.

Celia My problem is, all the men I fall in love with turn
out to be such terrible people.

Philip Oh. Do you think so?

Celia Not you, I don't mean you. That's what I'm trying

to say. I was never really in love with you because you aren't firm enough. I don't think I'm capable of loving anyone as weak as you.

Philip Do you prefer to be bullied then?

Celia I prefer to know where I stand.

Silence.

Philip Can't we . . . isn't there . . .?

Celia I don't think so.

Philip Are you sure?

Celia Yes. Yes, now I've made up my mind, I honestly don't know what it is I ever saw in you.

Philip Oh, well. Oh, well, then.

Celia No, don't misunderstand me. I'll always like you, I'll always be fond of you. It's just that we're not compatible.

Philip So you already said. I still can't see it myself, but I suppose I shall just have to take your word for it.

Celia Now I think it would be best if I went. (*She gets up.*)

Philip Don't.

Celia Yes.

Philip Please.

Celia I think it would be best.

Philip Stay and talk to me. I feel a bit suicidal.

Celia Oh, don't exaggerate.

Philip Well, you know. Stay and talk for a bit.

Celia Look, what have we got to talk about now? What could we possibly talk about?

Philip Anything.

Celia bursts into tears. Philip is amazed, he takes her in his arms and she sobs uncontrollably for a minute, then slowly recovers.

Celia Sorry.

Philip Are you all right, love?

Celia Yes. All right now.

Philip What's the matter?

Celia What do you think?

Philip But I mean . . . I mean, it's your decision.

Celia What difference does that make?

Philip All right, now, are you?

Celia Yes, thanks.

Philip Would you like a glass of water or anything?

Celia No, no. I really must go now. Good-bye.

Philip Good-bye. (*He takes her face in his hands and kisses her on the eyes and on the mouth.*) What now? Death, hell, destruction, madness, suicide, or will he come through smiling?

Celia Yes.

Philip When will I see you again?

Celia Not for a bit. Not until we've got over it.

Philip Soon.

Celia I expect so. (*She moves quickly to the door.*) Good-bye. (*Celia exits.*)

Philip Good-bye, love.

*He stands for a moment in the centre of the stage,
disconsolate. Then he sits at his desk, picks up a book,
and reads. He breaks off for a moment and stares into
the distance, then returns to his book. He makes a note.*

Blackout.

*The second movement of Albinoni's Concerto in D
minor for oboe and strings, Op. 9, No. 2.*

SCENE SIX

*A few hours later. Evening. Philip is now writing a letter,
apparently with some difficulty. After a time, he puts his
pen down and thinks for a moment, gazing vacantly into
space.*

Philip But I . . . (*He breaks off, gets up, goes over to the
bookshelf, takes down a book and looks something up.*)
Yes.
But I was thinking of a plan
To dye one's whiskers green,
And always use so large a fan
That they could not be seen.
Yes. (*He smiles, then, after a short pause, moves over to
the telephone and dials a two-figure number.*) Hello, Don?
. . . Yes . . . I wonder if you could just come round for a
minute, I'd like to talk to you . . . Well, yes, it is, rather
. . . it is, it's been a day of major catastrophes, and I . . .
Well, in fact, I want to ask your advice about something
. . . it won't take a minute, honestly . . . all right, thanks,
right.

*Philip crosses the room and pours himself a drink. A
knock at the door and Don enters. He smiles at Philip
and slumps into an armchair.*

Don Hello.

Philip Scotch?

Don Thanks.

Philip Sorry to drag you over here. Are you busy?

He pours a drink for Don, takes it over to him.

Don Well, no, not exactly, I . . . well, I'll tell you about it in a minute. First of all, what's your problem? You don't look very well.

Philip I don't feel very well. I mean, I feel a bit remote.

Don What do you mean?

Philip Distant.

Don Why? What's the matter?

Philip Well, Celia came round this afternoon and told me she didn't want to marry me any more.

Don Oh.

Philip Last night, Araminta stayed here under circumstances too appalling to relate.

Don Really?

Philip And this morning Celia came round here before Araminta had left.

Don Oh, I see.

Philip No. Because Celia admitted that she'd decided to leave me anyway.

Don Did she?

Philip She having spent the night with Braham.

Don (*bewildered*) Good God.

Philip Although she said that had nothing to do with it either.

Don With what?

Philip Her decision.

Silence.

Don How extraordinary.

Philip She said what you said when we were talking about it yesterday. She said she didn't think we were compatible.

Don Meaningless nonsense.

Philip But you said that as well.

Don Yes. But I was speaking theoretically.

Philip (*uncomprehending*) Oh.

Don You see, I always divide people into two groups. Those who live by what they know to be a lie, and those who live by what they believe, falsely, to be the truth. And having decided that Celia belonged to the first group and you to the second, I concluded that you weren't compatible, and that furthermore that was what attracted you to one another. But, I mean, trying to make elegant patterns out of people's hopelessness doesn't really work. It's only a frivolous game.

Philip Seems to have worked on this occasion.

Don What is wrong with the statement: 'all generalizations are false'?

Philip It's a generalization.

Don See, you're not as remote as all that.

Philip But why . . . why do you say I live by what I believe, falsely, to be the truth?

Don Because you do. Your whole behaviour is based on the assumption that everyone is like you.

Philip Isn't everybody's?

Don No. Of course not. Most people's behaviour is based on the desperate hope that everyone isn't like them.

Philip And why do you think Celia lives by a lie?

Don Because her vanity demands it.

Philip I'm not sure about that.

Don I am.

Philip Well, no doubt if you go on about it long enough, you'll persuade me to believe it. I haven't even got the courage of my lack of convictions.

Don Oh, I wish I'd said that.

Philip Why?

Don I don't know, it sounds good.

Philip That's not really why I said it, believe it or not.

Don Sorry. I'm sorry.

Silence.

Philip And which category do you belong to?

Don What?

Philip Of the two.

Don Oh, I live by a lie. In my case, the lie is that I am a teacher of English, when in fact I am paid a handsome sum by the college to perfect a technique of idleness which I hope will eventually become unparalleled in academic history.

Philip Oh, rubbish, you're not idle. You're famous for your conscientiousness.

Don Ah, well, that's part of the art. I perform, in fact I sometimes actually volunteer for, all those little administrative tasks, which require no effort or application whatsoever and which can be done quite automatically. In that way, you see, I acquire a reputation for conscientiousness, and also provide myself with an excuse in the unlikely event that I should be caught out not knowing something I ought to know.

Philip You're exaggerating.

Don Oh, no, I'm not. In my youth I might have been concerned about my idleness, I used to make feeble attacks on it by doing things like setting my striking clock an hour fast, but I think I knew all along what I was heading for. When I struggled through my finals in that cunning and devious way, I think I knew this was my destination. I worked hard my first year teaching, my God, yes. I took a couple of dozen index cards and noted down ten points about each of the subjects that might reasonably be expected to come my way. And now, twenty-four weeks a year, I simply select the relevant card and give my pupils the points they've omitted in their essays, or if they've got them all I say, wonderful, see you next week, and I recover from this strenuous activity with twenty-eight weeks a year of total inactivity, usually in some pleasantly warm climate. I've given up all ideas of writing books, research, all that nonsense, I'm just settling, settling into my character. I am more than half in love with easeful sloth. I'm . . . what's that word that means bloodless?

Philip Etiolated?

Don Etiolated. That's it, etiolated. Only fit for lying about on a sofa with the curtains pulled, listening to baroque music and occasionally dabbing at the temples with a damp flannel. Do you know that I'm capable now of emptying my head completely for two or three hours at a stretch? Not a single thought of any kind. Nothing. That's not easily done, you know.

Philip I'm sure.

Don I think that if one manages in one's lifetime not only to come to terms with one's own uselessness but to begin actually enjoying it as well, that's something, don't you think, something, some kind of . . . an achievement.

Philip Perhaps.

Silence.

Don I'm sorry, Philip.

Philip Why?

Don It's typical of you, you know.

Philip What?

Don You've had the most terrible day, everything has gone wrong, you ask me round to give you some support or advice or something and all that happens is that I talk about myself.

Philip That's all right.

Don I'll shut up now. You tell me what you want. What can I do for you?

Philip Well, when I was talking to Celia this afternoon, she asked me why I wanted to get married, I mean apart from wanting to marry her. It made me realize that she was right, that I did want to get married, that I was lonely, now that youthful hopes have faded in the usual way. I'm sorry, I didn't mean to get maudlin.

Don No, go on. What is friendship, if not a chance to indulge in mutual self-pity?

Philip And I was thinking what you said to me yesterday about Liz.

Don (*shiftily*) Oh?

Philip Yes, you remember you were saying you thought she liked me, and that she would be more suitable for me than Celia.

Don Well . . .

Philip Anyway, I've just sat down to write to her, I thought I'd ask her out or something, ask her to lunch, and I just wanted to ask you what . . . (*He breaks off, surprised by Don's obvious embarrassment.*) What's the matter?

Don Well, Liz is, she's in my room now.

Philip Is she?

Don She's been there since yesterday evening.

Philip Oh. Oh, that's . . . erm . . .

Don So I . . .

Philip Yes. Yes.

Don I've rather, you know, rather fallen for her.

Philip Oh, well, that's, er, isn't it?

Don Yes.

Philip I'm surprised, I didn't think you . . .

Don I'm surprised, too, in fact, I'm amazed. She's such a quiet girl, I mean, you don't expect her to be, I mean, it just sort of happened, and then for her to be, well, so passionate, I was very surprised.

Philip Yes.

Don I'm sorry, Philip, it's just the way things happen . . .

Philip That's all right.

Don The last thing . . .

Philip That's all right. Perhaps you should be going back to her now.

Don No, it's all right.

Philip I'd rather you did.

Don No, look, you're just a bit upset . . .

Philip Will you please get out!

Don Oh, all right, if you . . .

Philip Please go away!

Don exits uncertainly. Philip sits for a moment. Then he drains his drink, gets up, moves to his desk, crumples up the letter and throws it into the waste-paper basket. Next he moves back to the table, takes a cigarette from the cigarette-box and puts it in his mouth. Pause. Then he returns to the desk, opens a drawer and takes out a small pistol. He considers it for a moment, then puts it down on the desk. He lifts the telephone and dials two figures.

Hello, Don? . . . I'm sorry about all that . . . yes, I just, you know, well, I am sorry anyway . . . What? . . . Now? All right, if you're sure that's all right . . . are you sure? Yes, I am quite hungry . . . well, that's very kind . . . yes, I'm all right, now . . . no, don't let's get sentimental about it . . . well, anyway, I'm about to do something terrible . . . you'll see in a minute . . . I forgot to tell you, I thought of a new anagram today . . . 'imagine the theatre as real' . . . 'imagine the theatre as real' . . . it's an anagram for 'I hate thee, sterile anagram' . . . Yes, I thought so too . . . all right, then . . . yes . . . yes . . . see you both in a minute.

He hangs up, pauses a moment, then picks up the pistol. He turns it toward him and pulls the trigger. A small flame springs from the hammer. Philip lights his cigarette from it, inhales deeply, pockets the pistol and exits, leaving the door open.

Aria: 'Ich freue mich auf meinen Tod' from Bach's Cantata No. 82, 'Ich habe genug'.

Curtain.

ironic, considering
that a pistol is
what killed
John & Phillip
has been so
upset about

SAVAGES

For K. B.
and for friends in Brazil

A Note on the Quarup

The Quarup is the principal ceremony of the Indians of the Xingu. It is not necessarily an annual event but may be held in any year during which a chief or person of chiefly birth has died. Not that it is a funeral ceremony in any conventional Western sense of the term: for, apart from its social importance as a gathering together of all the neighbouring tribes, one of its central events is the bringing out of seclusion of the young girls who have menstruated for the first time since the previous Quarup, who have been strictly confined since their menstruation, and who are now ready for marriage with their betrothed. This makes of the Quarup a celebration of rebirth as well as a lament for the dead, a ceremonial of a richness and subtlety to which no brief account can do justice, a ritual drama of regeneration.

The host tribe spends weeks preparing for this – sending out messages to invite all the neighbouring tribes, clearing campsites for them and gathering enough food to feed them when they arrive. The day before the Quarup is spent setting up and decorating the Quarup posts, which represent those who have died, and which are decorated until they resemble the human body, at which point, in the eyes of the participants, they actually become those who are being mourned. In addition to this, there is dancing and flute-playing, and the members of the tribe decorate their own and each other's bodies.

During the night, as the mourners sit watching and lamenting the dead, representatives from the tribes camped round the village one by one rush into the village to steal firebrands in order to light their own fires.

The next day, the main ceremony unfolds. The messengers go out and lead the chiefs of each tribe into the centre of the village – and when they have taken their places, their tribesmen rush into the village, and the wrestling tournament begins with the strongest members of the host tribe each challenging the champion of one of the visiting tribes. This leads into a more general, less formal series of wrestling bouts, and then, after an exchange of gifts, the girls are brought out of seclusion, walking behind a kinsman of the dead chief, carrying a gourd cup containing 'pequi' nuts (a symbol of fertility), which they empty on the ground in front of the visiting chiefs. This is followed by general feasting and then by a dance in which pairs of fluteplayers (playing the special ten-foot Quarup flutes) followed by pairs of the now released girls visit each hut in the village in turn. After further celebration, speeches and a final distribution of gifts by the host tribe, the visiting tribes depart, leaving the host tribe to take the Quarup posts down to the lagoon at dusk and float them out until they sink and join the spirit village at the bottom of the lagoon.

The next morning, the chief gives every member of his tribe a new name.

C.H.

Characters

Alan West
Mrs West
Carlos Esquerdo
Miles Crawshaw
General
Attorney General
An Investigator
Ataide Pereira
Major Brigg
The Revd Elmer Penn
Kumai
A pilot, a co-pilot, Indians, guerrillas, etc.

The bombing of the Cintas Largas tribe during the performance of their funeral ritual took place in 1963; and the confession of Ataide Pereira was recorded shortly after this by Padre Edgar Smith, S. J.

The rest of the play is set in Brazil in 1970–1.

Most of the characters in this play are fictitious: most of the events are not.

The play was first performed at the Royal Court Theatre on 12 April, 1973. The cast was as follows:

Alan West Paul Scofield
Mrs West Rona Anderson
Carlos Esquerdo Tom Conti
Miles Crawshaw Michael Pennington
General Leonard Kavanagh
Attorney General/Investigator Gordon Sterne
Ataide Pereira Glyn Grain
Major Brigg A. J. Brown
Chief/Bert Frank Singuineau
The Reverend Elmer Penn Geoffrey Palmer
Kumai Terence Burns
Pilot Leonard Kavanagh
Co-pilot Glyn Grain
Indians George Baizley, Lynda Dagley, Thelma Kidger, Donna Louise, Eddy Nedari, J. C. Shepherd

Directed Robert Kidd
Designed Jocelyn Herbert and Andrew Sanders
Lighting Andy Phillips
Presented by the Royal Court Theatre and Michael Codron

'The "Indian problem" in Latin America is in its essence a problem of the economic structure of the national and international capitalist system as a whole.'

ANDRE GUNDER FRANK – *Capitalism and Underdevelopment in Latin America*

'. . . il s'ensuit que la morale immanente des mythes prend le contrepied de celle que nous professons aujourd'hui. Elle nous enseigne, en tout cas, qu'une formule à laquelle nous avons fait un aussi grand sort que "l'enfer, c'est les autres" ne constitue pas une proposition philosophique, mais un témoignage ethnographique sur une civilisation. Car on nous a habitué dès l'enfance à craindre l'impureté du dehors.

'Quand ils proclament, au contraire, que "l'enfer, c'est nous-même", les peuples sauvages donnent une leçon de modestie qu'on voudrait croire que nous sommes encore capables d'entendre.'

CLAUDE LÉVI-STRAUSS – *L'Origine des Manières de Table*

ONE

*Bare stage. In the centre, five or six blazing torches
inclined towards each other to form a pyramid with a
single head of flame. The theatre is entirely lit by this.
Indian music, flutes, drums, chanting. Shadowy forms.*

    After a time, **West** *appears. As he speaks,* **Indians** *enter,
one by one, from the wings, through the auditorium. Each
takes a torch and returns with it the way he came.*

West
Origin of fire.
In the old days men ate raw flesh
And had no knowledge of fire.
Also they had no weapons
And hunted the game with their bare hands.

A boy went hunting one day with his brother-in-law.
They saw a macaw's nest up perched on a cliff-ledge.
They built a ladder and the boy climbed up to the ledge.
In the nest were two eggs.
The boy took them and threw them down to his brother-
    in-law
But in the air they turned into jagged stones
Which as he went to catch them cut his hands.
He was very angry.
He thought the boy was trying to kill him.
He took the ladder down broke it and went away.

The boy was on the ledge for many days and nights
Dying slowly of hunger
Eating his own excrement
Until one day the jaguar passed by

With his bow and arrows
And seeing a shadow cast ahead of him on the ground
Looked up and saw the boy.
The jaguar mended the ladder helped the boy down
Took him back to his home and revived him
Feeding him cooked meat.

The jaguar loved the boy and treated him as his son
Calling him the foundling
But the jaguar's wife was very jealous of him
And when the jaguar was away she never missed a chance
To scratch him or to knock him over.
The boy complained to the jaguar that he was always
    frightened
So the jaguar gave him a bow and arrow
And taught him how to use them.
The next time the jaguar's wife attacked him
He shot an arrow at her and killed her.

The boy was terrified by what he had done.
He took his bow and a large piece of cooked meat
And escaped into the jungle.
After many days wandering he reached his own village
And told his people all the things that had happened to him
Showing them the meat and the bow.
The men were very excited by his discoveries
And they set off on an expedition to the jaguar's home
To steal his weapons
And to steal his fire.

What you take from people
They will never find again.
Now the jaguar has no weapons
Except his hatred for man.
He eats no cooked meat
But swallows the raw flesh of his victims.
And only the reflection and the memory of fire

Burn in his eyes.

Silence. The last torch has vanished. Embers. A strange cry in the darkness.

Blackout.

TWO

A comfortable bedroom with twin beds. West and **Mrs West** *are in evening dress, West struggling with his bow-tie, Mrs West ready, waiting.*

West God. I can never get these things to work.

Mrs West You've had enough practice.

West I know. What's the matter with it? I keep meaning to get one of those ones on an elastic strap. There we are. (*He makes a final adjustment, considers it in the mirror.*) Jesus, it looks ludicrous.

Mrs West (*sighing*) Start again. Concentrate.

He does so.

West Look, do we have to go to this thing?

Mrs West turns away, ignoring him.

Mm? Do we?

Mrs West I don't know why you always say that. You know perfectly well we have to. At least, I don't have to. You have to. That's the only reason you're going in the first place, because you have to. So why you always say that, I don't know.

West All right, there's no need to, I was just asking. (*Pause.*) I suppose there's always a remote chance there might be someone amusing or interesting there, never let it

193

be said I'm not an optimist. That's better. (*He inspects himself in the mirror.*) No, it's not, it's worse.

Mrs West It'll do.

West No, it'll come undone.

Mrs West We're going to be late.

West What you mean is, we're not going to be early. I can't think why you have this passion for always wanting to be the first person there. All that happens is you hear your name spoken so often you begin to think there's at least six of you, and you run through all your small talk before the soup. I won't be a minute.

> *He undoes his tie again and turns to the mirror. As he does so, the door bursts open and three young men enter. They are all wearing rubber Walt Disney masks. Two of them are holding sub-machine-guns, the third, Carlos, a pistol fitted with a silencer.*

Carlos Mr West?

West Erm, er, I don't think so, no. Why?

> *Carlos looks down at something in his hand and back at West.*

Carlos I know you are Mr West. Please put your hands up.

West (*doing so*) Oh.

Carlos Mrs West.

Mrs West Yes.

Carlos Please lie face down on the floor and put your hands behind your back.

> *She does so. Carlos gestures and one of the others lays his gun down, produces a rope, binds and gags her.*

West What is this?

Carlos Rag week.

West is nonplussed by this reply. With one hand he plucks at his tie.

Keep your hands still, please. (*Pause.*) Are you armed?

West Of course not.

Carlos Right. Now you are to come with us. Our car is parked just outside the front door. You must walk just in front of me, on my left, sort of arm in arm. If you make any disturbance I shall shoot you more or less in the liver. Now. Do your tie up.

West fumbles hopelessly with his tie.

West Easier said than done.

Carlos Do it!

West tries to. Time passes.

West Be with you in a minute.

Blackout.

THREE

A dark, dingy bedroom with a single bed. West is lying on it, tied to the frame, a black canvas hood over his head. He sits up with a start, in so far as this is possible, when Carlos comes into the room, holding a piece of paper.

Carlos How are you?

West Incredibly uncomfortable.

Carlos Yes. I'm sorry about this. I hope before the end of the day we'll be able to arrange something more satisfactory. Handcuffs.

West Sounds wonderful.

Carlos But we're very busy at the moment.

West Think nothing of it.

Carlos I've come to explain why this has happened to you.

West (*muffled*) Does it matter?

Carlos I beg your pardon.

West Does it matter?

Carlos Well, it matters to us. And so, I suppose, in the circumstances, it matters to you as well. (*Pause.*) We are members of the M.R.B., the Movimento Revolucionario Brasileiro, and we have kidnapped you in order to achieve certain political aims. We have asked for the release of twenty-five political prisoners . . .

West Twenty-five?

Carlos Yes.

West Is that all?

Carlos Well, yes.

West But you got forty for that German.

Carlos Yes, but he was the ambassador . . .

West And seventy for the Swiss ambassador . . .

Carlos You don't think we've asked for enough?

West No, I'm sure Her Majesty's Government will feel most affronted.

Carlos Well . . .

West (*muffled*) They probably take it as some sort of slight . . .

Carlos What?

West I say they're probably annoyed you didn't kidnap the ambassador.

Carlos The security . . .

West *I'm* annoyed you didn't kidnap the ambassador.

Carlos The security arrangements have become far more efficient recently.

West You can't be speaking of the British Embassy.

Brief silence.

Carlos We have asked, as I say, for the release of twenty-five prominent political prisoners, together with a safe conduct and facilities for flying them to Cuba. Then we have asked for 100,000 dollars, which is merely a formality, because, as you know, these people would rather give us their mothers than part with any real cash, so that's a kind of bargaining point. Finally, we've demanded, which is very important to us, that our manifesto (*he indicates his piece of paper*) is broadcast on TV and radio and released by the national and foreign press. I'm going to read it to you.

West Don't.

Carlos No?

West No, don't.

Carlos Well, we think it's very important for you to know and understand why we've done this to you, which is not a thing we like to do to anybody, you know? (*He reads some of the manifesto quickly through to himself, muttering.*) Hmm, hmm, yes, I'll miss out the first bit, this is about the heart of it, I think. 'We wish to draw the attention of the world to the fact that with the passing of the Institutional Acts, and in particular the fifth Institutional Act of 13th December 1968, the military dictatorship has transformed itself into the most regressive and repressive government anywhere in the world . . .'

West Oh, really!

Carlos 'The measures it has introduced include:

'The suspension of all political rights and banning of all political parties except for the hired lackeys of the official opposition.

'The imposition of blanket censorship and the silencing of all opposition newspapers by intimidation and compulsory withdrawal of advertising.

'The promulgation of a law whereby "non-conformity" although nowhere defined, is described as a crime against the State.

'The expulsion of one-quarter of the officer corps.

'The appointment of government stooges as labour leaders and the stipulation that only candidates approved by the political police may stand in union elections.

'The reorganization of the Supreme Court and the dismissal of those of its judges who expressed dissent. The suspension of habeas corpus.

'The cowardice and cynicism of the military dictatorship extends from the smallest and most ludicrous details, such as the replacement of the official Senate historian . . .'

West Have they done that?

Carlos Yes, they have.

West Good God.

Carlos '. . . the replacement of the official Senate historian, to the most cruel and squalid barbarities such as the reintroduction in September 1969, after seventy-five

years of abolition, of the death penalty, to give spurious
legality to the murders of Carlos Marighela, Mario Alves,
Joaquim Camara Ferreira and countless other comrades in
the struggle against Fascism.

'The military dictatorship has lined its pockets by selling
our country to the interests of U.S. capitalism, which it has
allowed to exploit our resources and steal our land, while
our people starve and suffer all the miseries of poverty and
unemployment. Meanwhile, anyone who utters the merest
whisper of protest risks joining the 12,000 political
prisoners, including university professors, doctors, writers,
students, priests and nuns, at present suffering detention
and brutal torture in the regime's jails and concentration
camps. Anyone who doubts this should visit the
Department of Political and Social Order, where the
corridors stink of burnt flesh, or confront the thugs of the
Death Squad, whose hands are wet with innocent blood.

'This is what we are fighting against, comrades, and we
shall fight, if necessary, to the death.

'Death to U.S. imperialism!

'Down with the military dictatorship!'

That's all.

West Quite enough.

Carlos What do you think?

West I could quibble with your economic analysis.

Carlos This is not an analysis. This is a simple expression
of the truth.

West Well, I suppose you could look at it that way.

Carlos We do.

West Well, what the hell do you expect me to say about
it? It may be true or it may not be, and if it is I'm very
sorry about it, but it's nothing to do with me.

Carlos It is now.

West Look, why don't you go away?

Carlos First I have to tell you that we've said our conditions must be met by 6 p.m. on Thursday. We've said that if they aren't, we would have to execute you.

West Ah.

Carlos What I wanted to say to you was that we don't expect the deadline will be met . . .

West What?

Carlos It hardly ever is, it's just an arbitrary date we pick on, it sometimes takes the government a long time to agree to our terms. So you don't need to worry if nothing's happened by Thursday.

West Well, I'm sure that's very thoughtful of you, but as a matter of fact, I've no idea what day it is, and even if I did, I couldn't see to look at my bloody watch, could I?

Carlos That's true, Mr West, all I wanted was to reassure you you're not really in any danger. We have no intention of harming you, we, most of us, don't believe in attacking civilians or foreign nationals, whatever interests they represent. And the government will certainly do what we ask before they allow you to be harmed – they may not care about their people, but they tenderly love their investors. So you shouldn't worry too much. I know this is very inconvenient for you, but when we let you go, everyone will be very nice to you, and you can go back to England and sell your story to the papers for a few thousand pounds. You'll be very famous.

West Well, it must be my birthday.

Carlos Someone will be in as soon as we can manage it to make you more comfortable and give you some food, I'm sure you must be hungry.

West Why did you pick on me?

Carlos For poetic reasons.

West (*surprised*) What do you mean?

Carlos We liked your name.

He exits quietly, without West hearing. West is silent for a moment, then he does the equivalent of drawing himself up to his full height.

West I wish to lodge a formal protest on behalf of Her Majesty's Government against this barbaric assault on a representative of the Crown, a premeditated act of violence contrary to all . . .

Blackout.

FOUR

Bare stage. The sound of rattles and a rhythmic stamping. Two Indians enter, dancing, spinning and playing rattles. Behind them, three Indians carrying the funeral posts on their shoulders, circling and stamping, until, at a sign from the **Chief***, they 'plant' them ritually at the back of the stage in silence. In the course of the play these posts will be gradually decorated with feather head-dresses, shell belts, straw arms, etc., until they finally come to resemble the dead chiefs they represent.*

West appears.

West
Origin of the stars.
The children were always hungry.

Their parents said: 'We give you all we can, why do you
    complain?'
But the children only cried and said again that they were
    hungry.
In the ashes of the fire their mother found the jaw-bone of
    a tapir and threw it to them.
They took what meat they could from the bone and
    divided it among the youngest.
When they saw there was nothing left, they knew that they
    would have to leave.
They joined hands, sang a song and climbed slowly up
    into the sky.
Their mother said: 'Come back, come back. We will find
    more food for you. Forgive us.'
And the children answered: 'There is nothing to forgive.
    We know you did what you could. We bear no grudge.'
They said: 'We are better gone. Here we can help you.
    Here we can help to lift the darkness from you.'
And they became the stars.

*Silence. Indian Girls cross to the posts and begin to
paint them. The drone of a light aircraft as the lights
dim to blackout.*

FIVE

West's house. West, Mrs West and **Miles Crawshaw**, *an
anthropologist, sit drinking coffee after dinner.*

West Well, of course, the first I heard of it was through
Mrs Hardcastle.

Crawshaw Who's she?

West Haven't I ever told you about Mrs Hardcastle?

Crawshaw I don't think so.

Mrs West (*drily*) Are you sure?

Crawshaw Yes.

West Mrs Hardcastle first wrote to the Embassy, what, two or three years ago. From Bognor Regis. She said she was a widow with a little surplus cash to invest in something adventurous, and that an ad in the personal column of *The Times* offering land for sale in Brazil had caught her beady eye. So, never one to do things by halves, as she rightly remarked, she had purchased a hunk of the Mato Grosso, slightly larger, according to her computations, than West Sussex. The company to whom she had handed over her nest-egg had come through with many a bland assurance about the excellence of the roads leading to her land, which was divided equally, it seemed, between arable pasture, potential oilfields and fabulous diamond and gold-mines. Was there running water, she demanded sternly, was there . . . sanitation? Good heavens, yes, the company replied, in precisely such items as these lay the miraculous value of the transaction. So would I be so kind as to investigate for her? Need I say more? What they had sold Mrs Hardcastle and no doubt many another hapless buffoon the length and breadth of the British Isles, the U.S.A. and the Bundesrepublik, was the most arid, inhospitable, impenetrable piece of land you could ever hope to come across. I wrote to her. All is not milk and honey, Mrs Hardcastle, I said, and if you want to visit the land of Hardcastlia, you should start the parachute lessons right away. Well, then all hell broke loose. And because the company was so elusive, it broke all over me. The air was royal blue with the plaints of Mrs Hardcastle. Well, when I began to get one or two other similar inquiries, I thought I'd better try to look into it a bit. What I discovered was that the land which was being sold to these hardy investors really only had one feature of any great interest – it was land which in more enlightened times had been ceded in perpetuity to various Indian tribes. Now the companies that were selling the land were of course quite well aware of this – and being men of the most scrupulous integrity and in many cases landlords themselves, they knew there could be nothing more serious than to infringe the sacred laws of property. Happily, before long someone came up with an extremely simple and efficient method of protecting the Indians from land-grabbers: extermination. And so that's what was happening. They were bombing them, machine-gunning them, poisoning them, infecting them with diseases, no expense spared. None of this of course was of any interest to Mrs Hardcastle, so I thought I wouldn't burden her with the details. I simply explained to her that though the terms of the original ad were to say the least somewhat fulsome, the company were doing what it could to improve the site. (*Pause.*) We still maintain a lively correspondence. She's not quite so incensed any more. She's done ever so much better in Nigeria.

Crawshaw Did you do anything about it?

West What?

Crawshaw When you found out what was going on.

West Well, there wasn't very much I could do. I mentioned it to a few people, you know? But I couldn't actually do anything unless what was happening was against the interests of British subjects. Which of course this wasn't. Quite the contrary. Quite the contrary. (*Pause.*) Rather more possible for someone in your line, I would have thought.

Crawshaw You must be joking. Anthropologists aren't supposed to make comments on political matters, you know, in fact they're not supposed to make comments about anything very much. They're supposed to forget that the people they're working with are human and treat them as if they were an ancient monument, or a graph, or a geological formation. That's what we call science. If I'm writing a thesis about marriage practices among the Bororo, for instance, and I get fed up with writing about exogamous moieties and say as a matter of fact it doesn't make much odds who they marry because the rate things are going they'll all be dead in ten years' time anyway, I'd be told that's not anthropology, it's journalism.

West I see.

Crawshaw So what'll happen is, I'll finish my thesis, which will be so boring and full of technical jargon they'll roll over with delight, and I'll get my fellowship and start inching my way up the hierarchy, and finally, in about thirty years' time, I might be able to heave my weary bum on to some decaying Chair of Anthropology. And in the meantime some enterprising fellow with a much more practical bent than me, and a far more modest objective will have paid a visit to the tribe I build my reputation on, and without paying the slightest attention to kinship structures, he'll simply give then a couple of bags of sugar mixed with arsenic, or a few gallons of cachaça, or a dose of measles. And I'll be saying to my students, they had a social structure every bit as complex as ours, when they were alive, their way of life was perfectly adapted to their environment, when they were alive, they were happier than we are, when they were alive.

Mrs West Oh, come on, Miles, surely it's not that bad.

Crawshaw Well, it is. I sort of hate anthropologists.

West I thought things were getting better now.

Crawshaw What gave you that idea?

West Well, ever since those revelations in when was it, '68 was it? When all those Indian Protection Service men were put on trial.

Crawshaw Ah, yes.

Lights down on West and Mrs West and up on a government office. The **General**, *in uniform and dark glasses sits behind a large, chaste desk, its only ornament a large granite crucifix. The* **Attorney General**, *who wears a sober dark suit, sits to one side, nervous. Dim light still on Crawshaw.*

General Senhor, as the Minister has seen fit to release to the press some of the details concerning the corruption of the Indian Protection Service, we have decided to appoint you the head of a full judicial inquiry into the matter.

Attorney General Yes, General.

General I want you to get right to the bottom of this, Senhor, I want the world press to see how seriously we in Brazil take our responsibilities in these matters.

Attorney General Yes, General.

Crawshaw Some months later.

General Well, Senhor, how is the inquiry proceeding?

Attorney General We have had the most extraordinary results, General. We have accumulated such a vast mass of evidence, we are becoming quite desperate. For lack of space to store it, I mean. (*He laughs obsequiously.*)

General And what are your general conclusions, Senhor?

Attorney General My general conclusions, General, are that, as you so wisely remarked, the Indian Protection Service is a sink of iniquity. Very few of them will be cleared. Apart from the cases of murder, rape and enslavement, we estimate that over the last ten years more than 62 million dollars' worth of property has been stolen from the Indians. We have 42 charges against the head of the service alone, the Major. Including the embezzlement of 300,000 dollars.

General Excellent, well done, Senhor.

Attorney General Thank you, General, but that's not all. You see, what we've discovered is that the Indian Protection Service really plays a very insignificant part in the whole picture. They're only small fry. The people who are really responsible are far more powerful, land-speculators and landowners, a large number of Brazilian companies and even some foreign corporations . . .

General I see.

Attorney General And furthermore . . .

General Thank you, Senhor, that will be all. Except for one thing. I happen to know there's an empty wing at the Ministry of Agriculture, so if you're having storage problems, please have all your documents sent there, will you?

Attorney General Yes, General.

Crawshaw Later still.

General Well, Senhor, you will be pleased to hear that we have decided to dissolve and abolish the Indian Protection Service, and replace it with a new body, the Fundação Nacional do Indio, FUNAI. This will be an entirely reconstituted and efficient organization, under the direct jurisdiction of the army. As you know, recruitment for these arduous and, it must be admitted, not particularly well-paid posts has never been easy, but on this occasion we have been able to solve the problem by transferring a large number of men from the Indian Protection Service.

Attorney General But, General . . .

General They have all determined to turn over a new leaf, Senhor.

Attorney General Even the Major?

General The Colonel, Senhor, as he now is, has been transferred to the Air Ministry. The new head of FUNAI is an excellent man, a personal friend of mine. A general.

Attorney General But, General, what about all the evidence we have collected?

General Ah, yes Senhor, I forgot to tell you. By some curious quirk of fate, there was a disastrous fire last night at the Ministry of Agriculture. The west wing was, alas, completely destroyed.

Attorney General But, General, what am I going to say to the Minister?

General Senhor, for some reason best known to himself, the Minister has seen fit to hand in his resignation. Now, if you'd be good enough to excuse me, I'm expecting a call from the American Embassy. Good morning.

Lights down on General and Attorney General and up on West and Mrs West. Silence. Crawshaw sits, smiling.

West (*smiling*) I'm sure it didn't quite happen like that.

Crawshaw (*his smile disappearing*) More or less. What's the difference how it happened?

West No, I . . . suppose you're right. (*Pause.*) Would you like a brandy or something?

Crawshaw (*nodding*) Thanks.

West What about you, dear?

Mrs West No, thanks.

To Crawshaw, as West moves over to the sideboard,
and pours out two glasses of brandy.

It keeps me awake.

Crawshaw (*turning away from her to speak to West*)
No, the thing is, a lot of good, young, idealistic people
are going into FUNAI, but they can't do anything.
They've got no resources, they don't get paid for months
on end, their wives leave them, they catch malaria,
everything is controlled by the army. All they can do is
try to follow the government line, which is don't
exterminate, integrate.

West Well, at least that sounds like some kind of an
improvement.

Crawshaw No, no, it's the same thing, only slower.

Mrs West Surely they've got to be integrated sooner or
later, they can't just go on living in the Stone Age.

Crawshaw That's it, you see, integration is such a friendly
word, no one ever remembers that if people do get
integrated, they get integrated into the bottom layer, which
in Brazil means they get integrated into the urban
proletariat, who are overcrowded, under-employed and
desperate, or into the peasantry, who in large areas of the
country are simply starving. Integrate them, give them the
benefits of civilization, the government says. What they
don't say is that the first two benefits of civilization the
Indians are going to be given are disease and alcohol. All
they mean when they say the Indians have got to be
integrated is that the Indians have got to give up their land
and a totally self-sufficient and harmonious way of life to
become the slaves of slaves.

West Well, that may be what happens, Miles, but I'm sure
it's not the government's intention.

Crawshaw What about BR–80, then?

Mrs West What's that?

West The road.

Crawshaw The Transamazon Highway. Look, almost the only place in Brazil where the Indians are protected, looked after and allowed to lead their own lives is the Xingu Indian Park. The road was planned to pass north of the park. Now they've decided, at great inconvenience and expense, to move it, so it goes bang through the middle. Why do you think they've done that?

West Didn't they offer a new grant of land to make up for it?

Crawshaw None of that land to the south can support life. They just want to get rid of the Park. It's no secret, they keep saying they want to get rid of it in their speeches. Listen, just the other day, the head of FUNAI, the Minister of Indian Affairs, said: 'We must remove these ethnic cysts from the face of Brazil.' That's what I call putting your cards on the table.

West Well, I don't know nearly as much about it as you do. As I say, I just got to hear about it in a roundabout way via Mrs Hardcastle. What I'm really interested in is their legends.

Crawshaw Legends?

West Yes, I publish, I mean I have had published, a few what we used to call slim volumes of verse, um, poetry, you know. Nothing very grand, just a small independent publisher . . .

Mrs West (*drily*) Thrust Press.

West Yes, and I want to do a collection, I mean I got very interested, and they seemed to me very beautiful, some of them, of Indian legends. You know, so I've been trying to collect them.

Crawshaw I see.

West (*laughing nervously*) You seem a bit dubious.

Crawshaw Well, I suppose I am, really. I don't really approve of the idea of presenting the Indian myths on their own like a lot of pretty children's stories, without trying to show that they're just an aspect of an extremely complex and sophisticated society. It's the kind of thing that reinforces people's prejudice.

West Well, I've approached them . . . I mean, to me they're just like er, Greek legends, or . . . something like that.

Crawshaw I'm sorry, it's very rude of me to judge them, without even having read them, I just . . .

West Well, I'll er . . .

Brief silence. Then Crawshaw rises abruptly.

Crawshaw Excuse me a minute.

He exits swiftly. A moment's silence.

Mrs West He's not a bit like James, is he?

West No, well, I shouldn't think our children would be anything like us. If we had any.

Mrs West What's that supposed to mean?

West Nothing. (*He crosses to the sideboard, pours himself another brandy.*)

Mrs West He wasn't very nice about your poetry, was he?

West You're not very nice about my poetry.

Mrs West I've never said anything about your poetry.

West Exactly.

Silence. West sips his brandy.

Mrs West You know something, we're going to have to get rid of Maria.

West Why?

Mrs West The dinner was disgusting. I've told her how to make rice pudding, I've explained it to her time and again; tonight it was so cold and full of lumps it was more like school porridge.

West I can't sack her for not being able to make rice pudding.

Mrs West Why not, that's what she's paid for, isn't it, you pay her enough.

West I pay her next to nothing.

Mrs West Well, it's a lot to them.

West sighs. Silence. Crawshaw returns, sits.

Crawshaw When I was in the lavatory just now, I thought of something that happened the other evening. I was at a dinner-party and there was a woman there who told a story she could hardly get out for laughing. Apparently she has an Indian servant, very unsophisticated, practically a savage, I think she said, but very good-natured and very willing. Anyhow, one day she'd asked him to put a new roll of lavatory paper in one of her bathrooms. An hour or so later, she wanted him for something else, but at first she couldn't find him. Eventually she discovered him in the bathroom. He was winding the new roll of lavatory paper very slowly and very carefully on to the core of the used roll. He just couldn't work out how else to do it, she said, and by this time she was laughing so hard I thought her teeth were going to drop out. He looked so funny, she said, hooting and spluttering, you can't imagine, bent over concentrating with his tongue sticking out. (*He shakes his head.*) Extraordinary story, I thought. Everyone else seemed to think it was hilarious.

Silence. Mrs West laughs abruptly.

Mrs West Well, you must admit it is quite funny, isn't it?

Blackout.

SIX

The guerrilla hideout. West no longer wears a hood and is handcuffed by his left hand to the bedpost with what seems to be a home-made handcuff designed to give him maximum flexibility. He is lying in the most comfortable position available to him, staring blankly out into space. The door opens and Carlos enters. West takes a brief glance at him, then jerks his head violently away towards the side wall.

Carlos It's all right, Mr West, you needn't worry.

West turns back slowly, looks at Carlos.

West What?

Carlos Doesn't matter now if you see me. My executive has decided that I am to accompany our comrades to Cuba and carry on my work there.

West So you're the bastard.

Carlos What? (*He grins broadly.*) Oh, yes, I'm the bastard.

West I won't forget you.

Carlos Well, I'm sure I won't forget you.

West Why are they sending you to Cuba, aren't you good enough?

Carlos This is none of your business, Mr West. (*Pause.*) I came to tell you that we are making some progress in our negotiations with the dictatorship.

West Oh?

Carlos Yes. Things haven't been going as smoothly this time as in the past, but it looks as if it's going to be all right now. We hope to have you out of here in a week or so.

West I'm glad to hear it.

Carlos (*smiling*) Patience.

Silence.

West Look, I know it's no good my saying this, but I really don't think this is the right way to go about things, you know. I mean, I realize everything's very bad for you at the moment, but this kind of thing isn't going to get you anywhere. It just puts um people's backs up. What I mean is, if you leave it alone for a while, I'm sure things will improve in the future.

Carlos The future is the only kind of property that the masters willingly concede to their slaves. Camus.

West I see.

Silence.

Carlos I wanted to ask if there was anything you wanted, any way we could make you more comfortable.

West Well. (*He reflects a moment.*) I was wondering if you could find something a bit lighter for me to read. (*He indicates a pile of books on a table by the bed.*) I mean, it's all very interesting, all this stuff you've left me, and not the sort of thing I'd normally have happened across, but I do find it, you know, all those statistics and so on, rather tiring.

Carlos I'll ask around the boys, see what we can dig up.

West Thanks. Oh, and there is just one other thing.

Carlos What?

West Can you let me have a pen and some paper?

Carlos (*hesitating*) What for?

West Well, I write poetry, you know, in fact I've had some published. What we used to call slim volumes of verse.

Carlos (*dubiously*) Oh, I see.

West In fact when you said you'd kidnapped me for poetic reasons, I thought for a moment it was because you'd taken against my work. I thought, very erudite class of kidnappers they have nowadays.

He laughs nervously. Carlos is frowning, not listening.

Carlos Well, I suppose that's all right.

West (*pleased*) Oh.

Carlos But you must write in Portuguese.

West Portuguese?

Carlos Yes, well, you can't expect us to let you write in English, can you? As far as the others are concerned, you could be writing anything. Anyway, your Portuguese is very good, it'll be good exercise for you, interesting for us.

West All right, then.

Carlos moves over towards the door. As he does so, West suddenly jerks upright, his expression ferocious.

You're never going to get away with this, you know.

Carlos startled, stops. Then bursts out laughing.

Carlos Oh, come on.

West (*hurt*) Well.

Carlos You play chess?

West Erm, yes, why?

Carlos Well?

West I enjoy it.

Carlos O.K., we must play. I'm very good. (*Pause.*) Maybe we aren't going to get away with it, but it doesn't matter. There are plenty of others to carry on with the work. They try very hard, but: no one can blot out the sun with one finger. Carlos Marighela.

Silence. West raises his handcuffed wrist.

West Man is born free, but is everywhere in chains. Rousseau.

Carlos laughs and exits. West alone, smiling.

Blackout.

SEVEN

An office. A desk, covered with papers and books, some of them pushed aside to make way for a tape-recorder. Behind the desk, an American **Investigator**. *Sitting at an angle, facing the microphone nervously,* **Ataide Pereira**, *wearing a check shirt and baggy trousers. In his lap a sweat-stained hat.*

Investigator Move a little closer.

Pereira does so.
Now you know what you're saying here is on your
honour.
Just as if you were in court under oath.

Pereira Yes sir.
Yes I do.

The Investigator switches on the tape-recorder.

Investigator How did you come to be involved in all this
In the first place?
Pereira Well.
Even after the bombing they were still causing some
trouble.
So the Company asked Senhor de Brito to hire some men
for an expedition
And I was one of them.

Investigator How did you feel about the mission?

Pereira O.K.
I felt fine.
Look at it this way.
Those Indians are on valuable land
Sitting there doing nothing
And sometimes they can be hostile.
There's no way you can move them out
So what else can you do?
To be honest I was quite looking forward to it.
Made a change.
And then there was the money of course.
I know it probably seems wrong to you
But to us it's just like going hunting.
You see we're taught to think of them as animals.
At least that's what the boss always calls them.
Animals.
He asked us to bring back a couple for him.

He likes to take then for what he calls
The trip to the dentist.
Open wide he says.
Say aah he says.
Then he puts his pistol in their mouth
And blows their brains out. (*Pause.*)
Myself I'm a very good shot.
That's why I was chosen.

Investigator How many of you were there?

Pereira Six.
Including Chico.
He was the leader.
That was the one thing we weren't too happy about.
Because Chico well
He'd cut your head off soon as say good morning.

Investigator Tell me about the expedition.

Pereira Well it was no picnic
I can tell you that.
First of all we travelled upstream for a few days.
Then we left the launch and set off into the jungle.
Chico had a compass
Japanese it was.
Didn't stop us getting lost.
We were wandering around for days
And by the time we found somewhere we recognised
We'd run out of food.
Luckily before too long the plane came over
And dropped us some more.
But it wasn't all that long
Before that ran out as well.
Eventually we found a village.

Investigator What happened then?

Pereira Well nothing really.

Somebody'd beaten us to it.
Nothing but corpses all over the place
And a terrible stench.
Still we did get some food there
Dug up some manioc
That kind of thing.
Then we pressed on.
By this time we were all pretty jumpy.
For one thing we were in diamond country
And you know what they're like
Shoot and no questions asked.
Also the rains had started
So every day we got drenched
And the insects that were just hatching out
Ate us alive.
Chico was in a really filthy mood.
So were we all.

Investigator Go on.

Pereira We knew we were warm
So we were very careful very strict
No talking
No smoking
Keeping several yards apart.
And finally
After all that time
One evening
We saw their village through the trees.

  Blackout.

EIGHT

*Ancient, scratchy 78 r.p.m. recording of Gilbert &
Sullivan – 'Selections from* The Pirates of Penzance' *or*

something like that. West sits, sipping a tall drink, on the veranda of a modest colonial bungalow, with its owner, **Major Brigg,** *a leathery old party, dressed in khaki shirt, shorts, long socks with a ribbon, in fact everything but the topee. Sundown.*

Brigg Well, nice to have some company for once.

West Yes.

Brigg Always enjoy this time of day the best, you know. Sitting down, bit of a drink. Doesn't last long, of course, it'll be pitch black before you know where you are. My wife always used to get furious, time for your drink, she'd say, and I'd say, just finishing up one or two things, be with you in a tick, and of course by the time I got out it was like the middle of the night and we'd both be in a temper all evening. (*Pause.*) D'you think I should go back home?

West To England?

Brigg Yes.

West Well, I don't know, I think you'd find it very different . . .

Brigg Oh, yes, I know that. Time of the General Strike I left, you know. Always like to think that was deliberate but actually it was a complete coincidence. Of course, I was there for some of the war, and I've been on leave a few times, but you don't get much impression. Don't suppose I could afford it, anyway.

West It has got very expensive.

Brigg Yes, and I never paid any of those stamp things, so I wouldn't get a proper pension. Can't think why I want to go back really, just a sort of an urge. (*Pause. The record has ended. Brigg gets up.*) D'you like Gilbert and Sullivan?

West Erm . . . I really don't know that much about them.

Brigg Remarkable pair. (*He crosses to the gramophone, winds it up and turns the record over.*) Damn difficult to get hold of the needles for this thing.

He looks expectantly at West, who, though embarrassed, refuses to take the hint.

West Yes, I'm sure.

Silence. Brigg sits down again and the music crackles out.

Brigg You mustn't think it's something new, you know, all this you've been telling me. They've been killing them off ever since I can remember and before, in fact, good God, they were killing off the poor beggars in Shakespeare's day. It's nothing new. But at least when I went into the Indian Protection Service, we actually did make some sort of a stab at protecting them. Now, as far as I can gather, it's the I.P.S. you go to if you want them done away with.

West There certainly has been a great deal of corruption . . .

Brigg Corruption? It may be. It may be they've just given up in despair. I did. You don't have the money, you don't have the equipment, you don't have the authority. At least when I joined the Service, after the war, you knew more or less what you were up against and you could do something about it. But by the time I left the whole thing had become so industrialized and so efficient, there was absolutely nothing to be done. And I suppose they all feel, well, if you can't beat 'em, join 'em.

West What exactly do you mean, industrialized?

Brigg I can remember, in about '47 I suppose it would have been, sitting up a tree on the Aripuanã, because we knew these fellers were trying to get rid of some Indians so that they could get at some diamonds or some damn thing or another. Anyway, sure enough, I hadn't been there very long, when these two chaps appeared in a boat. In those days the favoured approach was to get blankets from the smallpox ward of a hospital and distribute them, you see, among the Indians – that way, with a bit of luck, you could polish off the whole tribe. And, needless to say, the boat was full of blankets. So I shouted to them and told them to stand and deliver, as it were.

West And did they?

Brigg No, they didn't take a blind bit of notice.

West So what did you do?

Brigg Well, I shot them.

West Ah.

Brigg Shot 'em dead. Oh, yes. You see, that's what I mean, in those days there was something you could do about it, you could take some direct action. But nowadays, when they use bombs and machine-guns and I don't know what else, you could sit up a tree on the Aripuanã till you rotted, for all the good you could do. Ready for another?

West (*sipping at his still half-full glass*) In a minute.

Brigg Good, good.

   Silence.

West You must have seen some extraordinary things in your time.

Brigg Yes. (*Pause.*) You know the strangest thing I ever saw?

West No, what?

Brigg I found this body in the jungle, least it was more or less of a skeleton by the time I came across it. All his equipment and his knife and so on had been stolen, but he'd obviously been English or at any rate English-speaking.

West How do you know?

Brigg Well, this was the thing. He'd carved this message on a huge jatoba trunk, before he died. It said IMAGINEUS, all one word, IMAGINEUS. And underneath, a sort of a map.

West Good heavens, what did you do?

Brigg Well, nothing. I certainly wasn't going to take any notice of the map, that's always the first step to disaster, look what happened to poor old Fawcett. But the message was so intriguing, don't you think, imagine us. What could he possibly have meant, it haunted me for years.

West Did you ever think of a likely explanation?

Brigg Well, I did, yes. In the end I decided his spelling wasn't very hot, and that what he'd actually been trying to say, in a spirit of bitter irony, was, 'I'm a genius.'

West laughs, and Brigg looks at him sharply, then smiles.

Ready for another?

West Yes, thanks.

Brigg claps his hands loudly above his head. A moment later, an elderly Indian in an ill-fitting white suit appears, takes the glasses and shuffles back into the bungalow.

Brigg I told you he was the last surviving member of his tribe, didn't I?

West Yes. What did you say his name was?

Brigg Oh, I don't know, he has some endless unpronounceable name, but I call him Bert, after my late brother. The rest of the tribe all died of a 'flu epidemic, you know. Caught it off me. One of our many failures. He's been with me about twenty years, and I suppose he's the real reason I don't go back home.

West I wonder if he'd remember any of his tribe's legends. I think I told you I'm rather interested in collecting legends.

 The Indian reappears with the drinks.

Brigg Oh, it's no good asking him anything like that, I'm afraid he hasn't got much between the ears, poor old beggar.

 The Indian exits. Silence.

I must say, it's nice to have a bit of company. (*Pause.*) You know, one thing I never could get used to all those years was them not wearing any clothes. I know it's silly, but I never could get used to it. Bloody heathen habit, if you ask me.

West Oh, I don't know about that.

Brigg (*vehemently*) There's no hope for them, you know. No hope. Not a chance. Might as well be philosophical about it. I sometimes think the best thing is for them to get it all over with as quickly as possible. Let's have a record. (*He gets up and puts on another record, this time some gay number of the twenties. He sits down again.*) Cheers.

West Cheers.

 Silence except for the oppressively jolly record.

Brigg Quite good some of this modern stuff.

Silence.

West (*pensive*) Imagine us.

Blackout.

NINE

West
Origin of music.
One evening a strange boy arrived in our village.
He told us he came from the house of the sun.
He said he was here to bring us a great gift.
Then he sang for us and we felt for the first time
The beauty of music.

But before very long our men began to die
And we found that those who came back from the river
    ate their fish and listened to his song
Died in the night.
So we explained to the boy that we would have to kill him
And he asked to be burnt.

As he died in the flames he sang his most beautiful song
And from his ashes grew the paxiuba palm.
Now our men make their flutes from its wood.
And sometimes in the evening we have music
Strange and beautiful as the boy from the house of the sun
And sad as his dying.

*Flute solo. The Indians continue decorating the funeral
posts.*

Blackout.

TEN

The guerrilla hideout. West, still handcuffed, has been playing chess with Carlos. Now he contemplates the board, shrugs, makes a gesture with his free hand and pushes over his king. He looks up at Carlos, smiling and shaking his head.

Carlos Told you I was good.

West Yes. You are quite.

   Carlos smiles, executes a courtly bow, gets up and moves round the room, stretching.

Carlos Want another game?

West Oh, not just now, I don't think. Later on perhaps.

Carlos You very bored?

West Yes, I suppose you might say so, yes.

Carlos (*abstractedly*) Things move slowly. I get very bored as well.

West I hope you don't expect me to sympathize.

Carlos (*smiling*) No.

   Silence.

West Tell me, what's your position, I mean, I didn't see anything about it in any of that stuff you gave me to read, what's your policy as far as the Indians are concerned?

Carlos Indians?

West Yes.

Carlos What Indians?

West The Brazilian Indians.

Carlos Oh. Well, I suppose our policy is to protect them from exploitation just as we intend to protect the workers and the peasants.

West It's not so much that they're being exploited, it's that they're being killed.

Carlos Oh, yes, well, I know about that, of course. It's just one of the things we'd have to put a stop to, isn't it?

West Not so easy.

Carlos No, probably not, but then neither are a lot of things. I must say, compared with most of the difficulties we'd have to face, it is rather a marginal problem. Why do you ask?

West I'm just interested in them, that's all, I know quite a lot about them.

Carlos Well, so do we.

West Mm.

Silence.

Carlos You write some poems?

West No.

Carlos Oh, I'm sorry, why not? I was looking forward to seeing them.

West Well, I don't know, I haven't been feeling at my best for one reason or another. (*He indicates the handcuff.*) Also I'm left-handed.

Carlos (*seriously*) Oh, yes, well, that does make things difficult, I can see. (*Brightening.*) You can dictate them to me, if you like.

West Also I do find the idea of writing in Portuguese rather . . . inhibiting.

Carlos Well, sketch them out in English if you want to, then translate them into Portuguese, then give us the English so we can destroy it, you keep the Portuguese and translate it back when you get out.

West I'll see.

Carlos Listen, I wrote a poem yesterday, I'm going to read it to you, then when you write your poems you can read them to me and we can discuss them, it'll be interesting. All right? (*He produces a piece of paper from his inside pocket.*)

West All right.

Carlos It's called 'The New Beatitudes'. (*He considers his piece of paper a moment.*) 'The New Beatitudes'.

Blessed are the corporations: for theirs are the kingdoms
   of the world.
Blessed are the complacent: for they shall never mourn.
Blessed are the aggressive: for they have inherited the
   earth.
Blessed are they which do hunger and thirst after nothing
   but righteousness: for they shall be easily satisfied.
Blessed are the merciless: for they shall obtain power.
Blessed are the pure in race: for they shall see themselves
   as God.
Blessed are the armed forces: for they shall call themselves
   the children of the Revolution.
Blessed are they which persecute others for righteousness'
   sake: for theirs are the kingdoms of the world.
Blessed are ye when men shall revile you and say all
   manner of evil against you for the sake of the poor and
   starving.
      Send for the censor and secret police.
      Rejoice and be exceeding glad.
      Smear the electrodes and sharpen the knives.

Ye own the salt of the earth: but if the salt have lost his market value, invest in real estate.

He thrusts the piece of paper back into his inside pocket, looks expectantly at West.

West Erm . . .

Carlos Like it?

West (*hesitantly*) Yes. I mean, it's a little bit more direct and er crude than what I'm used to.

Carlos Yes, well, you see, we haven't time for all your old European bourgeois subtleties.

West I don't know if that's quite . . .

Carlos Myself, I think if anything it's too literary, not direct enough.

West Well . . .

Carlos The understanding of a poem should be not merely an intellectual advance, but a political advance. Fanon. And he also said the national culture of an underdeveloped country should take its place at the very heart of the struggle for freedom. He said that in the revolutionary phase many people who under normal circumstances would never have dreamt of producing literary work have a job to do – as awakeners of the people.

West I suppose it depends what . . .

Carlos You see what interesting discussions we can have.

Silence.

West Your people are against organized religion, are you?

Carlos No, not particularly. Why do you ask?

West Well, the poem . . .

Carlos Oh, no, that's . . . No, many of the priests in Brazil, and especially the young ones, are with us, which is very good for us, because they know how to speak to the people. Of course, there are plenty of the other sort and nowadays they're importing them from Spain, because they're so clever at explaining how dictators are the beloved of God and how the poor are the only ones who'll be admitted to heaven, except, of course, for those members of the ruling class who've kept up their subscriptions.

West Do they tell them to turn the other cheek?

Carlos Yes, yes, repeatedly. Are you a religious man, Mr West?

West Not at all.

Carlos Good, good. Let me see if I can get you a drink.

Blackout as he strides towards the door, beaming.

ELEVEN

The main room of the **Revd Elmer Penn's** *spotlessly clean bungalow. Everything is extremely tidy and strictly functional. Among the more prominent objects, a desk, filing cabinets, a deep-freeze unit and a harmonium. Penn enters, followed by West, who looks somewhat grim and strained. Hum of an air-conditioner.*

Penn Well, now, that's pleasant, isn't it? I don't know what we'd do out here without air-conditioning. I expect you'd like something to drink. (*He moves over and flips up the lid of the deep-freeze unit.*)

West brightens visibly.

I'm afraid we don't keep any alcohol in the mission; since

we don't allow the Indians to partake of any, we feel we have to ask our visitors to forgo it as well. We have Coke, 7-up, all kindsa soft drinks.

He helps himself to a Coca-Cola, which he opens with a device on the side of the deep-freeze unit, takes a straw and turns to look inquiringly at West.

West Er, no thanks, I won't.

Penn No? (*He closes the deep-freeze unit, moves over and sits in the chair by the desk, indicating the more comfortable armchair to West.*) Sit down.

West does so.

Well? What do you think?

West (*uneasily*) It's . . . very impressive.

Penn Glad you think so. Tell you the truth, we're very proud of it ourselves. It's not been an easy job, I can tell you. Five years it's taken to get to this stage, five years. And there's been numberless times I've wanted to give the whole thing up and go home. Numberless times. But I always used to say to myself, forgive me, Alan, but I really did used to say it, Moses laboured forty years as a shepherd, and our Lord Himself spent many years sawing lumber in a carpenter's shop. And that used to help some. But as I say, we've had our problems.

Brief silence.

West Why . . . why have you put, got barbed wire round the village?

Penn Well, Alan, I've been expecting you to ask about that, I could see you were surprised when you arrived, many of our visitors are. Believe me, it's for their own protection. You see, we felt when we arrived, and you must understand that when Maybelle and I arrived here

231

five years ago, it was so primitive, it was like something out of the pages of the *National Geographic Magazine* – we felt that what was very important was to make a clear distinction, clear enough to be unmistakable to the Indians, between what they had in the past and what we were offering them for the future. Well, now, after the first steps, when the only thing you really need is a little courage and frankly nerve, and believe me, if there's one thing even a Stone Age savage can understand, it's raw courage – you consolidate. Now when I say consolidate, that probably sounds quite easy to you, but what it really involves is more than three years of very very hard work, in which you have to learn their language, teach them the Gospel in terms they can understand, show them that your medicine is better and more effective than the shaman's, win them away from their own primitive beliefs and, well, I suppose one has to be honest about this, make them dependent on you. Well, when you have achieved all that, there comes a moment, and I suppose judging that moment correctly is the most difficult job we have in the civilisation process, there comes a moment when you have to move from the defensive to the offensive. And when that moment comes, you have to say to the Indian, look, either you must go forward with us, or you must leave the flock. You see, for a long time the new concepts you've introduced them to co-exist with a lot of the bad old ways and there just has to be a confrontation, when you say to them, if you don't want to renounce the stimulants and intoxicants that are preventing you from becoming a useful member of the community, if you don't want to accept what we do for you, why you're just going to have to go your own way. It's a very delicate task and it's really impossible to avoid stepping on a few cultural toes, but if as I say you choose the moment carefully, you'll only lose a very small number of them. And of the rest you can truly say:

The race that long in darkness pined
Have seen a glorious light.

West And the wire?

Penn Is to protect them from outside influence during this very critical period. I don't want you to think they're not free to come and go. Anybody can join the community providing he understands its rules and agrees to abide by them, and of course if anyone has a reason for wanting to leave the village for a few days, all he has to do is come and see me and I make the necessary arrangements. Hopefully it won't be too long before the stabilization phase is completed and then we'll be able to dismantle the wire – and I might be able to think about having myself a little vacation. (*He laughs heartily, then adds.*) The Indians put the wire up themselves, you know.

West Really?

Penn Oh, yes, sure they did. You see, Alan, alongside of preaching the Gospel, which is of course our primary task, there are other ways in which we have to change the lives of these savages. For instance, we have to instil in them a work ethic tied to a reward system, which is something quite new to them. Now, if you do that, naturally they're going to have to look at a whole lot of things in a new way, things like property and personal possessions, and they're going to want to preserve and protect them.

West I see.

Penn People have these very romantic ideas about the Indians. Give you an example, this thing about clothes, people always say the Indian doesn't like clothes, doesn't want clothes, he's proud to go naked. It's just not true. You should have seen the fighting and the quarrelling when we issued them with T-shirts. Course they had no idea how to put them on, it's one of the funniest sights I ever seen, all of them struggling with those things, you know, trying to put their heads through the armholes, my, we did laugh.

West But, Mr Penn . . .

Penn Elmer, Elmer . . .

West Elmer, do you think it's a good thing, I mean, fair to them, to change their way of life so radically?

Penn We have no choice, Alan. See, even if you leave aside the religious aspect of our work, these men have to be integrated into society, we have to bring them into our world, Alan, yours and mine. Otherwise they can never survive. I don't have to tell you there've been a lot of regrettable incidents in the last few years because the Indians have no understanding of the world as it is. The government knows that – that's why they're pursuing a policy of integration. You know, when I first came to Latin America in the forties, they wouldn't allow foreign missionaries into Brazil at all: thank heavens this government sees it differently and understands the value of what we're doing, so they couldn't be more helpful. For instance, just recently, they took around eighty Indians into Belo Horizonte and turned them into a crack police force. And what people don't understand is that the Indian wants this, he sincerely wants progress.

West Even if it means losing his land?

Penn Alan, there are ninety million people in this country, you can't expect them not to exploit its natural resources, how else are they going to make this into a prosperous country? They must have access to the land.

West It's a pity a few of the big landowners don't know about that.

Penn Well, Alan, I'm not going to talk politics with you.

All I know is that this government may have some terrible problems as of now, but it's working very closely with the United States government, and I think together we're going to be able to lick most of them.

Silence.

West Perhaps I will have a Coca-Cola.

Penn Sure, sure. (*He organizes this, hands West an open bottle and straw.*) A man must do what a man can do. (*Long pause. He consults his watch.*) My goodness, it's time for choir practice already.

West (*making to get up*) Oh, well, I'll . . .

Penn No, no, I want you to see this, Alan. (*He moves to the desk, presses a button. Chimes of an electric church-bell.*) I'm planning a little surprise for Maybelle, when she gets back from the States. You'll see what I mean in a minute. You're going to meet Kumai, you know, the one I was telling you about?

West Oh, yes, yes, good.

Penn He's a remarkably intelligent boy for an Indian. He's very quick-witted and kind of artistic, something of a rascal but very lovable. I've even been able to teach him a few words of English. We had a little bit of trouble with him a year or so back, but we got over that in the end.

West What sort of trouble?

Penn Well, Alan, alongside of all the other problems I was telling you about, one of the most difficult things for the savage to understand, and of course one of the things he must be made to understand, is the question of morals, I mean sexual morality. Now before we came, the custom was that a man would have a wife, but he'd also have a number of mistresses, in fact the whole tribe was extremely promiscuous, and quite openly so. Well, we made ourselves very very clear on that point and put a stop to it as far as we could. Then, after a time, Kumai came to me and told me he wanted to get married. Well, I thought the girl was rather unsuitable for him; frankly she was rather a stupid girl, but he insisted and so I agreed to marry them. Everything went along O.K. for a time, and then I noticed that his attitude toward us seemed to have changed, he became sullen and unfriendly, and looked kind of guilty all the time. Well, I looked into it, and sure enough I discovered he was paying less and less attention to his wife and had become involved with a girl who had given us nothing but trouble from the day we arrived. We weren't sure what to do, we thought about it and thought about it, and finally we realized we had to discipline him, we had no choice. What made it even harder was that Kumai understood as well, he knew he'd done wrong, and it darn near broke our hearts the way he accepted his punishment.

West What was it?

Penn We sent the two of them away. He came back a few months later. He looked terrible. Begged me to let him come back to stay. Well, of course, it was a very great joy to forgive him and accept him back into the flock.

West And what happened to her?

Penn I didn't ask him. As far as I was concerned, he'd been forgiven and the incident was closed. I've certainly never referred to it again. (*Pause.*) They should be here by now. You know, some of my more old-fashioned colleagues won't allow the Indians to even set foot in their personal quarters. I think that's very narrow-minded, don't you? The way I look at it, how are you going to win a man's confidence if you won't even let him see inside your home?

*A tentative knock on the door. Penn strides over to it
and lets in half a dozen Indians. By contrast with the
Indians as they appear in the other scenes, these seem
cowed and dejected, miserable in shabby, holed T-shirts
and tatty shorts. Their manner is painfully timid and
ingratiating. Penn grabs one of them and drags him over
towards West. The others cluster over by the
harmonium.*

This is Kumai. O senhor é inglês, Kumai.

West Hello, Kumai.

Penn Have you some little thing you could give them?

West Er . . . (*He searches in his pockets a moment, comes
out with a handful of small change.*) How about this?

Penn Yeah, that's O.K.

*He takes the money, gives some to **Kumai**, then
distributes the rest carefully among the other Indians.*

Kumai Ingiss.

West Erm . . .

Kumai Ingiss.

West Yes, that's right, English.

Kumai Sooba.

West What?

Kumai Sooba. (*He makes vigorous kicking movements.*)

West I . . .

Penn He means football. They can't manage fs, you know.

West Oh, football!

Kumai (*nodding and smiling, delighted*) Sooba . . . Nobistai.

West What?

Kumai Nobistai.

West I don't . . .

Penn Well, neither do I. What are you trying to say, Kumai?

Kumai Nobistai . . . Ingiss.

West Oh, I see!

Penn What?

West Nobby Stiles. He's trying to say Nobby Stiles.

Kumai (*nodding proudly*) Nobistai.

Penn I still don't understand.

West (*muttering*) He's an English footballer.

Penn Oh! (*He roars with laughter.*) Well, I'll be! He's a pack of surprises! I wonder where he could have picked that up. (*He laughs again, shaking his head.*) O.K., Kumai, let's go.

> *He shepherds Kumai over to the harmonium, sits him down at it. Meanwhile West, who is extremely upset, passes his hand unnoticed across his eyes.*

West Oh, my God.

> *Penn gestures to Kumai, who starts to play.*

Penn (*singing lustily*) The day . . . (*He breaks off.*) No, no, wait a minute. Again.

> *He gestures again. Kumai begins again and Penn booms out the hymn, the Indians joining in with vaguely approximate noises.*

(*singing*)

The day thou gavest, Lord, is ended,
The darkness falls at thy behest;
To thee our morning hymns ascended,
Thy praise shall sanctify our rest.

The sun that bids us rest is waking
Our brethren 'neath the western sky,
And hour by hour fresh lips are making
Thy wondrous doings heard on high.

So be it, Lord; thy throne shall never,
Like earth's proud empires, pass away;
Thy kingdom stands, and grows for ever,
Till all thy creatures own thy sway.

West, appalled, pulls disconsolately at his Coca-Cola.

Blackout.

TWELVE

The curtain rises on the long, melancholy cries which summon the Champion wrestlers of the visiting tribes to start the wrestling tournament. By now the funeral posts are fully decorated and the Indians themselves ceremonially painted. An Indian enters, circles the stage warily, acknowledges the Chief and gestures to his chosen opponent, who steps forward. They circle each other, drop to their knees, slap their right hands together and engage. The wrestling match is intense but graceful, and lasts until one of the wrestlers succeeds in touching the back of his opponent's thigh, after which they embrace and move to the back of the stage, arm in arm, while the Chief summons another pair to take their place. At the end of the second wrestling match, the Chief congratulates both wrestlers and the Men move into a tight group, discussing the contests and passing a gourd from one to the other.

West appears.

West
The coming of Death.
The creator wished his children to be immortal.
He told them to wait by the river.
'Wait for the third canoe,' he said.
'For in the first canoe or in the second canoe
Will be Death.'
After a time the first canoe passed.
In it a basket of rotten meat.
The men moved towards it and smelt the meat.
'This must surely be Death,' they said
And let the canoe pass by and vanish.
Time passed.
Until one day the second canoe appeared.
In it a young man.
Strange and alien, but who waved and greeted them like a
    brother.
They waded out and drew the boat in to the river bank.
Embraced the stranger, asked him who he was.
He was Death.
When the creator arrived in the third canoe
He saw there was nothing he could do for the men.
The trees had waited for him
They will never die.
The stones had waited for him
·They will live for ever.
The snakes had waited for him
And when they grew old they shed their skin and were
    young again.
But the men had welcomed Death like a long-lost brother.
And he, smiling, took them one by one into his arms.

West exits.
    The Indians pass the gourd around and drink,
laughing and excited, as the Women prepare the food.

THIRTEEN

The guerrilla hideout. West, handcuffed, alone, reading a
Portuguese edition of The Godfather. *Carlos enters,*
beaming, carrying two bowls of soup and some bread.

Carlos Good evening.

West Hello. You're looking very cheerful.

Carlos Yes, I've had a good day, very successful operation.

West Really?

Carlos Yes, I rang the police this morning and told them
the American Embassy was being attacked by a gang of
thugs disguised as an army unit and then I rang army
headquarters and told them the American Embassy was
being attacked by a gang of thugs in police uniform. Then
I went and watched from a safe distance. Most
satisfactory.

West You mean it worked?

Carlos Three dead, a dozen or so wounded and a certain
amount of damage to property.

Silence.

West Well, how nice for you.

Carlos Yes, it was.

West Why do you people always blame the Americans for
everything?

Carlos You know as well as I do the Americans were
behind the coup in 1964, and they were behind it because
their profits were being threatened, and now they bribe the
ruling classes to make sure their profits aren't threatened
again. The American public knows their government gives

aid to underdeveloped countries, unless they're communist of course, in which case they prefer to ship over a few tons of napalm, but what they don't know is that nearly all the aid has strings attached, and what they also don't know is that twice as much money comes out in profit as goes in in aid. Why do you think the corporations make two, three, sometimes ten times as much profit in Latin America as they do in their home markets? You may think all's fair in love and commerce, but some of us take it personally when our children starve to death so that somebody in Detroit or Pittsburgh can buy themselves a third car.

West That's a ludicrously oversimplified way of putting it.

Carlos Well, as it so happens, it's a ludicrously oversimplified process, starving. You don't get enough food to eat and, by an absurdly oversimplified foible of nature, it makes you die. And it can be very aggravating when you think to yourself that the excess profits which ought to have been ploughed back into your country so you might have stood a chance of getting a bite to eat have gone towards installing a telex in the interests of business efficiency. It can be a terrible setback to your notions of international brotherhood.

West Well, these things develop slowly . . .

Carlos We haven't got time for slowly. We need fast.

West But a lot of these things just can't be done fast.

Carlos They can't be done at all, as long as the Americans have their teeth in our neck. Don't think I'm so stupid as to be against them just because they're Americans. If it wasn't them, it'd be someone else. It's just that they're the most powerful at the moment. Before them it was you.

West Me?

Carlos You. England. You bled us empty all through the

seventeenth and eighteenth centuries. Or rather Portugal bled us and you bled Portugal.

West I thought Portugal was supposed to be our oldest ally.

Carlos Of course. If I had you round the throat squeezing you dry for hundreds of years, you'd be my oldest ally.

West Well, it's hardly my fault.

Carlos That's it. Nothing's ever anyone's fault. Millions of dollars flow out of the country, quite spontaneously, to the amazement of all. By some freak statistical whim, 3 per cent of the population of an underdeveloped country find themselves controlling most of the wealth and look on bewildered as it slips from their nerveless fingers and fortuitously lands in a numbered Swiss bank account. How can it be anyone's fault?

West None of it ever lands in my numbered Swiss bank account.

Carlos Think what you're missing, you silly man. My father has three.

West That's very interesting.

Carlos For you, maybe. Not for me. I don't get on very cordially with my father, he being well to the right of Caligula. Apart from counting his money, he has only two enthusiasms: Vasco da Gama football club and the Death Squad.

West What does he think about you?

Carlos He thinks I see everything exactly the way he does.

Silence.

West Somebody I know was killed by the Death Squad not so long ago.

Carlos Well well.

West So the story goes, anyway. He wasn't anyone we knew very well, a friend of a friend in England, we met him two or three times. He was a homosexual, so of course when the bank posted him to Rio, he thought it was his birthday. They just broke in one night, took him to some obscure favela and shot him. Because he was homosexual, we were told.

Carlos Oh, yes, the Death Squad disapproves of immorality.

West Well, in my opinion, their puritan zeal was rather undermined by the fact that they sexually assaulted him before they killed him.

Carlos It's a very tragic tale.

West Yes, I think it is quite.

Carlos Well, after all the things that have been done to friends of mine in the last year or two, you must forgive me if I'm not moved to tears by some garbled story about some foreign faggot.

West Oh.

Carlos Listen, I won't go into details about it . . . yes, I will, I will go into details about it, I will, I'll tell you what happened to a friend of mine, a girl of seventeen called Maria, a philosophy student, who had only the very remotest connection with us. She was a very quiet, thoughtful girl and she lived with her grandmother in Urca. Last September, they arrived in the middle of the night, and since it was a political offence she was suspected of, they naturally started off by raping her, right there in front of the old woman. Then they hauled her off for a few days on the Ilha das Flores and gave her all the usual treatment, more rape, electric shock, hanging her upside-down on the parrot perch and beating her, all that. She hasn't recovered from it and I don't think she ever will. She's still under treatment. She sent a message to us saying she never wanted to see any of us ever again. Mind you, it wouldn't do us much good if we did go to see her, because they gave her another piece of standard treatment, humorously referred to as the telephone, which consists of punching the ears of the victims as they hang upside-down. They broke her eardrums. She's completely deaf.

West Horrible.

Carlos You see, countries like ours operate their own version of the Welfare State. Instead of wasting a lot of money trying to reform and rehabilitate psychopaths, sex maniacs, thugs and sadists, we give them a uniform and a good salary and a title like the Death Squad, or the C.C.C., or the Metros, or the C.R.S. and let them use their skills for society's benefit. (*He sees West's dubious expression.*) Don't think there aren't hundreds of people in every country who'd jump at the chance to belong to that kind of organization, who'd love to spend an evening throwing beggars in the river or ramming a broken-off bottleneck up any pretty middle-class girl with a few vague ideals about improving the lot of the workers. And don't think there aren't thousands of people in every country who'd sleep more comfortably in their beds if they knew that kind of thing was going on. And the unity those people have, the unity of hatred, the wonderfully simple level of their ideas! Whereas we, my God, we poor old nit-picking intellectuals, I sometimes think we spend all our strengths and all our energy bickering over points of doctrine like a gaggle of old nuns discussing the Immaculate Conception in a brothel.

West I don't see how you can hope to achieve anything.

Carlos We will, in the end.

West You'd need a miracle.

Carlos Anything can happen. Suppose there was a nuclear war between America and Russia. I don't expect you know this, but by some quirk of the trade winds or whatever, Brazil would suffer less fall-out than any other country in the world. Then we might be able to make some progress, like we did in the First World War when the Imperialists got off our backs, we might even turn into that superpower the generals keep prattling about. You see, we always look on the bright side. We're not like Lady Britannia, sinking sedately beneath the waves and stolidly replacing one reactionary government with another even more reactionary government; our country is so vast that the most terrible things can happen without anyone even noticing – but it's also young enough to change in the most radical and unexpected ways.

Silence.

West I remember being in a little town on the Araguaia, sitting by the river, waiting for a boat which was needless to say several hours late. I was watching the children, who were going up and down the river-bank in groups of two or three, very active. I couldn't see what they were up to at first, but after a time I realized they were hunting out anything that was alive down by the river, small animals, reptiles, insects, anything they could find, and torturing it to death. Naturally I, sitting there like an idiot in my tropical ducks, was something of a centre of attraction for them, and they kept bringing me little offerings, like a worm sliced into six wriggling pieces or quite a large lizard with all its legs pulled off. They went on for hours, dozens of them, that's all they were doing.

He breaks off, reflecting. Brief silence.

Carlos Well, what else is there for them to do, comrade?

Blackout.

FOURTEEN

Ground plan as Scene Seven.

Investigator And you attacked did you
When you reached the village?

Pereira No.
Not right off.
We stayed where we were until nightfall.
Then during the night
We crawled to the edge of the village
And waited for the dawn.
Being the best shot
My job was to start the attack off
By killing the chief.
Well in the morning
They all got on with what they were doing
Which was building some hut
And more or less straight away
I picked out the chief
A tall man
Who was leaning against a rock doing nothing.
I got him first go.
Then Chico gave them a burst of his sub-machine-gun
And we all charged.
It was over in five minutes.
All that time struggling through the jungle
And in five minutes
It was all over.

Investigator All over?

Pereira Well not quite.
Not quite.

Investigator What do you mean?

Pereira Well now we get to the cruel part
Nothing to do with me
I tried to stop it happening.

Investigator What?
What did you try to stop?

Pereira There was a girl.
A young girl.
We thought we'd got everyone you see
Then we heard this screaming and yelling
And we found a child of about five
With this young girl who was trying to hush it up.
Chico was very pleased.
He led them out into the centre of the village.
Here we go he said.
I said we should take them back with us.
He shook his head.
No he said we're supposed to kill them all
All these animals.
Then he grabbed the little boy threw him on the ground
And shot him in the head.
She just stood there
Not making a sound
Stark naked
Pretty little thing.
All right he said he said Pedro
Give me your machete.
Listen I said don't kill her
I mean here's all of us
Not seen a woman for six weeks.
Find your own women he said.
He looked funny.

He led her over to a tree
And got Pedro to help him hang her upside-down
Legs apart.
Then he chopped her in half.
Afterwards he said you can have her now if you like
She's all yours.

Silence.

Investigator Then you left did you?

Pereira You bet.
We threw all the bodies in the river
And got the hell out as fast as we could.

Investigator And you got back all right?

Pereira Yes sure
But that's when all the trouble started
I was telling you about.

Investigator Tell me about it again.

Pereira Well when we got back
They were furious with us for having taken so long
And they refused to pay us.
They said they weren't going to waste their time with us
   any more.
They were going back to the old more efficient methods
Such as poisoned candy
And sending them infected blankets.
I said it was a scandal
But he said that was the Company's final decision
And it wasn't for him to query it.
Now I ask you be fair
It's not right is it?
All that sweat and slog and hard work
For nothing.
I'd have thought they might have given us a bonus

But no
The Company won't even pay me what it promised.

Investigator How much was that?

Pereira Fifteen dollars.

Blackout.

FIFTEEN

The Chief sits, alone, on a stool, in front of the central post, his bow across his knees.
West appears.

West
The life after death.
Long ago there was a boy who fell in love with a star.
He called to her every night and told her of his love
Until one night she answered him inviting him to join her
By climbing a certain palm tree.

The boy climbed the tree and reached the desolate fields of
    heaven
And for many weeks he was entirely happy
But sometimes as he lay with his love he was disturbed by
    strange sounds
The murmur of distant celebration.

The star begged him to take no notice of this distraction
But soon his curiosity overcame his love
And he set off alone across the fields
Towards the sound of the flutes.

What he had heard was the endless dance of the dead.
What he saw was the numberless tribe of the dead
Fresh corpses rotting bodies skeletons
Dancing to the cruel music of death.

The boy ran from the field of the dead in horror
Fled from the eye of the great hawk
Who sat in the dead bones of a dead tree guarding his
    prisoners
Eating their putrid flesh.

The boy ran to the palm tree and began to climb down
    towards the earth
But the star saw him and called after him: 'You cannot
    escape. You will soon return.'
And a few days later the boy had wasted away
And his body returned to the dance.

Before he died he told the people what he had seen
And now it is known
That although the stars smile down and speak of the
    beauty of heaven
There is no rest and no joy in the field of the dead.

    West exits.
      *Music. The Indians appear and dispose themselves on
either side of the stage, facing the centre. Then an
Indian carrying a bow enters, leading a Girl, who walks
with her right hand on his shoulder. The Girl, who has
just been brought out of seclusion, wears feathers in her
hair, beads and cloth binding round the upper part of
her calves. Her hair grows down covering her face. In
her left hand, she carries a gourd full of pequi nuts. The
Indian leading her stops when she is directly in front of
the Chief, and without taking her hand off his shoulder,
she leans back as far as possible in a graceful movement
and empties the nuts on the ground in front of the Chief.
They move forward a couple of paces and stop again. A
young Indian approaches and takes the feathers from
her hair, her beads and the binding from her legs. The
other Indians close in around the Chief and begin
helping themselves to the pequi nuts as the lights dim.*

SIXTEEN

The guerrilla hideout. West, handcuffed, kneels with his back towards the audience as Carlos finishes off cutting his hair with a pair of nail-scissors.

Carlos There we are. Very nice. I'm afraid we don't have any double mirrors so you'll just have to take my word for it.

West turns round carefully, sits on the bed facing Carlos. He pats at his hair.

West Thanks.

Carlos Well, we can't let you out looking like a tramp, can we? The bourgeois press would be saying we didn't know how to conduct ourselves like gentlemen.

West Now all I need is a bath.

Carlos More difficult to arrange, I'm afraid. (*He sniffs delicately.*) I think you'll be all right without. I'll give you a slosh of my capitalist after-shave.

West Well, thank you.

Carlos brushes a knot of hair off West's shoulder.

Carlos I must say I'm very pleased with that. Who says intellectuals can't work with their hands?

West Yes, if you fall on hard times in Cuba, you can always apply for a job trimming Fidel's beard.

Carlos frowns.

Sorry.

Carlos shrugs. Pause.

Are you looking forward to going to Cuba?

Carlos (*sharply*) Yes, of course I am. (*Pause.*) It's very serious to leave your country and not know if you will ever be able to come back. But it will be very good to wake up in the morning and not have to worry about whether you're going to get through the day without being arrested, tortured or killed.

West Why are you going exactly? If it's not a . . .

Carlos I don't think I can talk to you about that.

West All right.

Carlos I . . . The truth is, I'm not a very valuable guerrilla. First thing, I'm a terrible shot. We go and practise, you know, on those machines in amusement arcades, but it's hopeless, I'm no good, they all say I couldn't hit an elephant if it was sitting on my knee. And we have differences, sometimes, you know, about matters of principle. Certain disagreements.

West What about?

Carlos Matters of principle. Tactics. (*Longish pause.*) Some of us, some of us believe that excessive terrorist violence is counterproductive. For instance, you remember when McNamara visited, we set off a bomb outside Sears Roebuck in São Paulo. That did no good. I mean, who knows except for us that McNamara owns shares in Sears Roebuck? All people knew was that their nearest cheap store was closed for two weeks and they were very angry about it. I think we have to be very careful not to use the methods of the enemy to defeat the enemy. It's essential for us to use violence, of course, but we must be very sure that every act of violence we commit is clear and . . . progressive.

West I take it you aren't opposed to kidnapping.

Carlos No. Certainly, it's regrettable, but how else are we going to get our comrades out of the torture-chambers?

West Yes, I can see how trying it must be for you.

Carlos There's no point in our talking about this. You're an intelligent man, I know you understand.

Silence.

West So they're sending you off to have another think.

Carlos Well, we had a lot of arguments, discussions that is, and in the end they said, Carlos, you're a man who can't hit a brick wall at three paces, why don't you go and set your thoughts down in a book for us? (*Pause. Then, almost convincingly.*) We decided it would be more useful.

Silence.

West Tomorrow, then?

Carlos Yes, all being well.

West Amazing.

Silence.

Carlos I think I should tell you something, I was told not to mention it but I don't see what difference it can make. Your wife has gone back to England.

West Oh. Oh, well.

Carlos So you won't see her tomorrow. In a few days.

West I see.

Silence.

Carlos Are you, erm, happily married, are you?

West Very. (*Pause.*) Not very. So-so. All right, you know. We're used to each other.

Carlos Children?

254

West No. (*Pause.*) What about you, are you married?

Carlos (*laughing*) No. Not for me. I'm much too fond of women to get married. That's another thing that's caused some . . . disputes in the past. Some people think my private life is self-indulgent and dangerous. Too many books about Mata Hari, you see, they all think I'm liable to become besotted with some sinister foreign whore who'll make me pour out all my secrets. I explained to them that on the contrary comrades who weren't at all successful with women would be far more susceptible to that kind of thing, but many of them didn't seem to find that a sympathetic point of view. (*Pause.*) Of course, what they disapprove of most is that I have a terrible weakness for American girls.

West Well, that is rather heretical, isn't it?

Carlos Not at all. Infiltrating the enemy, I call it. No, the thing is, I just love American girls of about twenty. They're always so enthusiastic and fresh and responsive and eager, beautiful skin, wide eyes, wonderful mixture of alertness and ignorance. Always so healthy. Question is, what happens to them?

West I'm afraid I don't know anything about it.

Carlos If I had to give a definition of capitalism I would say: the process whereby American girls turn into American women.

West (*laughs*) Capitalism, there's a quaint old word. Don't hear it nearly so often nowadays. I remember when I was much younger, I was posted in Venice, at the Palazzo Dario. Used to hear a lot about capitalism in those days, and I used to think this is where it started and this is what it is: a lot of sinking palaces.

Carlos Well, that's very good. But it gives you away, you see, far too romantic. If you want a city that really tells you what capitalism is all about, look at Brasilia. Designed by a Marxist architect as a city for the people and a city without slums. Then the property speculators get going, and before you know where you are the workers can't afford to live in the apartment blocks they're building. Well, they don't want to dirty up that sparkling white city, so the answer is, build slums in a big circle twenty miles outside the city and bus the workers in every day and watch a city for the people turn into a city where the workers have to construct the class barriers with their own hands.

West I know you see the problems. The thing is, I just don't believe you have the solutions.

Carlos (*amiably*) You people believe in what you have. The rich believe in money, the intelligent believe in intelligence, the powerful believe in power, the Army believes in strength, the Church believes in morality. But you really mustn't expect that to apply to everyone. You really shouldn't expect the oppressed to believe in misery and the starving to believe in hunger.

West It's been a very long time since I expected anything.

Blackout.

SEVENTEEN

A bar, though what we see can hardly be dignified with that title. The customers are all Indians, 'integrados', drinking from bottles, dressed in shabby cast-offs. Some are lying senseless in the familiar attitudes of Skid Row. Others have that lost, remote, melancholy expression of the Indian for whom nothing has replaced the tribal organization from which he has been divorced. They swig morosely at their bottles.

256

American voice Take a gamble in the Mato Grosso!

For as little as twelve dollars an acre, you can join Prince
Rainier of Monaco, several famous Hollywood stars
and a host of international celebrities as the owner of a
fabulous Amazon Adventure Estate in Brazil's most
mysterious and exotic region.

You may find yourself the possessor of one of Brazil's
fabled diamond mines, an oil baron or a manganese
king – anything may happen as you stake yourself out a
share in the inexhaustible resources of this hitherto
virtually unexplored nation within a nation.

Brazil's new progressive government, friendly to the U.S.,
has accorded top priority to the development of these
vast jungle territories – and its new roadbuilding
program will open up the area as never before.

In the next few years the development of Brazil's interior is
going to be very big business indeed – and we want you
to have a piece of the action.

Don't forget, too, that labor is plentiful and can cost as
little as seven U.S. cents per unit per hour.

We all of us have just a little bit of the Frontier Spirit in
our bones, don't we?

Yours should be telling you now to invest in the land of
the future and find your own personal El Dorado.

Huge profits are to be made!

EIGHTEEN

Ground plan as Scene Five.

West So you really don't think things are improving at all?

Crawshaw Well, they may be. I can only go by what I've
seen myself. I mean, I was in the Xingu only a couple of
months ago, 25th May 1970, I remember the date because
it was the day before my birthday, and they flew in the

remnants of the Beiços-de-Pau tribe. They're called that because they wear those, you know, lip-discs. They lived up by the river Arinos, and as far as we know, that's to say at the beginning of the year, there were about 400 of them left. There had, of course, been far more than that, but a few years ago, an expedition came up the river and left them a few sacks of food mixed with arsenic. Anyhow, after a great deal of red tape and nonsense it was decided to fly them into the Xingu, as it was obvious they didn't stand a chance of surviving where they were. So then it began. The rescue operation. Phase one was the measles epidemic, because as chance would have it, one of the rescue party was carrying measles. Only 109 of them survived it, but there we are. Phase two was the publicity stunt, in which four of the Indians were flown to Rio to meet the press. Unfortunately that didn't work out too well either, because three of them died in Rio. Phase three was transferring them to the transit camp. Now that hadn't been thought out too thoroughly, because what they did was drive them down overnight in open trucks, not altogether taking into account the fact that the Indians were naked and it was the middle of the winter. As a result of which another 65 of them died. This made the logistics of phase four, which was actually flying them into the Xingu, a good deal easier, but even so they weren't as careful as they might have been, and the 41 survivors were bundled into an unpressurised cargo plane and set off on the last stage of their great adventure. I was there when the plane landed at dawn at Posto Leonardo. We lifted them all out and laid them on the ground, the corpses to one side and the living to another, although it was by no means easy to distinguish. In the end we found that 24 of them were what you might technically call alive. It was quite cold. They lay on the ground without moving, they didn't move at all even when the ants began crawling up their nostrils and into their eyes, but they didn't blink, and the eyes didn't move at all, they gave no indication of seeing. They were lost. They were all lost. (*Long pause.*) It just so happens I witnessed that, but I could have told you about any one of a dozen tribes, same story, different details. It's strange, when I was in England, I didn't seem to be able to turn on the television without seeing some impassioned programme about some threatened animal species. I mean, I've got nothing against that, it's just that everyone knows the blue whale and the white rhino are in trouble. But who's ever heard of the Beiços-de-Pau or the Pacaas Novas or the Trumai?

West People are sentimental about animals.

Crawshaw Well, God knows, people are sentimental about Indians as well, and that's no help either, all those Noble Savage boys. I mean, I'd be the first to admit they show as much aggression, greed, superstition and cowardice as the next man. It's just that in their own terms they've provided themselves with solutions to all their immediate problems, and that makes them very well balanced, very relaxed and very happy.

West And very innocent.

Crawshaw Not if you mean unsophisticated, no. Only if you mean free of guilt. (*Pause.*) I think it's partly the way the children are brought up. The tribe I was with must have used some method of contraception, possibly an abortifacient, although I never managed to find out how they worked it. Anyway, the women had children more or less once every four years and for the first four years of the child's life its mother was never out of its sight. I used to watch the women grinding manioc with their children slung on their shoulders, and the children would urinate or defecate right there, all down their mother's side, and the mother wouldn't react at all, she'd just smile sometimes or not smile and carry on working.

259

West Extraordinary.

Silence. Then Mrs West rises.

Mrs West Well, Miles, I'm sure you two will excuse me if I take myself off to bed now.

Crawshaw and West both rise.

Crawshaw I'm sorry, I've probably stayed too long and talked too much.

Mrs West Not at all. Please don't go on my account.

West No, have another brandy.

Crawshaw Erm . . .

He is about to refuse, but Mrs West advances on him, hand outstreched, as West splashes more brandy into his glass.

Mrs West (*shaking Crawshaw's hand*) It was very nice to see you this evening, Miles.

Crawshaw Yes. Thank you very much for dinner.

Mrs West I'm afraid the rice pudding was absolutely disgusting.

Crawshaw No, it was very nice.

Mrs West I expect we'll see you again soon.

Crawshaw Hope so.

Mrs West Good night then.

Crawshaw Good night.

West See you later, dear.

Mrs West exits. Crawshaw and West sit down, and Crawshaw sips nervously at his brandy.

Crawshaw I must be on my way in a minute.

West No, don't go. There's no need to go. I'm very interested.

Crawshaw The thing is . . . (*He breaks off.*)

West Go on. Go on talking.

Crawshaw The thing is they know it, they know what they've got and you haven't. (*Pause.*) A year or so ago, I spent some time, a couple of months, with one of the nomadic tribes. And they had, I mean they owned nothing at all. They kept moving, they fed themselves on what they could catch, lizards, snakes, rats, whatever. They cooked what they had in the evening, then they put out the fire and slept in the ashes, all huddled together in each other's arms to keep warm. They had no home, no clothes and no possessions. Eventually the time came for me to leave them, and I explained it to them; it was a very emotional moment, we were all very upset about it. I used to sleep, rather prudishly, in a sleeping-bag, a little way off from them and that night, half-an-hour or so after we'd all settled down, I heard them weeping. After a bit, I got up and went over and sat near them. I said: you mustn't cry because I'm leaving, I shall come back some time. Then one of them said: we are not sad for ourselves, that we shall be without you; we are sad for you, that you can bear to leave us. You see they look into your eyes and they know it all.

Blackout.

NINETEEN

The guerrilla hideout. West, handcuffed, looks furious. Carlos paces uneasily up and down.

Carlos Well, look, I'm very sorry, that's all I can say.

West It's not enough, I want to know why.

Carlos I told you, there's been a hitch. A minor hitch, which means we have to delay everything for twenty-four hours.

West Listen, I've been very patient cooped up here all these weeks listening to your dreary propaganda, but there's just so much I can take.

Carlos I'm very sorry, it was my fault, I should never have said anything to you about it yesterday. I thought you'd be pleased to know.

West I was, of course I was, I thought it was true.

Carlos It's only another twenty-four hours. I promise you you'll be out tomorrow.

West You'd better give me that in writing.

Carlos We all have to suffer for the cause, comrade.

West I don't see why I should suffer for your wretched cause.

Carlos Because it's essential.

West That's a matter of opinion.

Carlos It's a matter of fact.

West Look, as far as I'm concerned, there are causes in Brazil which are far more essential. Like, for instance the extermination of the people who used to own this country. That seems to me far more important than replacing one authoritarian government with another.

Carlos Is that what you think we're trying to do?

West Well, I hardly imagined you had parliamentary democracy in mind.

Carlos Whatever makes you think democracy would be any use to us? Mm? Democracy is a luxury for countries rich enough so it doesn't matter who they elect. You don't think we're risking our lives so we can put in some bumbling idiot who'll waste all his energy trying not to upset anyone? We're fighting this war on behalf of the people. What could be more democratic than that?

West Letting the people choose.

Carlos Don't be absurd. How do you expect people to choose when all they're worried about is where the next crust of bread is coming from? There are children of eight on the streets of Rio offering themselves to anyone in a suit, you think they're going to turn into good Democrats? You make me laugh. All this crap about the Indians, it's just romantic bourgeois sentimentality. Listen, there are ninety million people in this country, and there aren't enough Indians left to fill up Maracana football stadium. So you say, look after the Indians, after all, poor things, it used to be their country, didn't it, and they'll never cause much trouble, because there are hardly any of them left, and they're not interested anyway. Look after the Indians, you say, but for Christ's sake don't look after the ninety million, or you never know what they might start wanting. All your liberal hearts bleed at the thought of those poor naked savages fading away, but it never begins to dribble across your apology for a mind that half a million children under five starved to death in Brazil last year.

West That is a complete perversion of my point of view.

Carlos responds with sounds mimicking West's pomposity.

(*indignant*) You people are all the same.

Carlos (*enraged*) So are you people.

He storms out. West sits, frowning, staring blankly into space. A moment later, Carlos returns with the chess board.

Better we don't have any more discussions, don't you think? Better we just play chess. (*Pause. He begins setting up the board.*) You might even win this time.

West I don't really feel like it just now.

Carlos goes on calmly distributing the pieces.

Carlos I don't have anything particular against you. It's just I can't help trying.

West What do you mean?

Carlos Che said, if a man is honest, you can make a revolutionary out of him. You seem honest enough.

He selects two pawns and holds his closed fists out towards West. Long pause. Finally, West indicates one, and Carlos opens his fist to show the white pawn. West takes it from him.

Off you go.

West makes an opening move.

West I've a feeling I'm going to win.

Blackout.

TWENTY

The Chief and his Wife sit, waiting. West appears.

West
Origin of the masks.
In the middle of the night
After a bad day's hunting and hungry to bed

A man heard something moving around near his hut
And running out found a giant paca which he killed.

There was enough meat for everyone in the village
But two did not join in the feast
A woman who that night was giving birth
And her husband.

The next day when the men had set off hunting
A devil wearing a bark mask appeared in the woman's hut
He told her that the villagers had killed and eaten his son
And that he must be revenged.

She and her husband and child he said would be spared
And told her to gather the bark from a certain tree
That night the devils came and killed every villager
But the three who hid their faces behind the bark.

Now it is known that the wearing of the bark masks
Is certain protection against the devils.
For who seeing his own image his own skin
Could destroy his own kind?

West exits.

*Music. Two Indians appear, playing ten-foot flutes
and dancing. Behind them, with their right hands on the
Men's shoulders, two Girls dance in time. They circle
and weave around the posts and across the stage. The
chief rises and moves behind the posts. As he does so,
the other Indians rise and join the dance. The Chief
emerges from behind the posts wearing a mask, dancing
his own dance. The ceremony is reaching a climax of
excitement and exhilaration.*

*Cutting through this the sound of a light aircraft. The
Indians falter, continue, falter again, and, as the sound
of the aeroplane increases in intensity, gradually stop.
The plane is now overhead.*

It drops bombs.

Explosions, panic, chaos. The sound of the plane diminishes, then increases again as it turns and flies back over the village even lower.

More bombs.

Screams of pain and fear.

Blackout.

TWENTY ONE

The guerrilla hideout. West, handcuffed, contemplating the chessboard. Carlos watching him. A knock at the door. Carlos gets up and leaves the room. Long pause, during which West gives out a little grunt of pleasure and makes a move. Then the door bursts open and Carlos re-enters, white and tense. In his hand, though at first concealed from West, the pistol with silencer. West looks up, triumphant, indicates the chess-board.

West Pick the bones out of that.

Carlos I . . .

West I think I've . . . (*He sees the gun and breaks off suddenly.*) What's erm . . . ?

Carlos I . . .

He levels the pistol at West.

West (*feebly*) Don't.

Carlos Sorry.

He shoots West three times. West slumps grotesquely to the floor, still dangling from his handcuff. Carlos looks at him for a second, desolate. Then, from outside, the wail of a police siren. Carlos starts, then rushes out. A hail of machine-gun fire in the blackout.

Fanfares, reminiscent of the opening of a TV news bulletin. A white frontcloth drops in. On it are projected, one by one, overlapping, innumerable photographs of West, black and white, colour, family snaps, headlines in several languages, until the whole cloth is covered with images of West.

TWENTY TWO

The frontcloth rises to reveal a bloody heap of Indian bodies. Silence. Then a groan of pain.

Two Men enter with sub-machine-guns, one, as is clear from his goggles and flying-jacket, the pilot of the plane, the other his co-pilot.

One of the Indians in the pile of bodies onstage groans, and begins painfully to rise to his feet. It is the Chief, still wearing his mask.

One of the men shoots down the Chief and fires a burst into the heap of bodies, then they pass across the stage and off. A cry followed by another burst of machine-gun fire offstage. Silence.

The Men return, looking well pleased. The **Pilot** *pauses, tucks the gun under his arm, produces a packet of cigarettes, offers one to his companion, takes one himself and lights them. Pause. Then he throws the box of matches to his companion who nods and leaves the stage. A moment later, he returns without his gun, but with two torches headed with rags soaked in kerosene. He lights one and hands it to the Pilot, then lights the other. They leave the stage in the direction of the village.*

Silence. An animal cry, another soft groan, the light drone of flies.

The crackle of flames.

Effect of flames as the lights dim to blackout.

TREATS

For Peggy

I wonder, wonder, who,
Mbee-doo oo who,
Who wrote the book of love.
Lyrics from the song, 'Book Of Love'
(Davis-Patrick-Malone)

– it doesn't take much to see that the problems of three little people don't amount to a hill o' beans in this crazy world.
From the screenplay of Casablanca *by*
Julius J. and Philip G. Epstein and Howard Koch

Characters

Ann
Patrick
Dave

Ann's flat in London. August, 1974; or now.

Treats was presented at the Royal Court Theatre in February 1976 by the English Stage Company and Michael Codron. The cast was as follows:

Dave James Bolam
Ann Jane Asher
Patrick Stephen Moore

Directed Robert Kidd
Designed Andrew Sanders
Lighting Jack Raby

SCENE ONE

The main room of **Ann's** *flat in London. Rather severely
and (for reasons which will emerge) sparsely furnished.
The main item of furniture is a full-length, high-backed
sofa, facing front, with a coffee-table in front of it. The
rest of the room is divided into three principal areas: a
dining-recess, with a table and one chair; a desk, facing the
window, covered with papers and books; and a white
colour-T.V. set facing an uncomfortable-looking modern
leather swivel-chair pretty much out of keeping with the
rest of the furniture. No carpet: instead a couple of rugs
covering rather unexpected areas of the floor. Apart from
this, there is a telephone near the desk, a large ornate
mirror on the side wall and two sets of bookshelves, one
fairly full, the other empty except for two or three
volumes, lying on their sides. The main door, which leads
into a tiny hall is in the centre of the back wall; and there
are two other doors leading to the kitchen and the
bedroom respectively. Early evening in autumn.*

*Ann, who is in her mid-twenties and striking rather than
beautiful, sits on the sofa, leafing through* Vogue. *Next to
her, holding her hand, is* **Patrick.** *He is about ten years
older, and looks amiable enough, although faintly absurd
at present, as he is wearing large white headphones,
connected by a long lead to the amplifier, which is in the
fuller of the two bookshelves next to the door. He is
listening to the 3rd movement of Bruckner's 4th
Symphony, fairly loud, and clearly enjoying himself.*

After a time, he speaks.

Patrick Apparently, when Bruckner finally got to hear one of his symphonies performed, he was so chuffed he tried to tip the conductor.

Brief silence.

Ann How come you know all these things?

Patrick (*not hearing*) Or so it says on the sleeve. (*As he speaks, he realises Ann has said something.*) What?

Ann Nothing.

She smiles. Silence.

Patrick I think that's rather touching. (*He looks at Ann, who is smiling broadly.*) You obviously think it's pathetic.

Ann Not at all.

Patrick What?

Longish silence. Then, from outside, quite clearly, the sound of breaking glass. Ann looks up, startled.

What?

Ann shakes her head at him and he sinks back into the music. Ten seconds. Ann, looking worried, gets up and starts moving round behind the sofa. As she does so, the handle of the door turns and it begins very slowly to open. Ann freezes. **Dave** *appears in the doorway. He is a man of about 30, ordinary enough looking in the normal run of events, but possessed of a kind of malignant energy, which is at the moment particularly apparent. Ann seems about to cry out, or at least to speak, but Dave puts his finger to his lips so quickly he succeeds in checking her. He stands for a moment, assessing the scene, then moves swiftly to the amplifier and turns the volume up very loud indeed. Patrick leaps to his feet with a howl of pain, plucking ineffectually at his headphones as if they were a swarm of bees. Finally* *he manages to get them off and throws them down on the sofa.*

Christ Jesus!

At this moment he becomes aware of Dave, who is already striding purposefully towards him. They come together behind the sofa, where, without the slightest hesitation, Dave punches Patrick very hard on the nose. Patrick collapses behind the sofa, vanishing entirely from view. Ann screams. Dave turns and strides back to the amplifier, turns the volume down very low, then turns back to Ann

Dave Any messages?

Ann Get out!

Dave Any mail?

Ann Will you get the hell out of here!

Dave That's not very nice.

A groan from Patrick. His hand appears over the back of the sofa.

All I want to know is, is there any post for me?

Ann I sent it on to your mother's.

Dave You did what?

Patrick rises slowly from behind the sofa, very shaken. Dave glances at him briefly, then turns his attention back to Ann.

Why?

Ann I thought you'd be living there for the time being.

Patrick Look . . .

Dave I thought I was living here for the time being. And if

I'm not living here, I'm certainly not going anywhere near that old ginbag. You just sent my letters to her because you know she likes steaming them open. (*Pause. He looks around the room.*) Where's Arthur?

Patrick Look . . .

Dave Shut up. Where's Arthur?

Ann I gave him away.

Dave What did you say?

Ann I gave him away.

Dave You bitch.

Patrick Listen . . .

Dave Shut up. Who did you give him to?

Ann The newsagent.

Dave The newsagent?

Ann Yes, you know, our local newsagent.

Dave Well, you listen to me. You better have him back here by this time tomorrow or there'll be trouble.

Patrick Now, look here . . .

Dave Shut up, you. (*He turns back to Ann.*) Do you understand me?

Ann If you want him back, you'll have to go and get him yourself.

Dave I can't look after him at the moment. Not where I'm staying.

Ann Then he'll just have to stop where he is. He's perfectly happy there.

Dave I'm not having my dog dumped off on some bloody

wog newsagent. They'll be sending him out delivering before we know where we are.

Ann Just go away, will you?

Dave That is my dog!

Ann Go away!

Dave I'm going to hurt you.

Ann Call the police, Patrick.

Patrick What?

Ann Call the police.

Patrick begins to move hesitantly towards the telephone.

Patrick I'm sure . . . Are you sure . . .?

Ann He's broken in, assaulted you and threatened me. Tell them that.

Patrick 999, is it?

Dave Who is this creep?

Ann Tell them to come right away.

Patrick is now poised above the telephone, eyeing it uneasily.

Dave I shouldn't pick up that phone if I were you, son.

Patrick picks it up. Dave rushes towards him as he leans forward to dial. Their heads crash. This time it's Dave who has the worst of the encounter. He doubles up and staggers away, moaning and covering his eye. Patrick, startled, stands watching him a moment, then puts the receiver down, concerned.

Christ, bloody hell, watch what you're doing.

Patrick Sorry.

Dave Nearly had my eye out.

Patrick I'm very sorry.

Dave I should think so.

Patrick Are you all right?

Dave Fuck.

Ann Now will you go?

Dave Not until you tell me who this strange man is.

Ann None of your business.

Patrick My name is Patrick Archer.

Dave Never heard of you.

Patrick And you must be Dave Tilley.

Dave I want to know where you picked him up.

Patrick We work together.

Ann Look, Patrick, will you not stand chatting, I want him to go.

Dave Patrick, Patrick, hang on a minute . . . it's not, is it?

Ann avoids his eye, doesn't answer.

Patrick Not what?

Dave Not the famous office bore?

Patrick What do you mean?

Dave Not the one who's so dull he put that Arab *and* his interpreter to sleep during their meeting?

Patrick catches Ann's eye, then, when she looks away, speaks with some dignity.

Patrick They'd had a long flight.

Dave I can't believe this. I come back from three weeks in Nicosia, most of which I spent lying flat in the corridors of the Ledra Palace Hotel, waiting for some Turk to put a bullet up my Khyber, to find you've not only changed the lock, put my possessions into store and hired some idiot answering service so you don't even have to speak to me, but that you actually appear to be living with a man who's been a household joke for two years. (*to Patrick*) You are living here, aren't you? Aren't you married? You look married.

Patrick Yes, I am living here; no, I'm not married.

Dave (*to Ann*) What's the meaning of this?

Ann The idea was to avoid this kind of scene. After all, we've had enough of them over the last few months.

Dave Give me a drink.

Ann No.

Dave (*to Patrick*) Scotch.

Ann No!

Dave It's very probably my Scotch.

Ann It is not.

Dave Look, there are things to discuss, you know, financial matters, that kind of thing. I know you like to pretend none of that exists, but you can't have an amputation without a few bits and bobs need tying up. So why don't we all sit down – (*he does so in the swivel-chair, swivels round to face front*) – and have a drink?

Ann No.

Patrick Let me get him a drink, then you can discuss what you have to discuss and get it over with.

Dave That's the boy.

Patrick crosses to the dining-recess, opens a cupboard, takes out a couple of glasses, pours Scotch. Ann watches him, annoyed.

Patrick Like something, love?

Ann No.

Patrick comes down, hands a glass to Dave.

Dave Thanks, thanks. (*He takes a sip.*) It's upset me, punching you like that. I try never to do anything spontaneous.

Patrick I'm surprised it was spontaneous.

Dave It wasn't, no, in fact I'd planned the whole thing, but the after-effect is the same as if it had been spontaneous.

Ann I'm going.

Dave That's not going to be very helpful.

Ann Well, then, get on with it.

Patrick Do you want *me* to go?

Dave Yes.

Ann No!

Dave Make-your-mind-up time.

Ann Look, it's all settled, everything's settled, so I can't think why you're pissing about. I worked it all out very carefully, so as far as I can see, there's nothing to discuss.

Dave Sit down.

Patrick sits on the sofa. Ann remains standing.

There is, on the contrary, a great deal to discuss, and since you insist on washing our dirty linen in public, let me begin with something which is very near to my heart, not to say directly beneath my bum: namely, my chair.

Ann What?

Dave This is my chair.

Ann We bought it together.

Dave Precisely. For me. We bought it together for me.

Ann Listen, there are two pieces of furniture we went out and bought together. One was this chair and the other was the rug. And since the rug was considerably more expensive than the chair, I decided if I gave you the rug, you'd have nothing to complain about.

Dave The rug.

Ann Yes.

Dave Well, now, that's going to be very handy for sitting at my desk typing, isn't it?

Ann The desk is mine.

Dave I don't mean that ramshackle old heap, I mean *my* desk.

Patrick Are you sure you wouldn't rather I went?

Ann Oh, shut up.

Dave If you'd really wanted to be on the safe side, you would have given me the chair and the rug. However, since I'm a reasonable man, I propose you give me the chair and I'll bring you back the rug.

Ann No, I don't want you bringing it back. Have someone deliver it and collect the chair and send me the bill.

Dave Right. Excellent. Now. Next. Fixtures and fittings.

Ann You want half the curtains?

Dave Oh, very good, this is very good. No, no, as you well know, fixtures and fittings has very little to do with the curtains. It's a metaphysical, landlord's idea, the purpose of which was to secure, as you will remember, large and far from metaphysical sums of money.

Ann You want half the money.

Dave Well, I hadn't actually worked it out in detail, but . . . now you mention it, yes, all right, yes, I would like half the money.

Ann You shit.

Dave I wouldn't want to press you or anything, it's just I'm a bit short at the moment.

Ann I'll give it to you as and when I can get hold of it, I haven't got anything like that kind of money at the moment.

Dave Do you wonder the country is on its knees?

Ann Naturally I'll have to deduct for the pane of glass you broke in the door.

Patrick This is awful.

Ann Now why don't you go away? I don't know why you have to go through all this. For the last year, you've done nothing but threaten to leave me; all I did was the work.

Dave Work? I spent hours in Nicosia lying on my belly in the telephone queue, while you were in bed with a bore of international reputation, you call that work?

Silence. Dave suddenly looks defeated, his face collapses.

I want . . . to talk to you alone.

Ann No.

Dave I must, it's very important.

Ann No.

Dave Please. Please.

> *Dave bursts into tears. Longish silence, broken only by his sobs.*

Ann.

Ann Don't.

Dave You mustn't do this to me, Ann.

Ann It's too late for all this.

Dave I want to go on living with you.

Patrick Perhaps I'd better . . .

Ann No.

Dave It's so sudden. You shouldn't have done it just like that.

Ann Better quick.

Dave I'd made up my mind. I'd made up my mind I was going to ask you to marry me when I got back.

Ann That's not what you said on the phone.

Dave I was frightened. I got frightened. In Cyprus. I'd decided. I knew something had to be done.

Ann Something has been done.

Dave Let me come back. I'm sorry. I'm sorry. I know I was . . . I'm . . .

Ann I really think you must go now.

Dave All right.

Silence. Dave wipes his eyes, blows his nose, his face reassembles. He gets up.

Patrick Would you like me to call you a taxi?

Dave (*angrily*) I can't afford a taxi, I'm completely broke. (*He subsides, breathes deeply, is now just as he was before breaking down.*) I'll walk.

Ann Where are you staying?

Dave The Savoy.

Ann That's absurd.

Dave None of your bloody business.

Ann I'm surprised you don't go and stay with one of your mistresses.

Dave You know very well all my mistresses in London are married. (*He moves over to the door.*) I'll be in touch.

Ann shakes her head. Dave leans round her to smile at Patrick.

Pip pip, old fart.

He leaves. Silence. Patrick gets up, moves towards Ann as she comes away from the door. She avoids him, sits in the swivel-chair. He hovers a moment, then returns to the sofa, sits down again.

Ann He'll never forgive me now. (*Pause.*) Not that he would have done anyway. (*Pause.*) Jesus.

Patrick So that's him.

Ann Yes.

Patrick Can't ever remember such an unusual meeting.

Ann I told you he was a bastard.

Patrick Whatever made you put up with him for so long?

Silence.

Ann Expect he'll be back.

Silence.

Patrick Tell me . . . why did you tell him all those things about how boring I was?

Ann That's the kind of thing he used to enjoy.

Silence.

Patrick Fair enough.

'Runaway' sung by Del Shannon.

SCENE TWO

The next morning. Empty stage. The sound of a key in the lock, then Patrick enters, followed by Dave, who looks somewhat the worse for wear, but seems cheerful.

Dave Well, this is very civil of you, old sport. Any chance of a cup of coffee?

Patrick Sure.

He moves across the dining-recess and off into the kitchen; clatter of cups. Meanwhile, Dave settles himself comfortably in the swivel-chair. Patrick reappears.

Where is this undertaker's?

Dave Chalk Farm.

Patrick Bit out of your way.

Dave I decided to go and see a friend. As it turned out, she wasn't very pleased to see me. Wasn't my lucky evening for social calls.

Patrick smiles uneasily.

However, she was able to give me a bottle of Scotch. Then she made an excuse and I left.

Patrick To the undertaker's.

Dave Not immediately. I wandered about a bit and drank the Scotch. I was just thinking I couldn't possibly make it all the way back to the Savoy, when I spotted the shop. Could be I'm developing a taste for breaking and entering, anyway it was very easy, and I was just settling down for a kip in this very comfortable silk-lined casket when they arrested me.

Patrick How come?

Dave Apparently I left the door open.

Patrick It's the first time I've seen in the cells.

Dave It's all right. I was past caring. (*Pause.*) I'm sorry I had to get you involved.

Patrick That's . . .

Dave I couldn't very well tell them I was staying at the Savoy, could I, they'd have given me a proper kicking.

Patrick I'll fix the coffee.

He exits to the kitchen. Dave turns and shouts after him.

Dave White please. And white sugar. None of your poncy crystals.

Patrick returns with two mugs of coffee, hands one to Dave, who takes it without acknowledgement, moves across to the sofa, sits, sips. Silence.

Patrick I believe, I believe we have a friend in common.

Dave looks across at him, waiting.

Charles Peters.

Dave Charlie.

Patrick Yes.

Dave Mate of yours, is he?

Patrick Well . . .

Dave Because he's certainly no friend of mine.

Patrick Oh, really?

Dave Matter of fact, I think he's a fucking toerag.

Patrick Ah.

Silence.

Dave I suppose you have a lot of friends.

Patrick Fair number, you know . . .

Dave Yes. Don't believe in it myself.

Patrick Don't believe in what?

Dave Friends. Loyalty I believe in.

Patrick I don't um . . .

Dave What you going to do, marry her?

Patrick Well, I mean, eventually, maybe I yes will possibly.

Dave What's she said to you about me?

Patrick Enough.

Dave What I want to know is, how long have you been lurking around waiting for this to happen? (*Pause.*) Have you spent years admiring her from afar? Or were you the sympathetic shoulder for her to snivel on? Or have you in fact been giving her one twice weekly down amongst the filing cabinets?

Patrick Yes; to a certain extent; and no.

Dave What are you talking about?

Patrick Answering your questions.

Dave I see. (*Pause.*) In that case, what do you mean by to a certain extent?

Patrick I mean I tried to be sympathetic whenever she was obviously unhappy, which I think she appreciated. But she never told me what it was was making her unhappy.

Dave In other words she never complained about me?

Patrick No.

Dave That woman has no feelings.

Patrick Is that a joke?

Dave No, of course it isn't, you humourless berk.

Patrick It seems to me . . . if you're frightened what people are going to say about you, you should be careful how you treat them.

Dave And conversely, needlepoint mottos can make your thumb bleed.

   Silence. Patrick, puzzled. Dave, drinking his coffee.

Anyway, was it worth waiting for?

Patrick What?

Dave What do you think?

Patrick I don't think I have to talk to you about that.

Dave Reason I ask is, the age I am now, which is of course the age you were some years ago, can't remember the point of this remark . . . oh, yes, what I used to regret most were the women I couldn't have; now, as often as not, it's the women I do have.

Patrick Not a problem of mine.

Dave What I mean is, you've had the best of her now, from now on it'll be downhill all the way. She's not what I'd call sparky, you'll find it gets pretty boring, I used to have to put a record on or read a book. Why go through all that and upset yourself? Why don't you leave her to me, I'm all she's good for.

Patrick What do you expect me to say to that?

Dave Yes.

Silence.

Patrick Look, it's really no good talking to me about all this.

Dave I know that, I realise that, but I don't seem to have much alternative, do I? I mean, if you come back from abroad and find the person you've been living with for two and a half years has locked you out and refuses to speak to you, you have to grasp at any straw. Put yourself in my place. (*Pause.*) Mentally, I mean.

Patrick I know, well, I tried to persuade Ann this might not be the best way of going about things, but she insisted.

Dave You mean she doesn't do what you tell her?

Patrick You have a very aggressive way of putting a question.

Dave You have a very evasive way of not answering one.

Patrick I would have thought in your profession, not having your questions answered was all in a day's work.

Dave Right. Whereas for you . . .

Patrick That's right.

Dave I once frightened a man off by spending an entire evening violently attacking the Jesuits.

Patrick Was it a subject close to his heart?

Dave No, on the contrary, he knew as little about the Jesuits as I did. But once he'd ventured a tentative protest against some particularly outrageous assertion of mine, of course he was done. Hours of flabby footwork and judicious mumblings against the energy and passion of an apparently committed man. You can imagine the effect on the woman in question.

Patrick Yes.

Dave The contempt she felt for that poor bastard was something beautiful to behold. Of course, she was very stupid. I married them off in the end. I sometimes wonder how often and in what terms they speak of Jesuits.

Patrick Is this by way of being a warning?

Dave Only indirectly. The Jesuits wouldn't do for you and Ann. Whereas anything would have done for those two. Stock-car racing. I could have harangued him on stock-car racing, that would have been almost as good. Although the Jesuits did give me more . . .

Patrick Mileage.

Dave Scope. (*Pause.*) Where were you the night I got back, anyway?

Patrick Bristol.

Dave Bristol?

Patrick With my father.

Dave Terrific. (*Pause.*) I spent the whole night and most of the next day sitting on my suitcase in the porch.

Patrick Didn't you get the letter?

Dave Naturally I got the letter. But the letter didn't say you'd be skulking in Bristol for days. Nor did it say you were both going to take a lengthy holiday from the office. By the way, that must have caused some tittle-tattle among your colleagues.

Patrick I doubt it.

Dave Nor did it say anything about you, beyond referring to you as 'someone else', a more or less accurate but I thought not altogether flattering description. The only way I could find out who you were was to go and listen in to the tittle-tattle among your colleagues.

Patrick I see.

Dave I'm sorry I pretended not to know who you were last night. I thought it would be . . .

Patrick Jesuitical.

Dave Expedient, yes. Forgive me. But, you see, you can surely appreciate, it was a desperate situation. I mean, God knows, I've split up with enough people in the past, but it's always been a kind of ritual disembowelling. Never the guillotine.

Patrick Ann thought it would be better.

Dave Do you?

Patrick Well, I must say, judging by the image you've just . . .

Dave Then let me put it another way: it's always been a jump but there's usually been a parachute.

Patrick Well . . . listen . . . perhaps . . . you should come and have dinner with us this evening.

Dave Really?

Patrick Yes, I can understand . . . it would be a chance to clear things up.

Dave What time?

Patrick Eightish?

Dave Done. (*Pause.*) Ann'll be pleased.

Patrick Well, if she really doesn't think it's a good idea, I can always call you and cancel.

Dave Yes.

Patrick At the Savoy.

Dave Oh, yes.

Patrick Or at the paper?

Dave No, at the Savoy.

Patrick Good.

Dave My word, this is civilized. Now all that remains is for me to touch you for a loan.

Patrick I don't think so.

Dave No?

Patrick How much do you need?

Dave How much can you spare?

Patrick As far as I can gather from Ann, you make a great deal more money than I do.

Dave Yes, but I need a lot of money.

Patrick What for?

Dave To spend. What do you think for? To spend.

Patrick I see.

Dave You think you're underpaid?

Patrick Sometimes.

Dave Perhaps you should become a miner.

Patrick What?

Dave I'm sorry, it's just something I say to test people's reactions. If they laugh, I know they're shits.

Patrick I might easily have laughed. Out of politeness, say.

Dave Makes no difference, does it?

Silence. Patrick's hand goes to his inside pocket.

Patrick I . . . could probably manage something, just to . . . tide you over.

Dave Well. That's very handsome.

Patrick Erm . . .

Dave But no.

Patrick No?

Dave No, on mature reflection, I don't think it would be right.

Patrick Just as you like.

Dave Thanks all the same. Very generous of you. Shows there are more important things in life than women.

Patrick Ann tells me you hate women.

Dave She's a clever girl.

Patrick Why is that?

Dave My mum wouldn't let me have a bicycle.

Patrick I see.

Silence. Patrick gets up, looks at his watch, hovers indeterminately for a few seconds.

Dave Anything I can do for you?

Patrick Well. I'm afraid I have to go. I'm very late as it is.

Dave Don't let me keep you.

Patrick I thought . . .

Dave I just have to make one or two phone calls, if that's all right. In lieu of the loan.

Patrick Well, all right.

Dave I know you have to get on. This country may be on its knees, but others are on their faces in the mud, am I right?

Patrick Close . . . the door behind you.

Dave I've lived here for years, I know how to close the door.

Patrick Yes.

Dave See you this evening. You are going to be here this evening?

Patrick Yes, of course.

Dave Just wondered.

Silence. Patrick moves uncertainly towards the door.

How's your nose?

Patrick What?

Dave Your nose. (*He mimes swinging a punch.*)

Patrick Oh, fine, thanks.

Dave Terrific. (*Pause.*) Thanks for everything.

Patrick nods awkwardly, confused; and exits. Dave calls out after him.

Take care. (*He grins to himself, gets up, crosses to the desk and begins to rummage purposefully through the papers and letters.*)

'It's a Wonderful World' sung by Louis Armstrong.

SCENE THREE

An hour or two later. Dave alone, still at the desk. He holds a bundle of letters in one hand, and in the other hand a single letter, which he is reading. After a time, he grunts, replaces the pile of letters on the desk, pauses, reflects, looks at his watch, takes a small diary out of his top pocket and crosses to the telephone. He looks a number up, dials and waits.

Dave (*North Country accent*) 'Ello. Could I have the electrical department, please? . . . the electrical department . . . oh, is it? . . . oh, beg your pardon, mate, sorry . . . tara. (*He puts the receiver down, riffles through his diary, dials again, waits. This time, he speaks with his normal accent.*) Hello, Emma? . . . this is Dave . . . yes . . . yes, I know . . . what you up to this afternoon? . . . well, I thought you might like to pop round and visit me at the Savoy . . . that's right . . . oh . . . can't you put them off? . . . oh, well, never mind, perhaps next week sometime . . . well, I'm not sure, I'll ring you nearer the time . . . OK, love, have to run now . . . yes . . . speak to you soon . . . bye. (*He puts the receiver down, turns to another page in the diary, puts his hand out towards the phone, hesitates,*

then picks up the receiver, dials a number, waits.) Hello
. . . yes, that's right . . . well, I've been away . . . Cyprus
. . . can you make lunch? . . . (*With some relief.*) Well,
then, this afternoon . . . well, get your mother round . . .
about three would be good . . . the Savoy . . . the Savoy
Hotel . . . in the Strand . . . I don't know what tube it is,
get a taxi, I'll pay you back . . . yes, ask for me at the desk
. . . bring your wellies and half a pound of butter . . . it's a
joke . . . yes, all right . . . all right, love, see you later.

*He puts the receiver down, sighs, puts his diary back in
his top pocket, smooths his hair, crosses to the mirror,
combs his hair, puts his comb away, rubs his chin,
studies himself in the mirror. He stands looking at
himself for some time, expressionless. Then he moves to
the bookshelf, looks through the records and selects the
Bob Dylan L.P. 'Nashville Skyline'. He switches on the
record-player, puts the record on and sets the needle
down carefully at the beginning of the track 'I Threw It
All Away'. Then he sits down to listen to it. When the
song finishes, he gets up quickly and moves the needle
back to the beginning of the track, and, as the song
begins again, returns to the mirror.*

SCENE FOUR

*Ann, Patrick and Dave sit round the dining-table – Ann on
a kitchen-stool, Patrick on the chair from in front of the
desk and Dave on the regular straight-backed chair. On
the table, the remains of their dinner.*
Enormous silence.

Dave Did you know, I think this might interest you,
Patrick, as a detail of some consequence in the history of
your new home, that Dwight D. Eisenhower slept here?

Patrick Did he?

Dave Well, he came to a lot of meetings.

Patrick Is that true?

Ann Of course not, you buffoon.

Silence.

Dave This the kind of evening you normally spend?

Patrick What do you mean?

Dave Well, you know, full of fun.

Ann We don't normally spend our evenings under the malignant eye of a drunken journalist.

Dave You mean, Patrick doesn't.

Ann Nor do we usually spend our evenings with people who've had specific messages left for them, telling them not to come.

Dave Very remiss, those boys at reception.

Ann Why didn't you answer your phone all afternoon?

Dave *A* because I was busy and *b* because I knew you would call.

Silence.

I must say, that was a better bloody meal than you ever cooked me. Tell you what, why don't you move out and I'll live with Patrick. Mm? You could get somewhere cosy round the corner and Patrick and I could pop round to see you alternate evenings. After dinner. Then, you never know, one night, Patrick and I might strike it lucky and we need trouble you no further.

Silence. Dave gets up and moves into the body of the room.

Well, mine's a small coffee and a large brandy.

Ann You've had your free meal, now piss off.

Dave But, Ann, the discussion, Ann, our discussion.

Ann What's to discuss?

Dave Oh, dearie me.

Silence. Patrick rises.

Patrick I'll fix the coffee.

Dave I want this man to be the mother of my children.

Patrick steps into the kitchen, carrying plates. Dave moves to the bookshelf, starts looking through the records. Silence. Dave fetches out a John Lennon L.P.

This is mine.

Ann It is not.

Dave Well, look, I don't want to make an issue of it, but it is in fact mine.

Ann All right, take it.

Dave No, if you want it, of course, I wouldn't dream of taking it.

Ann I don't want the bloody thing, take it.

Dave OK.

Dave puts it in one of the empty bookshelves, facing front. Patrick comes out of the kitchen with a tray, puts it on the coffee-table in front of the sofa, arranges the cups. As he does so, the sound of chanting voices in the distance, indistinct at first, then swelling, so that the phrase 'Send them back' can be discerned.

Patrick What's that?

Dave Demonstration.

Patrick National Front?

Dave I.R.A. (*He gestures vaguely.*) The Home Secretary lives over there somewhere.

> *The chant changes to one of 'Murderer' which is heard clearly for a few seconds before beginning to die away to a murmur. Dave, meanwhile, has a glint in his eye, as a thought strikes him.*

Course it's nothing compared to the man downstairs.

Patrick The man downstairs.

Dave What, you mean to say you haven't heard the man downstairs? Practising his trombone? Listen, you have to be as insensitive as a warthog, like me, or more so, like Ann, to be able to put up with the man downstairs. I should have thought any normal person would find living over him absolutely intolerable. A few rounds of 'Twinkle, twinkle, little star' on that thing, and you'll be . . .

Ann Give up.

Dave Who's that? My God, you gave me a fright, I'd forgotten you were here.

Ann We all know our neighbour downstairs is a very sweet old lady.

Dave Are you going to sit on that penitential stool all evening? It's going to make our discussion unnecessarily diffuse.

> *Ann doesn't move. Dave, who has helped himself to coffee, settles himself comfortably in the swivel-chair, and turns to Patrick.*

Patrick Erm . . .?

Dave There is some brandy, isn't there?

Patrick Yes.

Patrick fetches some brandy, pours a glass in the dining-recess, exchanging a glance with Ann.

Dave Large as you like.

Patrick takes the glass over to him, sits down on the sofa.

Now.

Dave takes a sip, pauses. Ann gets up and crosses to the sofa, sits next to Patrick, pours herself some coffee.

Patrick.

Patrick Yes.

Dave Where do you live?

Patrick Here.

Dave Yes, I know that, I'm not talking about now, I mean usually.

Patrick Oh, at my mother's.

Dave Really? Do you mean with your mother?

Patrick Yes.

Dave Amazing.

Patrick Well, it's a big house. That's to say, I have a floor to myself. When my parents divorced, my mother kept the house in London.

Dave Good housekeeper, eh?

Patrick What?

Dave Nothing.

Patrick Oh, I see.

Dave So, divorced. I'm surprised. My old man died last year after 37 years of ecstatically happy marriage. Least, he'd spent so long telling everyone it was ecstatically happy, I think dying was the only method he could devise of getting out of it gracefully.

Ann If we're quite up-to-date with each other's family histories, perhaps now we could move on to the weather.

Dave Look, I'm just trying to get a full picture of the situation.

Ann Patrick's former domestic arrangements, if I may say so, have bugger all to do with the situation.

Dave Well, you never know, I thought he might have a nice cheap flat to rent me. Naturally, now I know it's a question of moving in with his mother, I shall have to think again, no disrespect to the poor old cow. (*Pause.*) Also, I couldn't help noticing there's nothing here that doesn't belong to you or, as for example in the case of this chair, me. And that made me curious.

Patrick Well . . .

Dave What I mean is, don't you find it inconvenient having to go back to your mother's every time you want to change your socks?

Patrick I have my clothes here. I've never accumulated very much in the way of possessions.

Dave Yes, well, very commendable. But you see now why I've been pursuing this tack. I mean, I can't really be blamed for thinking it all looks a bit temporary. Can I?

Ann You can be blamed for mixing it, which is what you're up to. If there's anything to discuss, which there isn't, it's not to do with Patrick. It's to do with why I decided to do what I have done, and what took me so long about it.

Dave All right, let's talk about that.

Silence.

Well, go on.

Ann What's there to say, except that for two and a half years you bullied and terrorized me to such an extent I could hardly open my mouth. I didn't dare to have an opinion you hadn't approved about anything. My friends pitied me and your friends despised me. The only peace I ever had was when you were away, and even then you were ringing up every evening snarling and taunting and threatening me about something or other. How's that to be kicking off with?

Dave Yes, well, I'm not denying it. I have erred. You're quite right. I have in fact erred.

Ann And that's not to mention that in the course of those two and a half years you had affairs or at any rate sexual relations with forty-two other women.

Dave Oh, you counted?

Ann No, you counted. I don't know or care whether you tell the truth about these things, but the mathematics is yours.

Dave I see.

Ann And judging by what I've been told since, things were not always as you described them.

Dave Told by whom? What have you been told? What do you mean?

Ann All I mean is people say just as unpleasant and probably more accurate things about you behind your back as you say about them behind theirs.

Dave (*to Patrick*) Doesn't speak very well, does she?

Ann And don't start that again.

Dave Sorry.

Ann Don't you bloody start on that again.

Dave All right.

Ann He used to save up clumsy sentences I'd said, and repeat them to me when we got home.

Patrick You told me.

Ann Well, I'm telling you again, it's relevant, isn't it?

Patrick Yes, I know, I'm not saying you told me, I don't want to hear it again, I'm saying you told me, I know about it and I can see why you said it.

Dave Your sentences aren't too elegant either, are they? (*Pause.*) However, I suppose grammar is the least of our worries.

Ann Ha.

Dave Two of those and you'd be laughing.

Ann scowls, Patrick laughs; Ann looks at him coldly.

Ann Enjoying yourself?

Dave Well, much more than I did during dinner. But then, if somebody'd thrown up it would have been a relief.

Ann I was speaking to Patrick.

Patrick Oh.

Dave Let's leave Patrick out of it for the moment, shall we, and see if we can't get back to what we were talking about. Our relationship. Now you were saying, if I read you correctly, that I bullied you and never allowed you to have any opinions of your own.

Ann Yes.

Dave Not true. When we met, you actually *had* no opinions of your own. Consequently, as time went on, the opinions you picked up tended to be mine, and if they weren't, they were sufficiently shaky and newly established to crumble as soon as I attacked them. Do you think I liked that? Do you think I liked hearing you parrot out all the things I'd told you to everyone we met? Do you think I liked the fact it was impossible to have an argument with you about any subject however neutral without you taking it personally? It's possible to disagree with someone about the ethics of non-violence without wanting to kick his face in. All that mute suffering you used to go through whenever we'd had some piddling dispute about the Common Market or the Stock Market or the supermarket or some other damn thing we didn't in fact give a toss about. I much prefer you the way you are now if you want to know.

Ann Nonsense, if I ever argued with you about anything, you used to go berserk. In the end, I just stopped bothering.

Dave I said I much prefer you the way you are now.

Ann I heard you. The only reason for that is you aren't living with me. If you were living with someone, you'd go home tonight and tell her how wonderful I was and abuse her for not being more like me.

Dave I never realised you felt so resentful about the other women.

Ann Didn't you, I thought that was half the fun.

Dave You never seemed to mind very much. Except your

friend whatshername, but that was a bit different. I mean, that's what we agreed at the beginning, isn't it, freedom and honesty. We could do what we liked as long as we didn't have to tell lies about it. Isn't that what we agreed?

Ann It's what you announced. I never believed for a moment that sort of freedom was supposed to apply to me.

Dave You didn't want it.

Ann That's not the point, is it?

Dave Of course it's the point, it's not my fault if you're temperamentally unpromiscuous, or however it was you described it.

Ann Anyway, if you're so bloody liberal, why did you split my lip that day I had lunch with Justin?

Dave I took against his name.

Ann Then why didn't you split his lip?

Dave He's bigger than you are.

Ann Very funny.

Dave What I want to know is, if I'm so appalling, how come you put up with me for so long?

Ann That's a really stupid question.

Patrick Sounds fair enough to me.

Ann Oh, does it?

Patrick Well, yes.

Ann Then you answer it.

Patrick I can't answer it.

Ann Then don't interrupt.

Dave Don't be horrible to Patrick.

Ann What are you up to?

Dave What do you mean?

Ann Why are you pretending to be so nice?

Dave I'm not pretending to be anything, I'm just sitting here waiting for the answer to a perfectly simple question.

Ann And I'm just sitting here waiting for you to piss off home.

Dave You see, Patrick, how years of living with me have taken their toll. She used to be so docile.

Patrick Really?

Dave Now I find that in leaving me she's taken with her several of my most unpleasant characteristics.

Patrick I wouldn't go so far as to say that.

Dave He's a goer, isn't he?

Ann Dave, there are two of us here. I don't know why you persist in speaking to us one at a time.

Dave Divide and rule.

Ann That's what I thought.

Dave All right then, since I've been unmasked, I may as well come to the point of this discussion, and I'll try and address it to both of you, although of course that was not at all my intention, and what I'm saying is for you and not for Patrick. I've always lived, privately and professionally, according to very simple principles, you know, with money and women, if in doubt say yes, with friends and neighbours, if in doubt say no, there's no business like show business, never trust a politician beginning with K, that kind of uncomplicated and reliable rule of thumb. I mean, I watch a few people doing their bit and thinking they'll stop the rot, but, like the majority, I don't really see much point in trying to dig steps in the side of the whirlpool. Better to go down smiling. So you'll appreciate that what I'm about to say is a betrayal of all my deepest instincts. Will you marry me?

Ann What?

Dave Will you marry me?

Ann Can I have a moment to think about it?

Dave No.

Ann In that case, the answer is no.

Dave In that case, you can have a moment to think about it.

Ann thinks for a moment. Silence.

Ann No.

Dave Look, if it's the women, if you're still worried about the women, I think I might be able to offer you certain concessions. I mean, most of the time, I can't say I enjoyed it all that much, having to put up with all their blather and misery, but I made sacrifices, you know, as we all have to. I think I could promise you to break all the, what, emotional entanglements, at any rate.

Ann It's not the women.

Dave Well, what is it then?

Ann It's you.

Dave I'm just explaining to you, I've decided to change.

Ann Oh, come on, next thing you're going to say is, you're only a humble reporter.

Dave Ann, this is less than reasonable. I don't think you're being quite fair.

Ann What's anything to do with fair, as you used to say.

Dave Patrick, I appeal to you now, I appeal to you as a neutral observer.

Patrick Hardly neutral.

Dave No, I know, but you know what I mean. What I mean is, is this right?

Patrick Seems perfectly all right to me. You asked her to marry you and she said no.

Dave No, Patrick, I don't think you're really with me. (*Pause.*) Look, let me give you a simple illustration of what we're talking about. There's a girl works at the paper, has the most enormous tits.

Ann Jesus.

Dave No, no, bear with me. You'll see the relevance of this in a moment. (*to Patrick*) Anyway, there she is, otherwise totally unremarkable, except, as I say, for these truly massive knockers. Well, one day, when Ann was away, I could restrain myself no further, and I invited her out to dinner. Afterwards, I brought her back here, and, after the usual dreary two hours of blabbing away, I managed to get her to bed. Once there, I confessed to her that all I really wanted to do, and indeed all I intended to do was to satisfy my curiosity as to the appearance and texture of her absolutely mesmerizing and exorbitant dongers. I just wanted to gaze, assess and generally fondle. Fortunately, she took it like a trouper and we're still the best of friends. Now, what I'm driving at, Patrick, is that that pleasant incident can't possibly have done the slightest harm to the girl, to me or to Ann, can it? Am I right or am I right?

Ann If I've heard about that poor wretched girl's tits once . . .

Dave Now, now, I'm asking Patrick. Fair dos.

Ann Fair dos!

Dave What do you think, Patrick?

Patrick Well. I'm not sure what . . . I mean, by and large . . . as a course of action in itself, I wouldn't particularly approve of it, but . . . you see, I don't know what your arrangement was with Ann, and if . . . that was your arrangement, I suppose there was no harm in it. I'm not sure I know what you're driving at.

Dave What I'm driving at is, that was the kind of thing that was held against me.

Patrick I see.

Dave That was the kind of thing she meant when she said I terrorized and bullied her.

Patrick Well, if that's the case, and I can't see how you should suppose I'd be in a position to judge whether it is or not, but if it is, and I still don't understand why you should want to ask my opinion about it, if it is, I suppose you're right.

Silence. During this last exchange, Ann has been looking incredulously from one to the other.

Personally, I've never really liked them all that enormous myself.

Ann Patrick.

Patrick Yes.

Ann I want you to do something for me. I want you to get in your car and drive Dave to a pub or a strip-club or somewhere, anywhere, away from here, so you can carry on your anatomical reminiscences with complete abandon. I've got other things to do. I can't think why you wanted to arrange this abysmal occasion in the first place, but since you did, I think it's up to you to get him out of here before he gets properly launched on the unending saga of his grubby love-life. Is that clear? There's no point gawping at me like that, I've made my mind up and I've had enough and I want you both out of here now.

Patrick stirs uneasily, then subsides. Dave permits himself a discreet smile. Ann looks from one to the other with mounting annoyance.

Go on, go!

Silence. Nobody moves.

'Book of Love' sung by the Monotones.

SCENE FIVE

The next morning. The John Lennon L.P. has vanished from the bookcase.

Patrick, alone, sitting on the sofa, looking through some papers, sipping at a cup of coffee. The radio is on, an early morning news bulletin, of which Patrick takes no notice whatsoever, unless a particularly appalling piece of news catches his attention briefly. He puts down the papers, finishes his coffee, looks at his watch, reacts, exits hurriedly to the kitchen. Sounds of washing-up. He crosses to the mirror, checks his tie, starts to move away from the mirror, stops, looks at himself again, dismayed, then exits to the bedroom. He returns a moment later doing up a minimally different tie. He finishes tying it in front of the mirror, then his hand moves to his chin as he notices he is unshaven. Back to the bedroom, to return with a battery shaver, already running. He shaves in front of the mirror, shining his shoes on the back of his trousers as he does so. He turns off the shaver, checks his chin dubiously, then puts the shaver into the briefcase which stands ready by the hall door. He looks at his watch again, then dives into the hall and returns a moment later, struggling into a light raincoat. He picks up the briefcase, stands thinking, then puts the briefcase down and crosses to the dining-recess, where he stands for a moment peering out of the window. He opens the window and stretches his arm out. Then he closes the window and hurries across the room, exiting to the hall. A moment later, he re-appears to fetch his briefcase, holding an umbrella. He picks up his briefcase, stands for a moment, a strained expression on his face, then exits by the hall door. The front door slams. Sound of receding footsteps. Silence. Sound of returning footsteps. Key in the lock. Patrick re-enters. He crosses to the sofa, puts down his umbrella, picks up the papers, fumbles them into his briefcase, picks up his umbrella and strides out to the hall, closing the door behind him. The door instantly re-opens, he appears, puts down his umbrella, crosses to the radio and switches it off. Back to the hall door, where he pauses, turns to contemplate the room and pats at his pockets with his free hand, making a final check. Then he exits, leaving his umbrella behind. The front door slams.

'Little Darlin'' *sung by* The Diamonds.

SCENE SIX

That evening. Ann, alone, curled up in the swivel-chair, facing front, reading. She looks up, thoughtfully, as she hears the key in the door. Presently Patrick enters, somewhat wet.

Patrick Hello. (*He looks around.*) Where are you?

Ann Here.

Patrick Oh.

He exits into the hall, peeling off his raincoat, having dropped his briefcase just inside the door. Ann swivels round slowly.

Ann Where are you?

Patrick (*off*) Taking off my coat.

Ann Ah.

Patrick re-enters, smoothing his hair. He smiles at Ann. Hiatus. Then he bends and fumbles with his briefcase, finally producing a record in a record shop carrier bag.

Patrick I bought you a present.

Ann What is it?

She gets up. Patrick holds out the carrier bag.

Patrick Guess.

Ann Erm, bunch of daffodils.

Patrick No.

Ann Too difficult, I give up.

Patrick It's a record!

Ann Never.

Patrick hands it to her, and, as she takes it, tries to kiss her, but bungles it. Ann slips the record out of the carrier bag. It is the John Lennon L.P.

(*coolly*) Thanks.

Patrick It is the one, isn't it?

Ann What?

Patrick The one Dave took.

Ann Yes. Yes, it is. Very sweet of you.

Patrick You do like it, don't you?

Ann Yes, it's, yes.

Patrick I don't think I know it myself.

Ann moves to the bookshelves, files the record, disposes of the carrier bag.

Ann Thank you.

Patrick Bad move, eh?

Ann Well, if it's supposed to be making up for last night's fiasco, perhaps it is a bit tactless.

Patrick Perhaps so.

Ann But it was very thoughtful of you.

Patrick I'm very sorry about last night.

Ann Yes, I know, don't let's talk about it.

Patrick It's just I thought perhaps he had the right . . .

Ann That bastard has no rights.

Patrick After all, he did ask you to marry him.

Ann That was a laugh, wasn't it?

Patrick Well, I don't know.

Ann No, you don't, and you shouldn't, it's none of your business.

Patrick I suppose not. But, I mean, I wouldn't like to think you'd get rid of me like that. Not without talking it over at all.

Ann Well . . . (*She breaks off. Pause.*) Your mother phoned.

Patrick Oh, did she?

Ann She wants you to call her back.

Patrick Oh. (*He moves towards the phone, then checks himself.*)

I'll do it later.

Ann Do it now if you like.

Patrick Later will do.

  Silence.

Busy day?

Ann Not remotely.

Patrick I came down to see you this afternoon, but Jane said you'd slipped out for something.

Ann There was so little doing today, I amused myself drafting a letter of resignation.

Patrick What?

Ann I think I've had enough.

Patrick But . . . you haven't said anything about it before.

Ann I only drafted the letter, I didn't send it.

Patrick All the same. This is a bit of a bombshell.

Ann I'm fed up with it there. It's true what Dave always used to say. Those people don't need an interpreter. They know perfectly well what they're saying to each other: nothing. I told you last week when I went out to lunch with Morrison and that Spaniard, all Morrison wanted to know was what the investment situation would be like when Franco died.

Patrick Yes, well, Dave told me all we were doing was

purveying to our hapless brothers overseas the educational ideas that had brought this country to its knees. It's very easy to be cynical.

Ann Dave's not cynical, he's puritanical.

Patrick I very much doubt that.

Ann Of course he is.

Patrick I don't see how he can afford to be.

Ann The first time I met him, I asked him what he did and he told me he wrote blistering reports in words of not more than one syllable in sentences of not more than five words for a newspaper that was guaranteed not to let the vinegar through.

Patrick I thought he worked for um . . .

Ann Yes, now he says he's allowed to write very considered and interesting articles and all he has to contend with is the fact that nobody reads them.

Patrick I don't really see what Dave's problems have to do with your . . .

Ann Nothing.

Patrick Anyway, I thought we weren't allowed to talk about him.

Ann What do you mean?

Patrick Well, every time I mention his name, you bite my head off.

Ann That's because you will insist on talking about him all the time, when you don't know the first thing about him. Not to mention defending him, that's what really gets up my nose.

Patrick I don't think I do, do I? It's just . . . I mean, I don't exactly like him, but I certainly don't mind him. I suppose you're right, I suppose I don't know all that much about him.

Ann Then shut up about him.

Silence.

Patrick All right, tell me why you want to leave the job.

Ann Because I want to leave you.

Silence.

Patrick No.

Ann nods.

You don't mean it.

Ann Yes.

Patrick But why?

No answer. Patrick has an idea.

Oh.

Ann No.

Patrick You want to . . .

Ann No, I do not. I knew you were going to say that.

Patrick You don't.

Ann I wouldn't dream of it.

Patrick Oh. (*Pause.*) Well, you must admit, it's the obvious conclusion.

Ann It's the obvious conclusion for a man, that one could only bear to leave him in order to go back to some other bloody man.

Patrick No, I didn't quite mean it like that. I meant, after seeing him again last night, that is, after seeing both of us together, it might have made you, you know, reawakened some, you know . . .

Ann The only thing it reawakened was a very strong and urgent desire to live on my own again.

Patrick I see.

Ann That was my mistake, Patrick, that was the mistake, I thought the only way to escape from Dave was to go off with somebody else. I used you. I'm very sorry about it.

Patrick Don't apologise, I'm very glad you . . . (*Pause.*) Anyway, don't you think this is all a bit radical after one bad evening?

Ann No.

Patrick After all, you put up with Dave for two and a half years, it seems a bit hard to give me the elbow on the basis of a single sticky dinner-party.

Ann You know I'm very decisive.

Patrick I don't call that decisive, I call it rash.

Ann How would you know, it takes you forty-five minutes every morning to decide which shoes to put on. And you've only got three pairs.

Patrick Well, I . . . (*He breaks off, stares morosely at his feet.*)

Ann I know it's a very trivial example, but that's the kind of thing I mean.

Patrick I may not know what shoes to put on, but I know what I want.

Ann You don't.

Patrick Of course I do, you can't say that, I should know, shouldn't I?

Ann You have wants the way other people have toothache. Kind of dull and general.

Patrick Look, are we talking about what I want, or are we talking about what you want?

Ann We're talking about what I want, and what I want I want because as far as I can see you don't want anything at all.

Patrick Let's have that again.

Ann You know perfectly well what I mean. You're so cautious and rational, anything as crude as a wish or a whim or a desire dies before you ever get your mouth open.

Patrick Balls.

Ann Patrick.

Patrick Well . . .

Silence.

Ann You know something, I think this is the first argument we've ever had.

Patrick It isn't.

Ann It is.

Patrick considers this a moment.

Patrick Is it?

Ann Oh, God.

Patrick Wait, I'm just trying to think . . .

He does so. Silence.

We did have that disagreement about Chinese restaurants, remember?

Ann Oh, for God's sake, what difference does it make?

Patrick Well, it obviously does make a difference, since you're reproaching me for it.

Ann No, I'm not, all I meant, the only point I was trying to make, was you must admit the whole thing has been rather passionless, joyless . . .

Patrick Painless.

Ann Yes.

Patrick Mm, I suppose that probably is my fault. At any rate, it's a familiar complaint. Someone else once accused me of being too happy.

Ann I don't see what that's got to do with it.

Patrick Well, by and large it's true that I'm a . . . happy man. Consequently, I don't expect anything very much from people, and consequently, I never quite know what it is they expect from me. To that extent, I'm totally maladjusted. That's why I find people, or at any rate women, so bewildering.

Ann You make a distinction, do you, between women and people?

Patrick No, don't let's get off on all that, you know what I mean. I mean, when someone says to me, I want this or that, or I feel this or that, I always try to respond accordingly. And it's only later I realise that's not what was meant at all. I'm an incurable optimist, that's the misery of it.

Ann An optimist? In this country? Now?

Patrick Yes, yes, I know it's all terrible at the moment, but I believe, I honestly believe, that in a hundred years' time or maybe two, all those problems, that's to say all the problems that can be, will be sorted out, more or less, and people will be able to start actually doing something with their lives.

Ann You mean, when we're dead?

Patrick Yes.

Ann You call that optimism?

Patrick Yes.

Ann Well, whatever may or may not be the truth of these philosophical speculations, the fact remains, I've had enough. I've made a mistake and I'm very sorry and now I've had enough.

Patrick Right.

Silence.

Ann If you were even vulnerable . . .

Patrick I'm sure I bleed as much as the next man.

Ann Maybe you do: but very neatly, I suspect.

Silence. Patrick suddenly plunges a hand up his trouser-leg, scratches his calf vigorously.

Patrick Excuse me scratching, terrible itch.

Ann watches him in silence.

Shall I, shall I not stay the night? Tonight.

Ann I don't really see the point, do you?

Patrick Oh. Well, then, perhaps I had better ring mother.

Ann Please yourself.

Silence. Patrick gets up. By this time, Ann is looking at him with something approaching horror.

Patrick This is all . . . very painful for me.

Ann (*coldly*) I'm sorry.

Patrick Reason I haven't . . . I mean, I don't want you to think it doesn't matter to me . . . it's just . . . the things we were talking about . . . I mean, you're everything *I* want . . . but what *you* want . . . I don't think I could ever . . .

Ann (*much warmer*) What do you mean?

Patrick You know . . . maybe I've misunderstood . . . I just wanted to make it clear . . . (*He breaks off, gropes around in his pocket, produces a key-ring.*) I'd better leave your key.

Ann Don't bother.

> *Patrick starts trying to get the key off the key-ring. He finds it very difficult. He tugs and fumbles at it with fierce determination.*

Don't bother.

> *Patrick perseveres, his face contorted with effort. Finally, he manages to wrench it free.*

Patrick There we are.

Ann You really needn't have bothered. Not right this minute.

Patrick Are you sure? (*He looks down at key and key-ring, begins to draw them together.*)

Ann Oh, leave it, now you've got it off, I couldn't bear to sit here and have to watch you fiddling the bloody thing on again.

Patrick All right. Erm . . .?

Ann What?

Patrick Where would you like me to leave it?

Ann Anywhere.

Patrick stands, holding the key, looking uncertainly around the room, from one possible location to another.

'Why Do Fools Fall In Love?' sung by Frankie Lymon and The Teenagers.

SCENE SEVEN

Two weeks later. Afternoon. Empty stage. Ann enters from the hall, backwards, protesting, followed by Dave, who has a large rug rolled up over his shoulder. They advance into the room.

Dave Right, where d'you want it, missis?

Ann I told you not to bring it round yourself.

Dave Well, you can't get the labour, guv'nor. (*He drops it off his shoulder on to the floor.*) Jesus, that's heavy. Give us a hand. (*He starts unrolling it, looks up at Ann.*) Come on, shift yourself.

Ann moves to help him. They unroll it and begin manoeuvring it into position.

Where's Patrick?

Ann Out.

Dave No, he isn't.

Ann Well, if you know, why ask?

Dave Just wanted to see what you'd say.

They start moving pieces of furniture to accommodate the rug.

it's a nice bit of rug. (*Pause. He straightens up, considers it.*) Perhaps I've been rash. What do you think?

Ann By all means, take it away again, if you want to.

Dave Very good for making love on, was that.

Ann I never thought much of it.

Silence. They move the furniture back on to the rug.

Dave By the way, I meant to ask you, what was Patrick like in bed?

Ann No worse than you.

Dave is momentarily shaken, recovers quickly.

Dave No wonder you got rid of him, then.

The placing of the rug is now complete.

There. Everything to your satisfaction, madam?

Ann looks up at him, nods.

Ann Except for one thing.

Dave I'm told you've left your job, as well.

Ann Yes.

Dave About bloody time. Perhaps now you'll use your qualifications for something more socially respectable. Dubbing pornographic movies.

Ann sighs.

No, I'm serious. Lot of money in that. I know a bloke . . .

Ann Look, why don't you take your chair, and get off back to wherever you've come from.

Dave I don't think it would go in my room.

Ann You're not still at the Savoy, are you?

Dave That's what my bank manager keeps saying.

Ann I'm sure.

Dave Question of waiting till I can afford to pay the bill.

Silence. Their eyes meet. Dave smiles.

Thirsty work.

Ann What?

Dave Cuppa tea would be most welcome.

Ann All right.

Dave Good gracious.

Ann exits to the kitchen. Dave looks around the room, his face serious. He moves over to the swivel-chair, is about to sit down then changes his mind and sits on the sofa.

Lonely?

Ann (*off*) What?

Dave Living on your own.

Ann (*off*) I like it.

Dave It has its advantages, doesn't it?

Ann (*off*) Yes.

Silence. Dave checks his watch, considers a moment.

Dave You're not having Arthur back from the newsagent's, then?

Ann comes in with two mugs of tea.

Ann No, I thought about it, but I decided against it. (*She hands Dave a mug, sits at the other end of the sofa.*)

Dave Thanks. (*He takes a sip.*) Oh, you remembered.

Ann Four large sugars is hard to forget.

Dave smiles. Ann sips at her tea. Silence.

Dave What made you get rid of Patrick?

Ann Didn't work.

Dave Nice chap.

Ann (*suspiciously*) Yes.

Dave Full of over-educated bullshit, of course. Otherwise, I liked him. I never thought he was quite your speed.

Ann Speed, of any kind, was not one of his strong points.

Dave His face, he looked like someone who'd just stepped into an empty lift-shaft. But then, so do most people nowadays, unless, like me, they actually enjoy dancing in the ruins.

Ann And what are you up to at the moment?

Dave Nothing much. I went round to see Millicent again, having managed to conquer my invincible distaste for her name, but she seems to have taken up with an Australian poet, if you can imagine such a thing.

Silence.

What are you thinking of doing now?

Ann I don't know, bit of a holiday, I should think, till the money runs out.

Dave Oh.

Silence.

Ann Well, I'd say that just about wraps up the conversational possibilities, wouldn't you?

Silence. Dave puts his cup down, looks across at Ann.

Dave Ann . . .

Ann No.

Dave I wasn't going to say that.

Ann What were you going to say?

Dave I was just going to say . . . what about another cup of tea?

Ann That wasn't what you were going to say.

Dave No, you're quite right. I was just . . . wondering if you'd given any thought to that proposition I made the other evening.

Ann What proposition?

Dave Proposal, I should say.

Ann Oh.

Dave Well?

Ann Yes, I have.

Dave I meant it, you know.

Ann Yes.

Dave And . . . what have you decided?

Ann I haven't changed my mind.

Dave Well, that's a relief.

Ann Oh?

Dave Yes, your instinct was absolutely sound, it would have been a catastrophe.

Ann I see.

Dave When I look around at the marriages of my friends, all I can see is . . . easy pickings.

Ann That's an exaggeration.

Dave True. (*Pause.*) Still, as long as it lasts, the bad conscience of the female middle-class mafia, I guess there'll always be a niche for me.

Ann Why do you hate women so much?

Dave I don't hate women.

Ann Then why did you treat me so badly?

Dave Question is, why did you allow me to treat you so badly?

Ann Do you mean you treated me badly because you hated me for letting you treat me badly?

Dave No, I mean I may have treated you badly because I thought you liked me to treat you badly.

Ann I can't believe that.

Dave Patrick told me you'd never complained to him about me.

Ann I didn't think it was any of his business. (*Pause.*) Were you pleased?

Dave No, I was rather annoyed. At first. Then I thought maybe I was on the wrong track all that time, since it doesn't seem to have had any effect. Still, I suppose we all make mistakes. As you no doubt said to Patrick.

Ann Not an apology, is it?

Dave I expect it's the nearest you'll ever get to one.

Ann Better make the most of it, then, hadn't I?

Dave It was what I was trying to tell you that evening I broke in.

Ann Even then it was too late.

Silence.

Dave No reason . . . no reason we shouldn't see each other from time to time, is there?

Ann What's the point?

Dave No point, I'd just like to know how you're getting on, that's all.

Ann You're unusually mellow this afternoon.

Silence.

Dave What I was going to say, I mean what I actually was going to say when you stopped me just now, was, why don't we go to bed?

Long silence.

Ann All right.

Dave What?

Ann All right.

Dave Ah.

Ann What's the matter?

Dave Nothing, you just, I don't know, caught me on the hop.

Ann Well?

Dave Well . . . terrific.

Silence. Neither of them moves.

Ann Then that'll be that.

Dave What do you mean?

Ann What I say.

Dave Well, we'll see, shall we?

Ann I'm telling you. (*Pause.*) I like things tidy.

Silence.

Dave OK.

Ann Right.

Dave It'll be; just a little treat.

Ann Yes.

Silence. They still haven't moved. Dave clears his throat.

Dave Well.

Ann gets up.

Ann Bedroom?

Dave smiles, recovered.

Dave Well, since I've gone to the trouble of humping this bloody great rug round . . .

Ann If you insist.

Dave I do.

Ann All right.

Dave gets up.

Dave Funny.

Ann What?

Dave I feel rather nervous. Reminds me of the night I lost my virginity, ha, what a card game that was.

He moves to Ann, takes her chin in his hand, looks at her for a moment, then turns away and crosses to the bedroom door, where he stops and turns back to Ann.

Get your clothes off, I won't be a minute.

He exits. Ann stands for a moment, then starts
undressing. After a time, Dave returns. He strides
straight across to her and slaps her face hard.

I've changed my mind.

Ann What?

Dave I've changed my mind. I don't know what it is
you're up to, but I don't want anything to do with it.

Ann What the hell are you talking about?

Dave Now, listen. I'm going back to the hotel now, and
you can think about it this afternoon and this evening or
however long it takes, and when you've made your mind
up, you can ring me. Or not ring me, whatever you decide.
Anyway, I'll be there. All right?

He moves over to the hall door. Ann watches him with
hatred.

Ann Is this what you planned, is it?

Dave I never make plans, I just live on my wits and try to
cover all the exits. (*He smiles at her triumphantly.*) You
just have to pick up the phone. (*He exits.*)

'Will You Still Love Me Tomorrow?' sung by The
Shirelles.

SCENE EIGHT

That evening. Ann, alone, in a dressing-gown, sitting on
the swivel-chair, facing front. She sits there for some time.
Finally, she gets up, crosses to the television and switches
it on. Instant picture. The actress should choose whichever
channel seems most dramatically appropriate. She wanders
back to the swivel-chair, turns it round and sits. She

watches television for quite some time, invisible. Then she half-swivels round so that she is visible in profile. She is weeping. She weeps for a long time, finally sobbing uncontrollably. She stops suddenly, waits a moment, then gets up, crosses to the phone, picks up the receiver and dials.

SCENE NINE

A week later. The room is now fully furnished, the empty bookshelf is full, there are more chairs, pictures on the wall. And so on. Evening.

Ann and Dave are sitting on the sofa, the remains of supper behind them on the dining-table, two glasses of brandy on the coffee-table in front of them. Ann is in her dressing-gown. Dave, in shirtsleeves, is listening, through the headphones, to 'God' from the John Lennon L.P. 'Working-class Hero'. Fairly loud. Enjoying himself.

After a time, from outside, the sound of breaking glass, followed immediately by frenzied barking. Dave looks across at Ann, takes the headphones off, gets up, crosses to the amplifier, puts the headphones down, takes the needle off the record, switches off and moves to the hall door. The barking continues throughout this. Dave opens the hall door and steps into the hall.

Dave Arthur. Arthur! Get down, boy.

After a moment, he returns, shepherding Patrick. Patrick's hand is bleeding. He stands just inside the door, hopelessly, white-faced.

Arthur didn't do that, did he?

Patrick No, no, the, um, glass.

Dave Oh, I was going to say, if it was Arthur, we'd better

332

get you down the doctor. Or him down the vet. You've given him a terrible turn.

Patrick I . . . (*He waves his bleeding hand at Ann.*) You see, not so neat, after all.

Ann What are you talking about?

Patrick You . . .

Ann Look, for God's sake, don't drip on the rug.

Dave Well, go on, get the poor bugger an Elastoplast or something, don't just stand there.

Ann hesitates, then exits angrily to the bedroom.

Patrick I've just dropped by to have a word with you about stock-car racing.

Dave What?

Patrick Nothing.

Dave Are you quite all right?

Patrick flaps his hand.

Patrick Apart from this.

Dave I think you'd better have a brandy.

He moves to the dining-recess, takes out a glass and pours a brandy. Ann returns from the bedroom with a bottle of T.C.P., cotton wool and a bandage. The two of them converge on Patrick simultaneously. He takes the glass and submits his hand to Ann with some confusion. Dave smiles, enjoying himself.

This is very trying, you know, we've only just had that pane replaced. The glazier will gossip. (*He swigs at his brandy.*) I must say, old bean, this shows a sad lack of imagination. Couldn't you have devised some other method? You could have bought a taxi and cruised around the area waiting to be hailed. Bit of originality, that's all we ask.

Ann Stop it, Dave.

She concentrates on bandaging Patrick's hand. He gazes at her miserably, speaks quietly to her.

Patrick I want to talk to you.

Dave We knew that, Patrick, but I have to tell you this is not a convenient moment. We can't even offer you any supper, alas, I'm afraid we've scoffed the lot. So when you're all finished there, I'm sorry, but I'm going to have to ask you to slosh down your brandy and get off home to mother.

Patrick I have a flat of my own now.

Dave Then what you breaking in here for?

Patrick I've told you, I have to talk to Ann.

Dave And I've told you, this is not the right moment. Now, don't force me to get heavy with you. An Englishman's home is his castle, you know.

Ann finishes bandaging Patrick's hand, breaks away from him.

And, not to put too fine a point on it, if you're not out of here in ten seconds, I'm going to call the police.

Patrick Look, I know it's difficult for you, but do you find it quite impossible to be serious?

Dave You'd be surprised, mate. (*Pause.*) I'm waiting. (*Pause.*) Right. (*He strides over to the telephone, lifts the receiver.*)

Ann Don't.

Patrick starts to move towards him, then freezes, panicked. Dave smiles at Ann, then dials 999. Moment of silence.

Dave Hello . . . oh, is there a choice? . . . I'll have to have a think about it, I'll let you know. Thank you. (*He puts the receiver down, smiling.*) Easy when you know how. (*Pause.*) Next time I'll get them round here.

Patrick I don't understand this at all.

Dave There are no certainties in this world, Patrick. I have a friend called Napoleon Bonaparte actually believes he's a lunatic.

Silence. Patrick bemused, Ann unhappy, Dave confident.

Ann I think perhaps you'd better go, Patrick.

Patrick looks uncertainly from Ann to Dave.

Patrick Are you going to get married?

Dave You're joking.

Patrick I just wondered.

Dave Look, in a couple of years' time or sooner or anyway sometime we shall probably make a very unpleasant mess of each other's lives and that'll be the end of it.

Patrick And is that . . . a reasonable basis?

Dave Of course it is, we just know in advance what catches most people by surprise, that's all. (*Pause.*) Look, I tell you what, I'm going away in a couple of weeks, why don't you wait and have another bash then? If you get anywhere, of course, you'll have to take into account the fact she's probably only doing it to get back at me, but if you think that's worthwhile, God bless you. Can't say

335

fairer than that, now can I? Alternatively, you could hang around until the whole thing's over, although I shouldn't if I were you, because I have to be honest with you, my money's on some third party.

Patrick Ann.

Dave Let's leave it for now, shall we?

Patrick Did you read my letters?

Dave She wouldn't, I'm afraid, she's very stubborn. So I did. They were most affecting.

Patrick I'm talking to Ann.

Dave I know that, I can see that, but is she talking to you? That's the question we should be asking ourselves.

Patrick Look, will you . . .

Dave Patrick, I'm sorry about this, I really am, I like you, believe me, I've grown to be very fond of you. I mean, I won't deny this whole situation has a certain, you know, well, as an old mate of mine, Charlie Peters, always used to say, there is no more subtle pleasure than to see your best friend fall off the roof. But I do have a genuine affection and . . .

Patrick Fuck off!

Dave Patrick!

Patrick I'm talking to Ann!

Dave The floor is yours. (*He moves abruptly to the sofa, sits down, puts his feet up and watches them over the back of the sofa.*)

Patrick Ann.

Dave The rug is mine but the floor is yours.

He laughs, having been unable to resist this remark. Patrick, however, takes no notice and moves closer to Ann, who has been growing increasingly tense, throughout these recent exchanges.

Patrick Is this what you want? That's all I want to ask you, love, I've done my best to be irrational this evening, but I can't understand, I can't bear to see this happening to you, so just tell me, it's all I want to know, is it, is this really what you want?

Silence. Suddenly, Ann bears down on Patrick, furious.

Ann Will you get the hell out of here, you stupid hopeless bastard, what the fuck do you think you're doing, can't you get it through your head, sod you, I want you out, understand that, can you, I want you out and I never want to see you again!

Silence. Patrick is stunned.

Patrick Well if you yes all right.

He turns, moves to the hall door, hesitates, turns back, shoots a helpless look round the room as if he thinks he's forgotten something, then exits into the hall.

A second's silence, then Ann suddenly runs after him into the hall, closing the door behind her.

Dave sits up, startled by this.

Long silence, during which Dave's face betrays a growing fear.

The heavy sound of a door closing.

Dave starts to get up. He looks terrified.

Ann opens the door, stands in the doorway.

Dave sits down again, looking at her.

Ann closes the door, advances into the room. She smiles at Dave.

Dave looks away from her, refusing to respond, stone-faced.

As she draws level with him, still smiling, he looks up at her again, very cold.